# Beyond the Risk Society

# Beyond the Risk Society

## Critical Reflections on Risk and Human Security

*Gabe Mythen and Sandra Walklate*

Open University Press

Open University Press
McGraw-Hill Education
McGraw-Hill House
Shoppenhangers Road
Maidenhead
Berkshire
England
SL6 2QL

email: enquiries@openup.co.uk
world wide web: www.openup.co.uk

and Two Penn Plaza, New York, NY 10121–2289, USA

First published 2006

A catalogue record of this book is available from the British Library

ISBN-10: 0 335 21738 9 (pb) 0 335 21739 7 (hb)
ISBN-13: 978 0 335 21738 0 (pb) 978 0 335 21739 7 (hb)

Library of Congress Cataloguing-in-Publication Data
CIP data applied for

Typeset by YHT Ltd, London
Printed in Britain by Ashford Colour Press Ltd., Gosport, Hants.

# Contents

# Contributors

**Alison Anderson** is a Principal Lecturer in Sociology at the University of Plymouth. She is the author of *Media, Culture and the Environment* (University College London and Rutgers University Press, 1997) and co-editor of *The Changing Consumer* (Routledge, 2002). Her recent articles on journalistic portrayals of nanotechnology, genetics, terrorism and war have appeared in *Sociological Research Online, Knowledge Technology & Society, New Genetics and Society* and *Science Communication*. She is currently conducting an ESRC study on nanotechnology and news production with Alan Petersen, Stuart Allan and Clare Wilkinson.

**Rob Flynn** is Professor of Sociology at the University of Salford. He is currently working on an EPSRC study of the socio-economic implications of transitions to a hydrogen energy economy, and public perceptions of risk and trust in experts. He is also collaborating in an ESRC study of the use of health outcome indicators in clinical decision-making. Previously he has researched and written extensively on health policy, health services organization and the regulation of medical professionals. He was the chairperson of the Editorial Board of *Sociology* and is a member of the Editorial Board of *Sociology of Health and Illness*.

**Jane Franklin** is Senior Research Fellow of the Families and Social Capital ESRC Research Group, and a Lecturer in Social and Policy Studies at London South Bank University. She was previously a Research Fellow at the Institute for Public Policy Research. Recently her work has focused on the relationship between social theory and politics, feminist theory in late modernity and on critiques of communitarian and social capital perspectives.

**Hazel Kemshall** is Professor of Community and Criminal Justice at De Montfort University, Leicester. She has research interests in risk assessment and management of offenders, effective work in multi-agency public protection and implementing effective practice with offenders. She has completed research for the ESRC, the Home Office and the Scottish Executive, and both teaches and consults extensively on public protection and high risk offenders. She has numerous publications on risk, including *Understanding Risk in Criminal Justice* (Open University Press, 2003). Hazel has recently completed an evaluation of multi-agency public protection panels for the Home Office and is currently investigating pathways into and out of crime for young people under an ESRC network.

**Deborah Lupton** is Professor of Sociology and Cultural Studies at Charles Sturt University, Australia. Her latest books are *Risk* (Routledge, 1999), *Risk and Everyday Life* with John Tulloch (Sage, 2003) and *Medicine As Culture: Illness, Disease and the Body in Western Societies* (Sage, 2003).

**Phil Macnaghten** is Chair in Geography and Director of the Institute for Hazard and Risk Research at Durham University. He is the author, with John Urry, of *Contested Natures* (Sage, 1998) and *Bodies of Nature* (Sage, 2001). He is currently researching the societal dimension of nano and emerging technologies.

**Jim McGuigan** is Professor of Cultural Analysis in the Department of Social Sciences at Loughborough University. He has published widely in social theory and cultural studies. His books include *Cultural Populism* (1992), *Culture and the Public Sphere* (1996), *Cultural Methodologies* (1997), *Modernity and Postmodern Culture* (1999, 2006) and *Rethinking Cultural Policy* (2004).

**Peter McMylor** is Senior Lecturer in Sociology at the University of Manchester. He is the author of *Alasdair MacIntyre: Critic of Modernity* (Routledge, 1994) and a number of articles on the connections between ethics, culture and social and economic transformations. His current research focuses on the civilizational aspect of religious and political transformations.

**Gabe Mythen** is Principal Lecturer in Sociology based at Manchester Metropolitan University. He has been researching in the area of risk perception and risk communication for several years, and has published articles in *The Sociological Review, Sociological Research Online, The British Journal of Criminology, Security Journal* and *Environmental Politics*. His critique of the risk society thesis is presented in *Ulrich Beck: A Critical Introduction to the Risk Society* (Pluto Press, 2004). Gabe is currently researching the social construction of 'new terrorism' and investigating the impacts of dominant discourses of terrorism on everyday life.

**Pat O'Malley** is Canada Research Chair in Criminology and Criminal Justice and Professor of Sociology and Anthropology at Carleton University, Ottawa. He is the author and editor of many publications on risk and security, most recently *Risk, Uncertainty and Government* (Cavendish, 2004) and an edited collection entitled *Governing Risks* (Ashgate, 2006). Pat is editor of the Cambridge University Press *Law and Society* series and he is on the editorial and advisory boards of various international journals in the field. His current research activity includes 'Government by fire: fire prevention and urban security networks', work on the nexus between security, risk and justice and a book manuscript, *Monetized Justice*.

**Teela Sanders** is a Lecturer in the School of Sociology and Social Policy at the University of Leeds and specializes in the sociology of crime and deviance. Her main research interests are in the female sex industry, examining the social organization of sex work. She has recently published in journals such as *Sociology; Urban Studies; Sociology of Health and Illness; Social Science and Medicine; Gender, Work and Organization*. Her first book *Sex Work: A Risky Business* (Willan, 2005) looks at the indoor sex markets in the UK. She is currently working on her next book *Paying for Pleasure: Men Who Buy Sex* (Willan, 2008).

**Steve Tombs** is Professor of Sociology at Liverpool John Moores University and Chair of the human rights charity, the Centre for Corporate Accountability. He has a long-standing interest in the incidence, nature and regulation of corporate crime and in particular the regulation and management of health and safety at work. Since 1999, Steve has been researching the control of corporate crime in Finland. His other current research interest is in the politics of knowledge. Recent publications include two co-edited texts, with Dave Gordon, Paddy Hillyard and Christina Pantazis, entitled *Beyond Criminology? Taking Harm Seriously* (Pluto Press, 2004) and *Unmasking the Crimes of the Powerful: Scrutinising States and Corporations*, with Dave Whyte (Peter Lang, 2003). He is co-author of *Corporate Crime* (Longman, 1999), with Gary Slapper, and *Toxic Capitalism* (Ashgate, 1998; Canadian Scholars' Press, 1999), with Frank Pearce. He also co-authored *People in Organisations* (Blackwell, 1996) and co-edited *Risk, Management and Society* (Kluwer-Nijhoff, 2000). Along with Dave Whyte, he is currently preparing *Safety Crimes* (Willan, 2006).

**Sandra Walklate** is Eleanor Rathbone Chair of Sociology at Liverpool University. Her recent publications include *Gender, Crime and Criminal Justice*, (Willan, 2nd edition, 2004) and a range of articles on criminal victimization. She is currently writing her third book on victims of crime, entitled *Imagining the Victim of Crime* (McGraw-Hill/Open University Press) and is the editor of the forthcoming *Handbook of Victims and Victimology* (Willan, 2007). She is Honorary Senior Research Fellow at the University of Bangor and Visiting Professor at the University of Stockholm.

**Dave Whyte** is a Lecturer in Criminology at the University of Stirling where he teaches and researches various aspects of criminal justice, with a specialist interest in the crimes of the powerful. His particular research interests include the politics of regulation, the criminalization of deaths and injuries at work and the regulation of the private military industry. He has recently completed a study on corporate corruption in occupied Iraq.

**Iain Wilkinson** is a Lecturer in Sociology in the School of Social Policy, Sociology and Social Research at the University of Kent, Canterbury. He is convenor of the British Sociological Association study group on Risk and Society. His publications include *Anxiety in a Risk Society* (Routledge, 2001), *Suffering: A Sociological Introduction* (Polity Press, 2005) and *Risk, Vulnerability and Everyday Life* (Routledge, 2006).

# Preface

Risk is ostensibly acknowledged as a cross-discipline issue, yet risk analysis has traditionally been centred within disciplinary paradigms. Indeed, this theoretical and empirical segmentation is reflected in the composition of existing social science collections on risk. Rather than promoting information interchange and the pooling of knowledge, risk theorists have gravitated towards distinct camps, leading to something of a critical impasse. With an eye to bridging this hiatus, this collection draws upon the expertise of leading thinkers on risk from a range of disciplines. The overriding aim of the book is to coalesce currently disconnected perspectives and inquiries to drive forward debates about the impacts and effects of living in the risk society. By chipping away at the boundaries between different social science disciplines, this text seeks to foster understanding and encourage dialogue by raising awareness of major developments and breakthroughs within particular areas. The title for the collection reflects our desire both to stretch debates in new directions and to assemble a fresh set of tools for thinking about risk. Bringing together a range of domain experts, this book marks a fresh departure within the social sciences and, we hope, acts as a first step towards establishing a holistic approach to risk and human security.

# Acknowledgements

The editors would like to warmly thank the authors for making this collection a pleasure to assemble. The vibrancy of their ideas has extended and invigorated our thinking about risk and we are indebted to them. Thanks are also due to Mark Barratt for his support in pushing the original idea through and to Chris Cudmore at Open University Press/McGraw-Hill for providing considered guidance.

# Introduction
## Thinking beyond the risk society

*Gabe Mythen and Sandra Walklate*

## The risk society context

In contemporary culture, risk is a ubiquitous issue that stretches over a range of social activities, practices and experiences. In Britain, current debates about welfare, crime, national security, food safety, employment and sexuality are all underscored by risk. Further, risk is a dynamic phenomenon that is constantly being cast and recast within the rhythms of everyday life. Despite its global omnipresence, risk remains an opaque and disputed concept, both in theory and in practice. In theoretical terms, risk has conventionally been approached as an objective entity, to be mastered by calculation, assessment and probability. However, in line with rising public concerns about unbounded techno-scientific development and the apparent ineptitude of expert systems in managing hazards, interest in risk has gathered momentum within the social sciences. Scholars of sociology, environmental studies, employment relations, social policy and criminology have all contributed to an expanding debate. The current fascination with risk is mirrored by an expanding number of research programmes, specialist centres and university courses oriented towards the subject. However, while the language of risk has become prolific, its material consequences remain uncertain and contestable, making it an irresistible subject for the social sciences.

In the 18 months in which this book has been conceived, a number of seismic events have taken place in different parts of the world. In one way or another, each of these episodes can be read through the prism of risk. There have been dreadful natural disasters such as the tsunami in South-East Asia, the devastating earthquake in Kashmir and the destruction wreaked by Hurricane Katrina in New Orleans. Alongside these 'environmental risks', concerns about the risks of terrorism have moved centre stage in the formal political arena. There has been a series of high profile attacks by groups purportedly practising 'new terrorism', the most notable of these being the Beslan siege, the double bomb attacks in Bali and the suicide bombings on the London Underground. Amidst – and, in many ways, connected to – the launching of the 'war against terrorism' by assorted Western superpowers, military conflicts continue to cause death and bloodshed in Iraq, Palestine and Chechnya. Since the occupation of Iraq by allied troops in 2003, over 30,000 civilians have perished. Back in the UK, there have also been notable health scares, such as MRSA – the so-called 'hospital superbug' – continued debate about the safety of the triple measles, mumps and rubella (MMR) vaccine for children, and fears about a possible pandemic resulting from the transference and mutation of avian flu. On a more mundane level, it is clear that people negotiate risks on a daily basis. Domestic violence in the home, uncertainty in the workplace and crime in urban areas are all salient examples of such 'routine' encounters with risk. There is also widespread recognition that potential risks of the future – global warming, genetic cloning and bio-terrorism – shatter national forms of regulation and demand global co-op-eration and control (Mythen 2005). Indeed, growing awareness of the transboundary nature of risk has led the United Nations to form its own Commission on Human Security. A recent report by the Commission (2003: 4) highlights a number of ways in which the security of people might be advanced – from humanitarian and military strategies through to economic, health and educational policies. While 'freedom from want' continues to be a pressing global imperative, in recent years, 'freedom from fear' has ascended the international political agenda.

In fast-moving, highly technologized Western cultures, risk has been eagerly seized upon as a focal theme by media outlets. Eye-catching risk in-cidents have taken their place in the news agenda alongside the less re-portable but nevertheless ruinous problems of drought, disease and famine in parts of East Africa. These are examples pulled out from a global geographic, about which we are informed through the cultural reach of the mass media. Yet while risk is undoubtedly *en vogue* in the media, 'risks' have always blighted human experience, well before the term assumed common currency (Bernstein 1998; Giddens 1998). Dangerous incidents and processes have marked the whole of history, from bubonic plague in the sixteenth century, to the potato famine and the eruption of Krakatoa in the nineteen hundreds to the virulent outbreak of Spanish flu in the early twentieth century. The common-sense assumption that contemporary cultures are materially more risky than previous eras needs to be scrutinized rather than uncritically ac-cepted (Mythen 2004). In absolute terms, indicators of mortality, health and longevity suggest that Western society is a relatively safe and healthy place in which to live (Furedi 2002; Pidgeon 2000).

In a culture that is increasingly characterized by hazards and un-certainties, it should come as no surprise that risk has been one of the de-fining themes of investigation in the social sciences in the last two decades. Sparked by Ulrich Beck's (1992, 1995, 1998) pioneering work, there has been an explosion of interest in risk in many disciplines. In the same way as there was a turn to culture in the social sciences in the early 1980s, so too there has been a turn to risk in the late twentieth and early twenty-first centuries. This 'risk turn' has manifested itself in various projects, studies, articles and texts. In light of the occurrences cited above, it is easy to see why academics, environmental campaigners and policy-makers have latched onto Beck's ideas and sought to cast the present epoch as a 'risk society'. Although the authors in this collection engage with the risk society thesis, they also seek to problematize the assumption that we are inhabiting a generic 'global risk society'. The prevalence of risk as a theme in the media, politics, popular culture and academia is called into question, with several authors injecting a note of caution about the political dominance of discourses of risk – and the uses to which they are put. Although we need to be wary of the threat of 'risk imperialism' – both politically and academically – it is indisputable that risk has become a mechanism for understanding and organizing social processes and experiences. Questions of risk and risk management have become ever more pertinent, leading to reflections on a number of different levels about ontological security. How do human beings manage their sense of well-being in a world in which less and less can be taken for granted? To what extent does the spectre of global risks interplay with more mundane insecurities which speckle day-to-day life? In a climate of seemingly routine indeterminacy, there is a need to continue to draw out the ways in which the social sciences can elucidate the dynamic relationship between risk, technological transformation and human security.

## Overview of the book

In this book, we present the work of a cast of experts, each with a particular interest in risk and each considered an eminent thinker in their respective fields. To a greater or lesser extent, the authors employ elements of the risk society thesis as a vehicle for elaborating key issues, themes and topics within their subject area. This said, we are not simply seeking to develop either an appreciation or a critique of Beck's work. These tasks have been adequately achieved elsewhere (Elliott 2002; Mythen 2004). Instead, we are bound up with responding to the question, 'What lies beyond the risk society?' For us, this is at once a conceptual, material, political, economic and cultural question. The diverse answers offered do allow us to take stock of historical and current debates about risk, but, more crucially, they also enable us to take the issues forward by considering the opportunity for greater cross- and interdisciplinary collaboration. By hooking into areas requiring expansion, our contributors reflect on the possible direction of future risk research and the multiple and mutable shape of the risk society. Meshing with this rationale, we have sought to provide an eclectic argument-based book on risk. To invite readers to think 'beyond the risk society', each chapter ends with a trio of study questions and suggestions for further reading. In addition to risk society theory, the respective authors in this volume also draw upon and utilize other perspectives, such as the governmentality thesis, the psychometric paradigm and the cultural/symbolic approach. Through this broad-based method, an overview of both past and present advances in risk research in different social science disciplines is elaborated. Some of the authors brought together here have been researching risk in close disciplinary proximity. It should be no surprise then that several chapters – such as those on culture, media and the environment – touch on overlapping areas of analysis and adopt parallel positions. Nevertheless, there are striking differences too, as one might expect over such an indeterminate concept as risk. Our intention in the editing process has not been to iron out or underplay opposing perspectives and contrasting stances. Rather, these differences are allowed to speak against one another, adding, we think, to the pulsating and stimulating rhythm of the text.

This collection is primarily interested in the way in which contests around the perception, communication, management, government and deployment of risk are set up and are played out. The book is structured in terms of three interrelated themes. The opening theme, 'Setting the Risk Agenda', acts as a framework for both the theories and issues that crop up later in the book. The first four chapters, penned by Lupton, Wilkinson, O'Malley and Kemshall, map out the impacts of risk – and, moreover, of *thinking* about risk – in sociology, psychology, criminology and social policy. Lupton begins this section by discussing the catalytic effect of the risk society thesis and goes on to contrast Beck's approach with the work of followers of Foucault and Douglas. As well as contrasting the theoretical paradigms which have been employed to study risk, Lupton also reflects on the extent to which applied research has illuminated the social dimensions of risk. Following on from this, Wilkinson reviews psychological studies into risk perception and summarizes the principal findings in areas of psychometric, optimistic bias and social representations research. Having criticized some of the assumptions underpinning these approaches, Wilkinson considers the terrain on which greater fusion may be achieved between sociology and psychology. In Chapter 3, O'Malley subtly shifts the focus from the social and psychological to the criminological aspects of risk. In order to evaluate the relationship between criminality and risk, he unpacks the inroads risk has made in areas of criminal justice, crime prevention and policing. Deploying particular cases, O'Malley elucidates how risk is an 'abstract technology' that can be put to both progressive and injurious uses and points towards the ways in which risk can best be used to improve justice and security. Dovetailing with O'Malley's reflections, Chapter 4 explores the evolving role of risk in social policy. Through the prism of welfare provision, Kemshall scrutinizes both the historical and the contemporary role of the state in providing safety and security. At this juncture, the consequences of risk-led social policy on the construction of the prudential citizen are considered. Echoing O'Malley's sentiments, Kemshall is critical of the way in which risk has been politically wielded as an instrument of blame and employed as a driver of responsibilization. Both authors point up the myriad of ways in which discourses of risk can be utilized in the strategic interests of government.

In so far as these contributions mark the impressions made by risk on popular social science disciplines, the next quartet of chapters embrace the risk agenda. Here the emphasis is on demonstrating how risk tools and concepts can be used and developed to improve social knowledge and enhance our understanding in complex areas. In Chapter 5, Flynn opens Part II by explaining how risk is intrinsically associated with health, centring on recent trends in medical provision and contemporary government policy. Proposing an alternative conceptualization of the relationship between risk and illness, Flynn posits that health risks are best understood through a hybridic framework of weak social constructionism and critical realism. Building on and extending Flynn's analysis, Sanders in Chapter 6 deftly unpicks the vortex of issues surrounding sexuality and risk, presenting an overview of the institutional tradition which has sought to label expressions of sexuality as moral lapse, pathological and disruptive of social equilibrium. Using case studies of HIV/AIDS and female sex workers, Sanders goes on to show both how risk discourses are attached to particular forms of sexual behaviour and how 'otherness' is constructed in relation to risk as a means of regulation, exclusion and blame. The shared focus in Chapters 7 and 8 is on environmental risk and, more precisely, how issues of environmental risk are represented and interpreted. Anderson's focus in Chapter 7 fixes firmly on media representations of risk. It is argued that the shifting character of media representation reflects both changes in the nature of risk and transformations in the structure and functions of the mass media. Reviewing the literature in media studies, Anderson comments on the significance of organizational news values, the production process, selectivity and market demand on shaping media representations of risk. Looking towards the future, she asks what the rising use of 'citizen journalism' by media outlets – for example, camcorder footage, mobile phone video clips and digital photos – might mean for the reporting of risk incidents, such as the London bombings and the Asian tsunami. The flipside of media representations of environmental hazards are considered in Chapter 8, in which Macnaghten addresses the way in which the general public interpret information about environmental issues. Adding vim to the debate, Macnaghten is questioning of dominant narratives of 'global nature under threat' and circumspect about the universality and cohesiveness of 'an imagined global community' of environmentally aware citizens. This chapter calls for greater attention to the heterogeneous ways in which the environment is embodied, assessed and experienced. Drawing on cutting-edge research, Macnaghten suggests that life in the risk society may be altering the ways in which people experience nature, with environmental risk becoming less associated with 'saving the planet' and more about how the environment 'meets me, head on, in here'.

We have playfully entitled Part III 'Putting Risk in its Place'. These final four chapters of the book are critical of the rapid rise in prominence of risk as a unit idea in the social sciences and sceptical about what may be obscured by the current emphasis on all things risky. In Franklin's words, these chapters are political 'with a capital P'. Each author puts risk in its place by assuming a polemical position on the significance of risk in contemporary society and emphasizing the limits of the risk society perspective. For her part, in Chapter 9, Franklin dissects the restless dynamic between politics and risk, and, like Kemshall, highlights the influence of risk-led social policy in New Labour's 'Third Way' politics in Britain. After assessing the way in which risk has influenced the political agenda, the chapter ends by speculating on the possible themes that might shape political discussions beyond the risk society. In Chapter 10, Tombs and Whyte lay out their critique of the risk literature through a critical examination of the workplace as a site of risk distribution. While the bulk of academic attention has thus far been directed towards the 'universal' spread of employment risks – for example, redundancy, job insecurity and short-term contracts – this offering reasons that risks are still filtered through existing forms of stratification such as class, age, ethnicity and gender. Tombs and Whyte tackle the presumptions of the risk society thesis head on, flagging up Beck's lack of attention to the negligence of employers in ensuring workplace health and safety and its deleterious consequences for individuals around the globe. Contending that the class-myopia of the risk literature means that risk is all too often *'defined* – rather than *informed* – by popular and political priorities', Tombs and Whyte call for a renewed understanding of risk that appreciates the significance of unequal resources, power and inequality in shaping social relations. McMylor in Chapter 11 is similarly unconvinced about the epochal shift into the risk society and in his account of the economics of risk he draws upon the classical sociology of Weber, Marx and Durkheim. McMylor's historical approach employs Polanyi's analytic model of the economy and his subsequent work on the 'great transformation' to make sense of the relationship between risk and modern global capitalism. The economy is also pertinent to McGuigan's final chapter, although here it is meshed with the cultural to unravel the risky nature of work in the creative industries. Bringing together many of the key issues raised in the book – media effects, environmental harm and individualization – McGuigan muses over the positive and negative implications of the cultural prevalence of risk. In the Conclusion, the editors encourage greater opening-up of interdisciplinary channels to foster new forms of dialogue about the risk society and what might lie beyond it. For us, thinking about this is not only a theoretical, but also a practical endeavour. If political and social policies are to produce meaningful and tangible effects on the individuals and groups that find themselves jammed up against the hard edge of risk, it is imperative that they are informed by rigorous and balanced inquiry. This book is but a small part of this ongoing process.

## References

Beck, U. (1992) *Risk Society: Towards a New Modernity*. London: Sage.

Beck, U. (1995) *Ecological Politics in an Age of Risk*. Cambridge: Polity Press.

Beck, U. (1998) Politics of risk society, in J. Franklin (ed.) *The Politics of Risk Society*. Cambridge: Polity Press.

Bernstein, P. (1998) *Against the Gods: The Remarkable Story of Risk*. London: John Wiley & Sons, Ltd.

Elliott, A. (2002) Beck's sociology of risk: a critical assessment, *Sociology*, 36(2): 293–315.

Furedi, F. (2002) *Culture of Fear: Risk-taking and the Morality of Low Expectation*. London: Continuum.

Giddens, A. (1998) Risk society: the context of British politics, in J. Franklin (ed.) *The Politics of Risk Society*. Cambridge: Polity Press.

Mythen, G. (2004) *Ulrich Beck: A Critical Introduction to the Risk Society*. London: Pluto Press.

Mythen, G. (2005) From goods to bads? Revisiting the political economy of risk, *Sociological Research Online*, 10(3).

Pidgeon, N. (2000) Take a chance, *New Scientist*, 12 August: 46–7.

United Nations Commission on Human Security (2003) *Human Security Now*. New York: United Nations Publications.

Wilkinson, I. (2001) *Anxiety in a Risk Society*. London: Routledge.

# PART I
## SETTING THE RISK AGENDA

# 1 Sociology and risk

## Deborah Lupton

## Introduction

In sociological research and theory, the concept of risk has excited a great deal of interest in the past decade or so. Much of this interest resulted from the publication of German sociologist Ulrich Beck's *Risk Society: Towards a New Modernity* (1992) and contributions by such well-known theorists as Anthony Giddens have also added to the debates. So too, writers drawing on Michel Foucault's perspective on governmentality have applied this perspective to analyse the role of risk in modern societies. The anthropologist Mary Douglas's work on risk and danger has also been taken up by some sociologists in their research on risk. Each of these theorists offer a different perspective on risk as it is understood, dealt with and experienced in contemporary Western societies. Each has not only instigated interesting theoretical investigations into the social and cultural aspects of risk but also underpinned empirical research into how people conceptualize and experience risk. This chapter will explore both the theoretical ways of understanding the role played by risk as part of modern consciousness and also how social researchers have investigated risk empirically. The chapter begins with an overview of major theoretical perspectives on risk in sociology, each of which draws upon the theorists referred to above. I then give some examples of applied research studies undertaken which have elucidated the social and cultural aspects of risk that are emphasized by sociologists. The chapter ends with some comments on the possible directions for further research in this field and suggests how sociologists might productively collaborate with other social science disciplines.

## Major theoretical perspectives on risk

Elsewhere (Lupton 1999a, 1999b), I have identified three major theoretical perspectives in sociological writings on risk. These are the 'risk society', 'cultural/symbolic' and 'governmentality' perspectives. Each of these approaches is based upon a different body of literature and has a particular way of viewing risk and social responses to it. The risk society perspective draws upon the writings of Beck, and to a lesser extent, those by the English so-ciologist Giddens (1990, 1991). Beck's *Risk Society* and his other related works (1995, 1999) have received a great deal of attention from sociologists in the Anglophone world. The main tenet of Beck's theory is that contemporary Western societies are moving from an economy and way of life shaped by industrial processes – the era of early modernity, as he terms it – to a late modern period in which dangers and hazards have proliferated as a result of industrialization, urbanization and globalization. The prevention and mini-mization of 'bads' have therefore become a central problem for contemporary societies. Both individual personal lives and the political area are dominated by concerns and debates about risk.

Beck and Giddens argue that while all societies in human history have been challenged by threats and dangers, these have largely been the outcome of the natural world, such as infectious diseases, famine and natural disasters. The difference in this late modern era is that human responsibility is now attached to risk. People are seen to both cause risks and be responsible for their minimization. The dominant risks affecting communities are global and wide-reaching in their effects, and they are regarded as the product of human endeavour. These risks include environmental pollution, ionizing radiation and the contamination of foodstuffs. Even such natural catastrophes as landslides and floods are now viewed as caused by human action such as excessive land clearing. As Beck and Giddens argue, such risks often require expert identification and calculation, so that lay people must rely on expert advice in many cases about what risks are prevalent and how to deal with them. They are no longer so easily able to rely on such structuring phe-nomena as traditions, local knowledge(s), religious beliefs or habits to shape their decisions about risks. However, lay people have become more and more suspicious of expert judgements on risk as they know that experts disagree, governments often fail to act and that science and other products of early modernity themselves often generate risks. As a result, lay people are chal-lenged by continual uncertainties about what information or advice to trust and what to do about risk – a point Flynn touches on in Chapter 5 in relation to the disjunction between lay and expert views on health. In late modern societies, therefore, risk is a highly political concept, often inspiring grass-roots political action.

The cultural/symbolic approach draws upon the writings of Douglas (1966, 1985, 1992). Her work has not had quite the same influence in so-ciology as that of the risk society theorists, perhaps because, as a cultural anthropologist, she is writing outside the discipline of sociology. None-theless, Douglas's work has had some impact on sociological theorizing and empirical research on risk. Douglas's central belief is that ideas about risks are part of shared cultural understandings and practices that are founded on social expectations and responsibilities. Pre-established cultural beliefs help people to make sense of risk, and notions of risk are therefore not individualistic but rather shared within a community. For Douglas, as for Beck and Giddens, risk is a political concept, as it is used to attribute blame and responsibility for ill events. Unlike Beck and Giddens, however, Douglas is at pains to emphasize that contemporary responses to risk are not founded in distinctively new social, political or economic conditions, but rather are continuous with earlier Western responses as well as those found in traditional societies (Wilkinson 2001: 3).

Douglas's thoughts on risk stem from her earlier theorizing on the cultural meanings associated with concepts of purity, pollution and Otherness (Douglas [1966] 1969). She argues that communities are conceptualized symbolically by their members as human bodies, in which flows from inside to outside and vice versa must be policed. Both bodies and communities have borders and boundaries and protection from threats issuing from outside. Douglas sees risk as a cultural strategy whereby communities or subgroups make sense of danger and threats they perceive from outsiders, or Others. Risk beliefs and practices are ways, therefore, of maintaining social cohesion, stability and order and dealing with deviance. From this perspective, risk ideas function to protect symbolic boundaries and manage threats to social order. What is selected in a community to be labelled as 'risks' are phenomena that in some way threaten moral principles. Those individuals or social groups who are identified as posing this threat are deemed to be responsible and therefore subject to opprobrium and demands for restitution. As Wilkinson, O'Malley and Franklin argue in later chapters, risk ideas are therefore moral and ethical as well as political.

The governmentality perspective on risk draws on Michel Foucault's writings on how modern societies are controlled and organized in ways which invite voluntary participation from their citizens. Foucault himself did not write extensively about risk, but the general approach he takes to governmentality has been adopted by writers such as Castel (1991), Ewald (1991) and Dean (1999) to specifically discuss the role played by risk in the regulation of modern societies, which they describe as 'neo-liberal'. Neo-liberal societies are characterized by an approach to political rule which champions individual freedom and rights against the excessive intervention of the state. Expert knowledges are central to neo-liberal government, providing the guidelines whereby citizens are assessed, compared against norms and rendered productive.

Like writers from the risk society perspective, those within the governmentality perspective see risk as a central concept emerging from modernization. They are particularly interested in the discourses that surround and construct risk, or the organized ways of talking about and acting upon risk that are shared within social groups. The crucial aspect of risk, as regarded from the governmentality perspective, is that it is a major apparatus through which individuals in a society are encouraged to engage in self-regulation. Foucault discusses disciplinary power, or the ways in which citizens are regulated by states and their apparatuses. As he argues, in modern societies, citizens are not often overtly regulated by oppressive strategies; rather, they are encouraged to adopt certain practices voluntarily, as 'good citizens' and in pursuit of their own interests. External government of citizens is thereby internalized to become self-government. These practices may include wearing a seat belt while driving or eating a healthy diet so as to avoid risk of poor health.

As discourses on risk proliferate, more and more risk-avoiding practices are required of the 'good citizen'. Risk avoidance has become a moral enterprise relating to issues of self-control, self-knowledge and self-improvement. It is deemed people's own responsibility to take note of risk warnings and act on them accordingly. Those people who fail to engage in such behaviours may thus often find themselves stigmatized and subject to moral judgements. Like Douglas, therefore, writers adopting the governmentality perspective on risk are concerned with the moral meanings underpinning risk discourses, the ways that risk discourses and strategies are used to deal with social disorder and to regulate and order members of communities. They also seek to draw attention to the ways in which governments are increasingly devolving the responsibility for protection against risks upon the individual, and how this process affects how we view ourselves and others.

Each of these major sociological perspectives has a different way of conceptualizing risk as a phenomenon. The risk society theorists tend to take a fairly realist approach to risk in their emphasis on how risks have proliferated in late modern Western societies. From their perspective, risks are objective and real, although how we respond to them is always mediated through social and cultural processes. The cultural/symbolic perspective takes a somewhat more strongly social constructionist approach in emphasizing to a greater extent the role played by social and cultural processes in identifying what is risk. The governmentality perspective adopts the strongest social constructionist approach of the three perspectives. Nothing is seen to be a risk in itself; rather, events are constructed as risks through discourse. While all sorts of potential dangers or hazards exist in the world, only a small number of them are singled out and dealt with as 'risks'.

From a sociological perspective, therefore, risk is inextricably intertwined with social and cultural norms, concepts and habits. In contrast to the psychological views on risk discussed by Wilkinson in Chapter 2, the sociological and anthropological perspectives reviewed above do not see risk perceptions as the products of certain types of cognitive behaviours or the results of personality traits. Individuals' notions of and responses to risk are instead viewed as shared understandings emerging from membership of and acculturation into social and cultural groups. Unlike in the hard sciences, where risk is separated from its socio-cultural context and treated as an autonomous phenomenon, sociologists argue that risk can never be separated from the social and cultural lens through which we view it and understand it. Indeed, exactly which phenomena are deemed to be 'risks' – that is, dangers or hazards – and which are ignored or deemed to be safe, is the result of certain kinds of value judgements and decision-making. So too, risk knowledges are regarded as dynamic; changing in time and space. What are perceived to be 'risks' in one region or nation may be ignored in another; new risks emerge all the time, often to subside in the public's consciousness or be replaced by others. Other priorities, themselves based on cultural understandings, may enhance perceptions of risk or otherwise eclipse them.

One aspect of the socio-cultural differences that different cultures or groups may have in relation to perceiving risk is the views of lay publics compared with those of experts. Members of the lay public often conceptualize and experience risk as part of their everyday lives in entirely different ways from those whose profession involves the calculating of risk and how it will affect lay people. As is shown below, this is an area of research that has intrigued several sociologists of risk. Researchers have pointed out that experts often represent lay views on risk as ignorant, ill-judged, or adversely influenced by bias, cultural forces or emotional responses. Yet, for sociologists, expert views themselves cannot be isolated from the wider social and cultural milieux in which such people construct their own judgements about risk. Both lay and expert risk knowledges are the products of the pre-established beliefs and assumptions that individuals bring with them in making their judgements on risk.

## Empirical research into risk

Having elucidated key sociological theories of risk, I now wish to discuss some examples of empirical inquiries in the field which bring these theories to life. Over the past decade or so, an increasing number of empirical research studies have been carried out into the sociologies of risk: that is, investigating the ways in which people conceptualize and cope with risks as part of their lives and as members of particular social groups. Most of this research has tended to focus on a limited number of topical areas: environmental risks, health risks and risks associated with technologies. One example is a study of how people living in English rural communities conceptualize risks related to unpasteurized milk (Enticott 2003). Unlike the tendency in Western cultures to fear and disdain bacterial contamination as 'dirt' which could cause illness and disease, individuals supporting the continued sale of unpasteurized milk maintained that the 'purity' produced by pasteurization was in fact bad for one's health. Pasteurization was represented as 'unnatural' by changing the essential nature of milk, including destroying enzymes and protein structure which aid digestion. Unprocessed milk, in contrast, was portrayed as part of a strategy of natural immunology to prevent and cure illnesses, because of its unchanged molecular structure and the 'good' bacteria it was believed to contain. Consuming such milk was seen to be an important benefit of living in rural communities where it was available. This research demonstrates the importance of understanding the cultural and social belief systems underlying notions of risk and danger, as well as the importance of geographical location and local identities: in this case, rural regions of England, in which people held quite different views on unpasteurized milk compared with those held by experts and people living in urban areas. It emphasizes how such binary oppositions as clean/dirty, natural/artificial, rural/urban, pure/contaminated and Us/Them often underpin risk beliefs.

In further demonstrating the cultural differences in perceiving risk, this time on a national level, Korthals (2004: 185) discusses the case of cheeses made from unpasteurized milk. In France, he argues, such cheeses are considered an important part of the national culture and its cuisine: to be French is to eat such cheeses as part of one's everyday habits, and therefore questions of risk rarely arise. In countries such as the United States, in contrast, which has no such cultural link with these cheeses and also in which there is a great anxiety about hygiene and cleanliness, there is a heightened concern about the possible bacterial contamination inherent in the cheeses. They are therefore banned from import and sale. Such studies have been insightful in demonstrating how risk knowledges are constructed and how they affect people's everyday lives. Moving away from personality-based understandings of risk – for example, the notion that some people are inherently more predisposed towards risk taking than others – or psychometric analyses which focus on the mental processes of decision-making, this research emphasizes the importance of acknowledging the social, cultural, historical and geographical influences on how certain social groups or subcultures think about and respond to risk. It reveals that differences in conceptualizing and dealing with risks are predicated on cultural background, basic assumptions, expectations and lifestyles, all of which may differ from nation to nation or even regions within a nation.

I noted above that one area of research interest among sociologists of risk is in exploring lay compared with expert notions of risk. Wynne's (1996) research, for example, explored how English sheep farmers in Cumbria responded to warnings about the radioactive contamination caused by fallout from the 1986 Chernobyl nuclear accident. After hearing the views of scientific experts on how they should manage their livestock, the farmers were struck by the experts' ignorance of the farmers' practices and sheep behaviour. The farmers knew that unpredictability was part of dealing with their livestock but yet they had to deal with experts' pronouncements of prediction and control which were based on unrealistic assumptions. Lay knowledges based on years of experience and knowledge of the local conditions, including their unpredictability, were therefore denigrated and ignored in favour of scientific knowledge, which was seen to be more accurate by the experts, despite their lack of knowledge about the practicalities of their suggestions. A key point made by Wynne based on his findings is that neither lay risk knowledges nor expert knowledges should be viewed as lying outside social and cultural influences. Further, lay knowledges may often be more valid than expert knowledges in the assumptions they make about risk.

Sociologists have also been interested in the ways in which expert discourses that position people as being 'at risk' affects such individuals' views of their bodies and their selves. Medical and public health discourses have played an integral role in nominating which individuals are considered to be 'at risk' by virtue of belonging to certain socio-demographic groups or engaging in particular 'lifestyle' activities. Thus, for example, pregnant women who are over the age of 35 are deemed to be at higher risk of bearing a child with a genetic defect, or people who smoke cigarettes or drink alcohol to excess are singled out as being at higher risk of health problems and early mortality. Sometimes one's genetic predispositions are cause for being placed in an 'at risk' group, such as women who carry a gene that makes it more likely for them to develop breast cancer. In all these situations, being designated as 'at risk' can often become an important part of the way individuals view themselves.

Being categorized as 'at risk' from a medical problem means that one is placed in a liminal category of wellness: neither actually ill (yet) nor fully well. Such people may feel the need for constant reassurance that nothing is wrong, and indeed often actively seek out medical testing or other interventions to protect themselves from the imputed risk and gain some measure of certainty about what the future may hold (Lupton 1995, 1999c; Scott et al. 2005). Here, then, expert discourses derived from medical testing technologies may have a profound effect on lay people's risk awareness and their sense of the wellness of their bodies. While they may feel no illness physically at all, a test result has revealed incipient illness and thus generated a sense that an apparently well body is in fact harbouring disease.

As Anderson shows in Chapter 7, the mass media have been identified by sociologists as a central vehicle for conveying information to the lay public about risk. It has been argued by researchers that in many cases, the public would have no knowledge of certain phenomena designated by experts as 'risks' were it not for mass media coverage, particularly in the news media (Kitzinger 1999). Blame is also often a key aspect of media coverage of risk. The individuals, social groups or institutions that are identified as being responsible for risk are frequently castigated and treated as outsiders. In line with Douglas's emphasis on the threat posed by the 'Other', those deemed to be responsible for risk are often out-groups seen by mainstream groups as deviant. In the case of HIV/AIDS, for example, gay men, intravenous drug users and heterosexuals with many sexual partners were singled out for public opprobrium for being 'risk carriers' (Lupton 1994).

Lack of appropriate action to minimize risk or attempts to hide the extent of risk on the part of government agencies or politicians are also often portrayed in the mass media as being to blame for causing risk to the wider population, as in the case of BSE ('mad cow disease') as it was reported in the British press (Miller 1999). But responsibility for reducing one's own exposure to risk is also often sheeted home to the individual in media reports. Thus, for example, people who are overweight and thus seen to be subject to a higher chance of health risks such as diabetes and heart disease are often portrayed in the mass media as culpable for their risk exposure because of lack of self-control and greed, while parents are represented as responsible for controlling their young children's body weight (Lupton 2004).

While the news media do frequently report on risk issues, and often in a very dramatic and attention-attracting manner, it is important to emphasize that heightened news media attention to a risk issue does not necessarily translate into concern on the part of lay audiences of those media. People respond to media in complex ways, and indeed may challenge or resist the dominant messages to which they are exposed, arguing that the messages are inaccurate or do not apply to them (Wilkinson 2001; Davin 2003). For example, an English study on mothers' responses to media coverage of alleged health risks for infants and young children associated with the measles, mumps and rubella vaccination found that while the media were identified by the interviewees as important sources of information on these health risks, social networks and interaction with health professionals were also very important in helping the women to make up their minds about whether or not they should allow their children to have the vaccination (Petts and Niemeyer 2004).

In my own research on the reporting of food risks in selected newspapers in Australia (Lupton 2004, 2006), I found that many topics raised as concerns in the press accounts were hardly or not at all mentioned by the people who were interviewed about food risks around the same time as the press reports were published. Nonetheless, the major topics on food risks reported in the media, the health risks caused by obesity in children and in adults, were concerns shared by the lay audiences who were interviewed. Further, people saw these risks as under their own control, and thus their own responsibility, in a similar way to which the press had represented these risks. Clearly audiences' concerns are not simply generated by exposure to the mass media. People may receive information about the risks of obesity, for example, from personal experience, friends, medical practitioners, commercial advertising, and so on. People are also often quite knowledgeable and cynical about the way in which the media sensationalize risk to attract audiences (Petts and Niemeyer 2004; Lupton 2006). There is no doubt, however, that the news media act as an important voice in setting an agenda for which phenomena are identified *qua* risks and how serious they are seen to be. The media also to some extent control what kinds of meanings and messages are publicly disseminated on risks.

While most sociological research on risk has thus far focused on environmental, health and technological risks, a number of intriguing studies conducted by sociologists have examined other aspects of risk. For example, while Beck has largely concentrated his writings on environmental, technological and employment-related risks, with Beck-Gernsheim he has published a book-length examination of how risks are conceptualized in relation to intimate relationships (Beck and Beck-Gernsheim 1995). An important concept emerging from this work is that of individualization. This concept relates to the ways in which people perceive their selves and their relationships as requiring constant 'improvement' and 'work', including frequent decision-making. In a social context in which traditions can no longer be relied upon to shape personal biographies, the individual must take action to shape her or his own destiny. Risks are related to the choices people make: whether or not to get married to a particular person, have children, and so on. Here again, the notion of human agency and responsibility for risk is accentuated. Rather than being able to see outcomes as a result of fate, as was the case in earlier eras where tradition dictated actions such as marriage and child-bearing, people are now held responsible for outcomes in their lives: whether or not, for example, their marriage or career succeeds.

One example of the current emphasis on personal responsibility for life outcomes is a recent debate in Australia about to what extent, and at what age, IVF treatments for infertile couples should be funded by the government rather than the couples themselves. Public debate on this question often centred on what was seen to be women's life choices. Those women who had deferred childbearing until their mid-to-late thirties or early forties and then found that they had problems conceiving were represented by some commentators as not deserving of governmental financial support for infertility treatment because they had decided to leave conception until it was too late to occur naturally. These commentators argued that these women should have taken steps to attempt to conceive when they were younger and less in need of medical assistance. According to the commentators, it was therefore these women's 'fault' that they were infertile, and hence the women should bear the burden of any costs associated with fertility treatment. Rather than the issue of female fertility being viewed as part of a wider social, cultural and economic web – including, for example, changes in marriage patterns that have resulted in people marrying at a later age, women's participation in the workforce, with its own constraints on their decisions about childbearing, and men's attitudes to childbearing – individual women were held responsible for their fertility problems. The problem had become individualized.

Little sociological research has explored how people conceptualize risk across the broad range of phenomena that have been labelled 'risks'. In my own research on risk and everyday life with John Tulloch (Lupton and Tulloch 2002; Tulloch and Lupton 2003), we were interested in understanding how people understand and describe the notion of risk in general, and what kinds of risks they saw as affecting their lives across the lifespan. One important aspect of risk and everyday life that we discovered in our research was that while people tended to be wary of risk and to take steps to avoid it, they were also at pains to emphasize that voluntary risk taking is an integral part of life, and indeed, of selfhood. As our interviewees noted, voluntary risk taking might include engaging in dangerous sports such as surfing or rock-climbing, but it also includes such actions as getting married or separating from a partner, deciding to have children, taking on a mortgage, changing cities or countries or leaving an old job and seeking a new career. Risk taking, therefore, permeated many aspects of ordinary daily actions and choices.

In our research, the positive aspects of risk were seen to be threefold. First, risk taking was viewed as a way of moving out of a 'rut', to progress in life rather than allowing oneself to stagnate. Risk-taking was viewed as a means of achieving self-actualization and accomplishment, a chance to improve the self by taking on challenges and demonstrating to oneself that one could meet and conquer these challenges. Second, risk taking was a means of engaging in heightened emotional states, of perhaps experiencing fear or trepidation but once, having met the challenge posed by taking a risk, of experiencing exhilaration, 'getting a buzz' or a thrill. This heightened emotion was pleasurable in its sheer intensity and its ability to transport people from the mundane nature of the everyday. Risk taking, therefore, was viewed as a means of distraction and release from the demands of normal life. Third, and in contrast to the previous discourse of emotional release, risk taking involving physical activities was described as a means of exerting control over one's body and self. People saw engaging in risky activities as allowing them to push the boundaries of their bodies, to conquer negative emotions of fear and feelings of vulnerability and, through use of their skills, to maintain control over a situation that threatened to descend into chaos.

Such research is able to demonstrate that 'official' notions of risk, including those in expert discourses that represent people who deliberately take risks as ignorant or reckless, often fail to recognize the multiple meanings around risk that underpin people's everyday lives. It is in such findings that sociological research can be so valuable: by challenging accepted 'official' or expert notions of risk or showing that the phenomena of risk taking and risk perception are far more complex than is often realized.

## Conclusion: beyond the risk society

While sociological (and in the case of Douglas's work, anthropological) theory has much to contribute to an understanding of how risk is conceptualized and understood in modern contemporary societies, it also has its weaknesses. One of these is a tendency for the grand theorizing of writers like Beck, Giddens and Douglas to lack a firm grounding in empirical research which is able to support their propositions. Several researchers, including those referred to above, have stepped in to fill this breach, but writings on risk which are able to cogently and thoroughly link the two aspects of risk scholarship remain quite rare. Any comprehensive understanding of the socio-cultural underpinnings of risk would ideally incorporate both a grasp of the grand theories and how empirical findings support or challenge these theories. Here then, remain opportunities for scholars of risk to fill this hiatus in socio-cultural research.

It is important to bear in mind that risk concepts are fluid and dynamic over time and space. It therefore remains vital for researchers to carry out empirical studies that are able to map the complexities, contradictions and changes in risk understandings, on the part of both lay publics and experts. In particular, research which investigates the meaning of risk in people's everyday lives and which can identify any differences between social groups, including those grounded in geographical or national differences, offers directions for future research. There are still gaps in understanding how people conceptualize risks in relation to intimate relationships, financial decisions, engaging in paid work, bearing and raising children or migrating to a different city or country, for example. It is possible that such research may identify challenges to the grand theorists in such a way as to stimulate new debate on what may lie beyond the 'risk society' and alternative ways of theorizing risk from a socio-cultural perspective.

One way to achieve advances in risk research is to engage in interdisciplinary collaboration within the social sciences. To some extent this has already taken place. I have commented above on the importance of the anthropological ideas contributed by Douglas to sociological risk theorizing. So, too, I have emphasized the role played by the mass media in influencing the development of risk beliefs. Here researchers in the fields of media and cultural studies have provided research findings of great interest to sociologists and will continue to do so in future risk research. Further, I have drawn attention to the way in which the area or country of residence may influence risk beliefs and to the potential to explore further how such beliefs are formed. Cultural geography offers the potential for an intermingling of sociological concerns with the meanings of risk and geographers' interest in the integral role played by space and place in people's views of risk. For example, how does type of dwelling (high rise flat versus large suburban house) and place of residence (for example, urban versus rural locations) influence the ways in which individuals conceptualize risk from various sources? How do socio-demographic factors such as gender, age, nationality and ethnicity then interact with place and space in people's risk concepts and behaviours?

Less common in the literature is research that combines a focus on how individuals mentally assess and process risk, how they order risks from important to unimportant, as is common in social psychological research studies, with exploring the ways in which these people are influenced by their social milieu, as is the concern of many sociological studies. Such research would be valuable in both acknowledging the importance of the social settings in which risk ideas are developed and of such psychological factors as personality traits which may influence risk assessment and risk-taking behaviour. While interdisciplinary collaborations are not limited to these examples, they provide some ideas about the ways in which sociological risk research could move forward by engaging with researchers working in other social science disciplines.

## Study questions

1. How do sociological perspectives on risk tend to differ from psychological perspectives?
2. What are the similarities and differences in the three major theoretical approaches to risk within sociology?
3. What is a social constructionist perspective on risk?

## References

Beck, U. (1992) *Risk Society: Towards a New Modernity*. London: Sage.

Beck, U. (1995) *Ecological Politics in an Age of Risk*. Cambridge: Polity Press.

Beck, U. (1999) *World Risk Society*. Cambridge: Polity Press.

Beck, U. and Beck-Gernsheim, E. (1995) *The Normal Chaos of Love*. Cambridge: Polity Press.

Castel, R. (1991) From dangerousness to risk, in G. Burchell, C. Gordon and P. Miller (eds) *The Foucault Effect: Studies in Governmentality*. London: Harvester/Wheatsheaf.

Davin, S. (2003) Healthy viewing: the reception of medical narratives, *Sociology of Health and Illness*, 25(6): 662–79.

Dean, M. (1999) Risk, calculable and incalculable, in D. Lupton (ed.) *Risk and Sociocultural Theory: New Directions and Perspectives*. Cambridge: Cambridge University Press.

Douglas, M. ([1966] 1969) *Purity and Danger: An Analysis of the Concepts of Pollution and Taboo*. London: Routledge and Kegan Paul.

Douglas, M. (1985) *Risk Acceptability According to the Social Sciences*. New York: Russell Sage Foundation.

Douglas, M. (1992) *Risk and Blame: Essays in Cultural Theory*. London: Routledge.

Enticott, G. (2003) Lay immunology, local foods and rural identity: defending unpasteurized milk in England, *Sociologia Ruralis*, 43(3): 257–70.

Ewald, F. (1991) Insurance and risks, in G. Burchell, C. Gordon and P. Miller (eds) *The Foucault Effect: Studies in Governmentality*. London: Harvester/Wheatsheaf.

Giddens, A. (1990) *The Consequences of Modernity*. Cambridge: Polity Press.

Giddens, A. (1991) *Modernity and Self-Identity*. Cambridge: Polity Press.

Kitzinger, J. (1999) Researching risk and the media, *Health, Risk and Society*, 1(1): 55–69.

Korthals, M. (2004) *Before Dinner: Philosophy and Ethics of Food*. Dordrecht: Springer.

Lupton, D. (1994) *Moral Threats and Dangerous Desires: AIDS in the News Media*. London: Taylor and Francis.

Lupton, D. (1995) *The Imperative of Health: Public Health and the Regulated Body*. London: Sage.

Lupton, D. (1999a) *Risk*. London: Routledge.

Lupton, D. (1999b) Introduction: risk and sociocultural theory, in D. Lupton (ed.) *Risk and Sociocultural Theory: New Directions and Perspectives*. Cambridge: Cambridge University Press.

Lupton, D. (1999c) Risk and the ontology of pregnant embodiment, in D. Lupton (ed.) *Risk and Sociocultural Theory: New Directions and Perspectives*. Cambridge: Cambridge University Press.

Lupton, D. (2004) 'A grim health future': food risks in the Sydney press, *Health, Risk and Society*, 6(2): 187–200.

Lupton, D. (2006) Lay discourses and beliefs related to food risks: an Australian perspective, *Sociology of Health and Illness*, 27(4): 448–67.

Lupton, D. and Tulloch, J. (2002) 'Life would be pretty dull without risk': voluntary risk-taking and its pleasures, *Health, Risk and Society*, 4(2): 113–24.

Miller, D. (1999) Risk, science and policy: definitional struggles, information management, the media and BSE, *Social Science and Medicine*, 49: 1239–55.

Petts, J. and Niemeyer, S. (2004) Health risk communication and amplification: learning from the MMR vaccination controversy, *Health, Risk and Society*, 6(1): 7–23.

Scott, S., Prior, L., Wood, F. and Gray, J. (2005) Repositioning the patient: the implications of being 'at risk', *Social Science and Medicine*, 60: 1869–79.

Tulloch, J. and Lupton, D. (2003) *Risk and Everyday Life*. London: Sage.

Wilkinson, I. (2001) Social theories of risk perception: at once indispensable and insufficient, *Current Sociology*, 49(1): 1–22.

Wynne, B. (1996) May the sheep safely graze? A reflexive view of the expert–lay knowledge divide, in S. Lash, B. Szerszinski and B. Wynne (eds) *Risk, Environment and Modernity: Towards a New Ecology.* London: Sage.

## Further reading

Beck, U. (1992) *Risk Society: Towards a New Modernity.* London: Sage.
Boyne, R. (2003) *Risk.* Buckingham: Open University Press.
Douglas, M. (1992) *Risk and Blame: Essays in Cultural Theory.* London: Routledge.
Lupton, D. (1999) *Risk.* London: Routledge.
Tulloch, J. and Lupton, D. (2003) *Risk and Everyday Life.* London: Sage.

# 2 Psychology and risk

## Iain Wilkinson

## Introduction

I write this chapter as a sociologist with an interest in the existential conditions of individuals in modern societies. My research involves an attempt to expose the social conditions and cultural processes that shape the ways we *feel* about ourselves and towards others; and, further, the extent to which matters of personal feeling impact upon the institutional dynamics of cultural production, political consciousness and social change. I am interested in the psychology of risk in relation to the ways in which researchers study social perceptions of potentially hazardous events, and more specifically, in connection with the distressing feelings aroused by the anticipation of possible danger, injury and harm. My approach to this subject derives from a critical engagement with the ways in which social theorists account for the *lived experience* of risk in modern societies; particularly when matters of risk are framed for public attention via graphic portrayals of human suffering (Wilkinson 2005).

I am interested to bring analytical attention to bear upon the ways in which social theorists incorporate generalizing assumptions about popular modes of consciousness and feeling within their writing upon the relative impacts of risks upon society (Wilkinson 2001a). Accordingly, one might say that in relation to the sociology of risk, my critical focus is directed towards the implicit accounts of human psychology contained within sociological representations of the shared thoughts and emotions of people faced with risks in everyday life. It is helpful to make clear some of the political and ideological motives that appear to be incorporated within writers' favoured accounts of the popular experience of a risk society and in common cultures of risk consciousness. Moreover, the existing empirical research evidence is examined that can be used to either develop or challenge theoretical conceptualizations of people's thoughts about, feelings towards and individual responses to various types of risk (Wilkinson 2001b).

Such interests permit reflection more broadly upon the relationship between psychology and sociology. In this regard, I may be more sympathetic than some of my colleagues towards the suggestion that, at various points in its history, sociology has been inclined to promote an 'over-socialized' conception of human drives and motives (Wrong 1961). Under the influence of writers such as Horney (1937; 1950), Fromm (1942, 1956), and Craib (1989, 1994, 1998), I am prepared to recognize a complementary role for psychoanalysis and psychodynamic conceptualizations of human subjectivity within sociology (Vogler 2000). Nevertheless, while I am prepared to admit that there are limits to a sociological account of 'the self', I still place a greater emphasis upon social rather than individual factors when it comes to explaining personal outlooks, affective states and forms of behaviour. To this end, there is good evidence to suggest that our individual personalities and life chances are much more a product of our social, economic and cultural circumstances than they are a matter of genetic inheritance or parental influence. I am generally inclined to place an accent more upon the social determining the individual according to relative conditions of material wealth and cultural opportunity, rather than the individual shaping the social according to the vagaries of psychological make-up, traits of personality and neurophysiology (Wilkinson 2001a: 15–84).

My sympathies lie with those who might be described as working towards a 'critical psychology'; that is, a 'psychosocial' approach, that works to make clear the lived reality of the personal domain within the dynamics of social, economic and political processes (Frosh 2003). In so far as I am prepared to incorporate references to psychological research within my accounts of our social subjectivity, I would always have us recognize the ideological investments that are placed in this discipline's professional commitments to 'methodological individualism' and the empirical veracity of research within a 'laboratory paradigm' (Rose 1998). I am much more inclined to locate the source of personal distress and unhappiness in socio-economic and cultural processes than in individual factors and deeply suspicious of the interests of power and privilege that stand to gain from the work of adjusting people to cope better with the prevailing status quo as though this is some kind of 'impersonal necessity' that is beyond our collective powers to change; the great majority of our discontents are more social than individual and any adequate 'treatment' of personal neuroses should begin with a questioning of society (Smail 1984, 1998, 1999).

In this chapter the current state of psychological research into matters of risk perception is reviewed and some analytical commentary upon the possible ways in which sociologists might engage with this work is provided. The first section describes some of the working hypotheses that shape the ways in which psychologists study perceptions of risk. Summaries of research findings are also provided that reveal a considerable diversity of ways in which individuals appear to acquire and create meanings for risk. In the second section, two distinctive sociological responses to the psychology of risk are outlined. The first of these proposes to marry sociology with psychology so as to advance a 'meta-analysis' of risk geared towards the enhancement of strategies of risk management and communication. By contrast, the second holds to the view that sociologists should stand at a critical distance from this work, on the grounds that the practice of psychology coupled with the language of risk is inextricably bound to an ideology of individualism that obscures the socio-economic determinants of people's life chances and cultural outlooks. In the concluding section, the suggestion is raised that, at the very least, the cumulative findings of the psychological research into risk perception serve to cast doubt upon any attempt to reduce the complexity of people's thoughts and feelings about these matters to a simple and one-sided account of risk consciousness. In this regard, as Lupton has already intimated in Chapter 1, many of the most celebrated social theories of risk, while championing their favoured accounts of cultural character of our times, might be criticized for making little attempt to engage with the many nuances, contradictions and varieties of risk perception in the contexts of everyday life. Moreover, readers are urged to consider the possibility that the failure of social theorists to engage with these matters may not only take place as a result of their apparent reluctance to develop theories from the findings of empirical research, but further, that this might also be related to the ways in which risk discourse and analysis tends to be rooted in a highly individualistic world-view. Accordingly, if we are to engage in debate over what lies 'beyond the risk society', I argue that as a point of departure we should be far more circumspect with regard to the possible ways in which the adoption of risk as a unit of sociological analysis serves to divert attention away from the *social* reality of lived experience.

## The psychology of risk: an analytical summary

The concept of risk is now used to describe a considerable diversity of social problems, cultural experiences and forms of behaviour. It is increasingly the case that any mention of risk requires careful qualification; given the variety of analytical, heuristic and ideological investments placed in this term, we must be careful to work at identifying the precise ways in which it is being put to use as part of the terminology of social science. For the purposes of this chapter it may be useful to begin by noting some of the key differences between sociology and psychology over the interests that tend to feature as the rationale for risk research.

In the contexts of sociology, a great deal of attention has been directed towards the variety of ways in which people are inclined to codify 'danger' as 'risk' in order to cast a negative *moral* judgement upon the desirability of scientific and technological innovations as well as the trustworthiness of expert opinion. Accordingly, by noting the widespread – and relatively recent

– adoption of 'risk' as a popular pseudonym for 'potential hazard' or 'impending catastrophe', sociologists understand themselves to be witness to a transformation in cultural outlooks that lead some sections of society to display an aggravated hostility towards the progressive claims of modern state-sponsored science. There are many disagreements within the sociological community as to the social meaning, lived consequences and political ramifications of emergent forms of risk society; and these are further complicated by the ways in which the language of risk is at the same time appropriated as a 'governmental' technique of Western nation-states. However, notwithstanding many conflicts of interpretation, the majority of sociologists share in the basic understanding that the popularization of risk discourse signals a fundamental shift in the ethical character of public debates that shape the social conduct of individuals and institutions in modern societies. On these grounds, sociological engagements with this subject tend to be inextricably bound to more broad-ranging questions concerning the social origins and cultural formations of 'risk' *ideologies* and their relative impacts upon the institutional dynamics of social change. In most cases, sociological inquiries into matters of risk are distinguished by a concern to explain the experience and exercise of *power relations* in contemporary society (Freudenberg and Pastor 1992).

By contrast, psychological studies of risk largely take place out of a concern to expose people's common-sense approaches to *the estimation of probabilities*. For the most part, psychologists have not been interested in generalizing debates over the cultural formation of moral character or the direction of social change, but rather, have been preoccupied with 'scientifically' documenting the ways in which individuals *visualize, encode* and *mentally process* information relating to a select range of 'natural', 'social' and 'technological' hazards. Psychological interest in matters of risk perception tends to be concerned with the rule of thumb measures or mental heuristics by which individuals cast judgements upon the magnitude of possible dangers and calculate the likelihood of experiencing harm. In the psychological domain, risk research is overwhelmingly committed to understanding how individuals estimate risks so as to expose their relative capacities for forms of mathematical reasoning. In this context, questions relating to the ways in which social power is exercised tend to fall outside the remit of scholarly concerns; psychologists tend to display little regard for the extent to which subjective perceptions of risk – as well as the assessments of scientific experts – are ideologically stylized in support of sectional interests. The tone of psychological research tends to be set to appeal to standards of 'scientific rigour' and the generally stated aim is to acquire an 'objective' (i.e. politically neutral) understanding of the cognitive techniques by which individuals work at presenting 'rational' explanations for their estimations of risk.

It is possible to group the psychological work on risk into three distinct bodies of research: (1) the 'heuristics approach', which is otherwise known as the 'psychometric paradigm'; (2) the 'optimistic bias approach'; and (3) the 'social representations approach'. While the work conducted under the auspices of 'psychometrics' and 'optimistic biases' may be more readily identified with my characterization of 'the psychology of risk', the social representations approach moves psychology to the threshold of sociology. Before I outline some of possible ways in which sociologists might respond to this work, I offer a brief synopsis of each approach.

## The psychometric paradigm

The psychometric paradigm is probably the best-known body of psychological research on risk and is heavily associated with the work of Slovic (2000) and his various collaborations. Drawing inspiration from Tversky and Kahneman's (1974) earlier research on the cognitive biases and mental heuristics that govern individual approaches to probabilistic thinking, Slovic and colleagues have been overwhelmingly concerned to document the taken-for-granted assumptions that seemingly determine the ways in which people perceive technological risk. The presentation of this work tends to be structured around a comparison between 'expert' assessments of various technological risks and 'lay' perceptions of their relative chances of being negatively affected by those risks. On this account, the 'objective' dimensions of risk are set in accordance with official records of annual accident and fatality rates associated with a host of risky behaviours and technological interventions. These 'objective' measures of risk are then compared to lay people's intuitive perceptions of risk, with research being focused upon the attempt to explain the discrepancies between the former and the latter. The overriding aim is to contribute to the development of a more scientifically 'rational' consensus with regard to the reality of the risks we face.

Lay people may be asked to categorize and estimate risks in various ways, but most research follows the 'classic' design of the earliest studies by requiring them to judge the severity of a particular type of risk according to scales indicating the extent to which it evokes a sense of 'dread', is judged to be 'known' or 'unknown', is perceived to be 'new' or 'old' or is assessed as 'voluntary' or 'involuntary'. Researchers typically find that, while expert assessments of risk are in line with evidence presented by technical estimates of annual fatalities, lay judgements tend to be heavily influenced by factors beyond the actuarial domain, such as their understanding of the catastrophic potential of hazards, their relative sense of control over risky activities and their perception of the threat posed by a particular technology to future generations. These differences between expert assessments and lay perceptions of risk are particularly marked in the case of technologies associated with the nuclear and chemical industries. Psychometric researchers have consistently found that, while experts categorize the risks associated with nuclear power and chemical processing plants as extremely low when compared with those of most other social activities and technological practices, lay persons tend to identify these as among the most dreadful and unknown of risks.

Such findings are understood to reveal that most people are not very good at estimating probabilities. However, researchers such as Slovic are not so crude as to then label the typical lay person as 'irrational' or 'phobic'; rather, an explanation for this fact is developed in terms of an analysis of the mechanics of cognition alongside a critical focus on the quality of information about risk made available to individuals within the public domain. Accordingly, lay perceptions of risk are understood to be both a product of the mental heuristics that are typically deployed in everyday life to deal with risky situations and a result of the 'stigmatized' ways in which matters of technological and scientific risk are portrayed in the news media (Heimer 1988; Flynn et al. 2001). On these grounds, it is argued that experts in the field of risk communication must both work at correcting 'inaccuracies' in the portrayal of scientific technologies in the public realm, and at the same time find ways of presenting 'the truth' of matter that are in tune with our intuitive capacities for processing such information. The overriding contention here is that it is possible to bolster the scientific rationality of popular understandings of the social costs and benefits of modern technologies; but this requires governments and scientists to concentrate their attentions upon improving the quality and production of public information about risk (Powell and Leiss 1997; Slovic 2000). However, on this matter it is also important to note that few are prepared to place much confidence in existing practices of risk communication as the ideal means to achieve this goal. The hopes invested in public education as the immediate 'solution' to problems of risk perception are not matched by any good evidence to suggest that this is the most positive and reliable means to bring about the major changes in an individual's expressed thoughts and feelings about technological hazards (Fischoff 1995; Leiss 1996; Jallinoja and Aro 2000; Scholderer and Frewer 2003).

More recently, the attentions of Slovic and his colleagues have turned to the moderating role played by emotions within judgements of risk. In this context, they have been interested to establish the ways in which an 'affect heuristic' motivates the ways in which people reason about risky decisions (Alhakami and Slovic 1994; Finucane et al. 2000). So far, major findings have concerned the extent to which judgements about risk appear to be structured by the quality and intensity of the negative feelings that individuals hold regarding potential hazards. Moreover, in working to understand precisely how such feelings are acquired, the suggestion had been raised that societies develop a common 'affective pool' of evaluative responses to risk; but to date, no serious research has been conducted into the conditions by which such a phenomenon is established and sustained. Ultimately, however, this research aims to piece together a more precise account of the interrelationships between cognition and affect, so as to arrive at a clearer understanding of how feelings might 'mislead' reason (Slovic 2000). Once again, the principal objective is to enable the development of a more scientifically informed cross-societal understanding of technological risks that promotes a greater consensus with regard to their relative costs and benefits.

### The optimistic bias approach

The various works that can be grouped together as examples of 'the optimistic bias' approach share some of the basic interests of the psychometric paradigm, namely a commitment to understanding the ways in which mental capacities for estimating probabilities may be rendered 'deficient' by the intuitive rules of thumb that govern everyday perceptions of risk. However, there is a major difference between these two approaches when it comes to the particular types of cognitive 'errors' that they aim to explain. Where the focus of the psychometric paradigm is fixed firmly upon the task of understanding lay people's psychological disposition to *overestimate* the risk of harm and exaggerate the catastrophic potential of various forms of technology, by contrast 'the optimistic bias' approach is more concerned to highlight the ways in which individuals are inclined to *underestimate* risks to themselves as compared with the ways in which they perceive risks for others. A key matter for concern here is the discovery that, while people may well be inclined to judge risks to be high *for society*, they are far less likely to identify themselves to be *personally* at risk. In individual minds, societal level and personal level judgements about risk are separated; where an individual may express a great deal of pessimism with regard to the risk-related prospects of society in general, they are far less likely to associate themselves with such a judgement. Indeed, researchers tend to be particularly concerned to highlight the ways in which the majority of individuals tend to be overly *optimistic* when it comes to assessing their own chances of avoiding harm.

While a great deal of psychometric research concerns the disjunctions between expert assessments and lay perceptions of risk in connection with the technologies of the nuclear and chemical industries, researchers with an interest in optimistic bias have tended to be more concerned with everyday risks relating to matters of health and safety (Weinstein 1980, 1982; Taylor 1989; McKenna 1993; Taylor and Armor 1996). For example, it has featured as a means to explain why individuals, despite being informed about the risks of contracting sexually transmitted diseases, still fail to practise safe sex (Taylor et al. 1992; Sheeran et al. 1999). In these instances, considerable disagreements remain as to how one should interpret the psychological significance of such a phenomenon. Optimistic bias has been attributed to 'information processing errors' connected with people's lack of personal experience with particular hazards, as evidence of the existence of an 'illusory' sense of control over one's life chances, as an illustration of the moderating force of negative affective states on individual capacities for estimating probabilities, and further, as a sign of self-efficacy which under most ordinary circumstances is a positive sign of mental health (Weinstein 1987; McKenna 1993; Taylor and Brown 1994; Weinstein and Lyon 1999; Helweg-Larsen and Shepperd 2001). While it is a widely documented phenomenon, the psychological explanation for optimistic bias remains open to debate.

Along with a focus upon optimistic bias, researchers tend to be preoccupied with a set of 'managerial' concerns, which, again, are notably different from those of the psychometric paradigm. Where Slovic and colleagues have been concerned with the task of allaying people's apparently excessive anxieties concerning potentially catastrophic risks to society, in studies of optimistic bias the general aim is to find ways to make people *more* preoccupied with the personal risks they face. A great deal of this research takes place as part of health promotion campaigns, where the aim is to persuade people to adopt precautionary behaviours designed to improve their overall quality of life and prospects for longevity (Kreuter 1999). While studies of risk perception within the psychometric paradigm tend to debate processes of risk communication out of a concern to attenuate people's worries about technological hazards, for those with an interest in 'optimistic bias' the focus is placed upon the potential to provoke people to worry more about what they can do to avoid potential hazards; the major difficulty here concerns the art of persuading individuals to take measures to minimize their personal risk of harm. The point on which researchers all agree is that established procedures of risk communication fail to match their ambitions; either in opposition to or in support of cultures of precaution, experts remain frustrated by the extent to which public perceptions of risk resist technical management and change.

### The social representations approach

The social representations approach within risk research is largely associated with the work of Joffe (1999, 2002, 2003). However, it should be noted from the outset that Joffe's studies are rooted in a much broader tradition of French research inspired by Moscovici's psychological elaboration of Durkheim's essay 'Individual and collective representations' (Durkheim 1974; Moscovici 1984). Such work rejects the conception of individual motivations and behaviours as primarily driven by a rational process of decision-making. Within this tradition, cognitive psychology, as displayed within the psychometric paradigm and optimistic bias approach, is understood to provide us with an overly mechanistic account of human thought and feeling, and further, is held to be methodologically misguided in its overall approach to the study of risk perception (Joffe 2003: 56–60). As far as Joffe is concerned, we should not be so much preoccupied with an account of risk perception that presents individuals as cognitively deficient or heuristically misguided, but, rather, should concentrate upon the ways in which individuals interpret the meaning of risk in accordance with *social forces* of moral solidarity and group belonging. On this account, individual perceptions of risk are more intricately related to the ways in which social groups use cultural symbols to interpret the psycho-social meaning of threatening circumstances than a result of the quality of scientific information and public education they receive about potential hazards.

In the social representations approach we are urged above all else to understand individual perceptions of risk to be shaped as part of a collective defensive reaction to the anxieties aroused by the shocking information about potential hazards that is presented to us via the mass media. In Joffe's (1999: 8) words, it is always the case that 'the "we" is sedimented in the "I"'. The common experiences and world-views of the social groups to which an individual belongs are a major influence over the forms of interpretation they give to new knowledge about risk. Understandings of new potential threats are always coloured by the ideas that a group associates with past dangers. Accordingly, for the purposes of scientific analysis, matters of risk perception should always be framed and understood as part of a broader cultural history of interpretations of, and responses to, hazards. Perhaps more importantly here is the further contention that people are always quick to associate the source of dangers with 'others' outside their group, and that once this association is made, the task of dealing with 'risk' is commonly reduced to strategies of exclusion and avoidance; group psychology appears to work according to the assumption that so long as 'the other' can be kept at bay, the potential hazard can be avoided.

Joffe's favourite examples of the responses 'not me' and 'others are to blame' are drawn from cross-cultural comparisons of social representations of the risk of contracting AIDS. She maintains that while the majority of South Africans tend to associate the disease with sinful practices of Western populations, in Britain one finds a common association of the origins of AIDS with the 'alien' sexual practices of African tribes (Joffe 1999: 40–2). On this account, social representations of the risk of contracting AIDS function both to shore up a group's sense of solidarity and self-righteousness as well as a means to portray this as a problem for 'others' who are not like 'us'; differences in 'risk perception' are much more a reflection of a group's defensive reactions against anxiety than a product of mental heuristics in the estimation of statistical probabilities.

Clearly such an approach has much in common with Douglas's (1985, 1992) cultural/symbolic perspective. Indeed, they are both rooted in the same

Durkheimian premises. Here psychology stands at the threshold of a particular sociological tradition of thinking about risk, namely that which locates
the social meaning of risk in terms of a blaming device that functions to
maintain group solidarities. Researchers such as Joffe are interested not so
much to discern the mechanics of thought processes within individual minds
as to expose the ways in which the psychology of risk develops as part of a
cultural (and moralizing) dialogue between individuals and social institutions. On this understanding, the task of effectively 'managing risk' is
doomed to fail if it is envisaged as simply involving finding the correct 'for-
mula' of information to offset common errors in probabilistic thinking; rather, this should begin by questioning the social boundaries of belonging
across which cultural dialogues about risk take place. People's judgements
about risk are understood above all as a reflection of their social identifications, moral practices and commitments of *trust*.

## Sociological assessments

How might sociologists respond to these various fields of research? The answer to this question very much depends upon the type of sociologist in
question. There is certainly no overall agreement among the sociological
community as to how one should engage with the psychology of risk. For the
purposes of this chapter, I shall outline two 'ideal-types' of response. The first,
though seeking to question and debate many research premises and findings,
aims to encourage the development of an interdisciplinary forum of debate
about risk. In this context, risk research is represented as a distinct field of
study that aims to produce a common account of risk for social science. The
main premise here is that, while divisions remain between sociology and
psychology in methodology and intellectual outlook, nevertheless, in the
context of risk research, they share the same object of study and both stand to
gain from a combined effort at understanding. The second response adopts a
far more critical stance towards any moves to marry psychology with sociology. On this account, psychological research on risk is more interesting
for what it reveals about the politics of knowledge within psychology than for
any claims it makes to have advanced our understanding of the social reality
of risk perception. Moreover, in this more critical setting, the 'methodological
individualism' and forms of laboratory research that characterize a psychological approach to the study of human behaviour are understood to obscure
more than they reveal about the ways in which people perceive and respond
to risks in the *social contexts* of everyday life. Indeed, such methods and
practices are held to betray an *ideological* commitment towards individualism
that fails to bring critical scrutiny to bear upon the socio-economic causes and
socio-cultural explanations of our personal anxieties and discontents.

Examples of the first approach can be found among the various edited collections of readings on risk that are marketed towards a managerial audience and among the policy-oriented articles published in journals such as *Risk Analysis* and the *Journal of Risk Research* (Royal Society 1992; Loftedt and Frewer 1998; Pidgeon et al. 2003). In this context, researchers such as Renn and Sjoberg make explicit attempts to summarize the relative merits of contrasting disciplinary approaches to the study of 'risk perception' and its 'social amplification' with the aim of piecing together an overarching perspective on these matters for a collaborative project of social science (Renn et al. 1993; Sjoberg 2000; Renn 1998). Critical questions may be raised with regard to limitations in the design and practice of psychometric research, particularly where this displays little concern for the extent to which the social characteristics of respondents, such as 'gender', 'socio-economic class', 'age' and 'nationality', appear to have a determining effect upon patterns and distributions of risk perception (Sjoberg 1998). Indeed, at this point attempts are made to build bridges between the domains of cognitive psychology and cultural theory so as to elaborate upon the social functions of risk perception (Sjoberg 2000). Moreover, by encouraging further reflections upon the social meaning of risk, it may well be the case that some recognition is given to the mediating role of cultural values within the *social construction* of collective perceptions of technological hazards as well as technical accounts of 'objective' risk (Royal Society 1992: 89–134). However, it is important to note here that the radical potential of such insights is not developed to a level where any ideological schisms are permitted to disrupt the overall task of advancing a 'meta-analysis' of risk (Rosa 2003). On this account, a shared commitment to the advancement of governmental and corporate techniques of risk management and regulation appears to override the potential for ideological and political conflict; rather, researchers predominantly concentrate their attentions upon existing opportunities for integrating psychology and sociology within a broad framework of risk research.

A strong example of a more critical sociological response towards psychological research on risk is to be found in the works of Rose (1996, 1998, 1999). Rose argues that sociologists should be highly sceptical of any claims that psychology is advancing towards a more 'objective' account of the inner dynamics of human thought and feeling, particularly where this is linked to policies and practices of risk management. In this context, he maintains that the ideological interests expressed in the social practices of psychology and the language of risk are deeply antagonistic towards a proper *sociological* understanding (and truly *social* account) of human reality. Rose (1998) advises that the cultural stock of psychology (along with psychiatry and psychoanalysis) is rising in so far as its inclination to reduce the analysis of cognition, motivation and affect to *individual* factors complies with the logic of 'liberal modes of government' that have vested interests in popularizing the notion that societies essentially comprise 'autonomous individuals' all 'striving for self-realisation'. He claims that: 'today, psychologists elaborate complex emotional, interpersonal and organizational techniques by which the practices of everyday life can be organized according to the ethic of autonomous selfhood' (Rose 1999: 90). The language of risk is presented as a technique of 'governmentality', that is, part of a strategy by which attempts are made to enforce more rigid standards of 'self-discipline' and 'personal responsibility' upon society. For Rose, the expert monitoring of lay people's capacities for risk perception, along with attempts to enhance practices of risk management and risk communication, are all part of an ideological move to redefine the rationality and morality of Western government. The expert-labelled social problems as types of 'risk', social behaviours as 'risky' or types of people as 'at risk', are all held to comply with efforts to govern societies according to the principle that individuals should '*take upon themselves* the responsibility for their own security and that of their families' (Rose 1996: 341–2). A key point of governmental understanding is that, once a warning about risk has been officially authorized and disseminated in public, individuals will monitor and adjust their behaviour accordingly so as to minimize their chances of experiencing harm. Moreover, it is further assumed that such efforts at communication serve as part of the means to legitimize the use of more authoritarian measures to 'persuade' reckless individuals to become more self-responsibly risk averse.

From this critical sociological perspective, the great danger here is that where social problems, social attitudes and social behaviours are addressed in terms of 'psychologies of risk' – or 'risk consciousness' – then the *social* component of these phenomena is eclipsed in favour of factors pertaining to 'the individual'. The risk society is hereby portrayed as comprising an aggregate of disparate individuals all sharing in a common cultural experience of risk and all bearing a personal burden of responsibility for their fates. Questions about existing possibilities for social change are divorced from matters of political economy, and rather, are presented solely in terms of need for education and moral reform. Rose tends to portray the language of risk as now so firmly attached to an ideology of individualism that it almost always works to divert social attention away from class divisions in experiences of health, economic opportunity and access to cultural and social resources. On this account, any enthusiastic endorsement of 'risk' as a unit of sociological analysis may well be identified with the promotion of a 'post-social' account of human dispositions and discontents; if sociology and psychology are to join forces under the auspices of risk research, then this is bound to be to the detriment of proper *social* understanding and *social* critique.

One way to begin the task of evaluating the differences between these two types of sociological response is by noting a basic division in the ways in which they handle the concept of risk. In the first response of writers such as

Renn and Sjoberg, the tone of discussion is characterized by political detachment and value-neutrality. In this context, 'risk' has a largely *descriptive* function; it is used primarily as a means to describe modes of perception, forms of affectivity, types of behaviour and categories of social problems. To represent human thoughts and behaviours in terms of 'risk' serves as a point from which to initiate further processes of sociological and/or psychological analysis of specific value orientations, cognitive processes and cultural outlooks. In managerial risk research, the concept of risk is used principally as a means to frame disciplinary concerns and the objects of research. By contrast, in the second approach, Rose understands power relations to always be at work in the ways in which the concept of risk is used to categorize individual attitudes and life problems. On this account, an ideological and political motivation is held to always be at work in the labelling of social problems, modes of consciousness and states of feeling in terms of risk. For Rose, research and debate on risk can never stand outside of an exercise in power and politics.

At the very least, readers might be prepared to acknowledge that the presence of writers such as Rose within these debates requires them to adopt a point of view on risk as 'power knowledge'. Moreover, perhaps it is inevitably the case that as ever-increasing numbers of research papers are published under the auspices of the sociology and psychology of risk, then we shall find the meaning of key terms of analysis being subjected to critical conflicts of interpretation; and where scholars are prepared to enter into borderland debates over the relative merits of their particular fields of research and disciplinary concerns, then this may be still more pronounced.

## Conclusion: beyond the risk society

Social theories of risk society almost invariably incorporate generalizing accounts of dominant modes of social consciousness and feeling. Indeed, I would be inclined to suggest that the overall coherence and logic of the majority of theoretical works on this topic rest extensively upon crude idealizations of our social subjectivity. For example, writers such as Beck (1992, 1995, 1999) can be seen to elaborate in the broadest terms on the dynamics of social change by reflecting upon the possible social and political implications of a particular representation of risk consciousnesses. Where sociologists have ventured to explore the *empirical* reality of risk perception, then much of what is written at the level of grand theory is exposed as no more than 'castles in the air'; in the social contexts of everyday life, individual perceptions of risk are far more nuanced, varied and contradictory than the 'realities' portrayed in some of the most popular theories of risk society (Irwin et al. 1999; Wilkinson 2001b). Moreover, it is still the case that, in empirical terms, very little is known about the ways in which expressed perceptions shape actual social behaviours (Sjoberg 2000). While a great deal of the existing psychological research on risk may be lacking in *social* insight, at the very least it serves to highlight a considerable variety in individual attitudes towards risk, and as such must serve to cast doubt upon any attempt to reduce the complexity of these phenomena to a simple and one-sided account of risk consciousness.

In this chapter, I have provided a brief overview of some of the principal areas of psychological research on matters of risk perception. While highlighting some of the shared understandings that characterize a psychological approach to this topic, I have also worked to draw attention to the research discoveries and categories of understanding that lead psychologists to disagree among themselves as to the factors that determine the ways in which people think and feel about risk. Certainly, there is much more to analyse in this state of affairs, but I hope that the above provides sufficient information to encourage more critical thinking. At the same time, some comment has been made on the possible terms of engagement between sociology and psychology in these domains. In this context, I have sought to bring more critical scrutiny to bear upon the ways in which the concept of risk is used by sociologists and psychologists to frame dimensions of human experience, thought and behaviour. More directly, readers are urged to enter into debate over the ways in which the language of risk shapes the thought of social science; and indeed, if thinking in these terms can ever be conducted without an exercise in power relations or outside expressions of political interest.

If we are to take seriously the arguments of writers such as Rose, then we might also approach the widespread sociological adoption of risk as a means to categorize cultural outlooks and social behaviours as a sign that sociology is more prepared than at any other time in its history to adopt an individualistic and individualizing world-view. On these grounds, perhaps some of the traditional divisions between psychology and sociology over the relative importance of social factors are decreasing? Is it on the topic of risk that sociology and psychology are advancing *together* towards a 'post-social' account of life problems and interests? Beyond the current debates on risk society shall we find the further demise of sociological thinking, or might efforts to expose the ideological motivations of risk discourse lead to the re-discovery of 'society'?

## Study questions

1   How would you summarize the principal discoveries of psychological research on risk?

2   What kinds of interests tend to distinguish a 'sociological' as opposed to a 'psychological' study of risk?
3   In what ways might the study of risk in contemporary social science be identified with a 'post-social' account of human thought and behaviour?


# References

Alhakami, A.S. and Slovic, P. (1994) A psychological study of the inverse relationship between perceived risk and perceived benefit, *Risk Analysis*, 14: 1085–96.

Beck, U. (1992) *Risk Society: Towards a New Modernity*. London: Sage.

Beck, U. (1995) *Ecological Politics in an Age of Risk*. Cambridge: Polity Press.

Beck, U. (1999) *World Risk Society*. Cambridge: Polity Press.

Craib, I. (1989) *Psychoanalysis and Social Theory: The Limits of Sociology*. London: Harvester Wheatsheaf.

Craib, I. (1994) *The Importance of Disappointment*. London: Routledge.

Craib, I. (1998) *Experiencing Identity*. London: Sage.

Douglas, M. (1985) *Risk Acceptability According to the Social Sciences*. London: Routledge and Kegan Paul.

Douglas, M. (1992) *Risk and Blame: Essays in Cultural Theory*. London: Routledge.

Durkheim, E. (1974) Individual and collective representations, in E. Durkheim *Sociology and Philosophy*. New York: The Free Press.

Finucane, M.L., Alhakami, A.S., Slovic, P. and Johnson, S.M. (2000) The affect heuristic in judgements of risks and benefits, *Journal of Behavioural Decision Making*, 13: 1–17.

Fischoff, B. (1995) Risk perception and risk communication unplugged: twenty years of process, *Risk Analysis*, 15(2): 137–45.

Flynn, J., Slovic, P. and Kunreuther, H. (eds) (2001) *Risk, Media and Stigma: Understanding Public Challenges to Modern Science and Technology*. London: Earthscan.

Freudenberg, W.R. and Pastor, S.K. (1992) Public responses to technological risks: toward a sociological perspective, *The Sociological Quarterly*, 33(3): 389–412.

Fromm, E. (1942) *The Fear of Freedom*. London: Routledge.

Fromm, E. (1956) *The Sane Society*. London: Routledge.

Frosh, S. (2003) Psychosocial studies and psychology: is a critical approach emerging? *Human Relations*, 56(12): 1545–57.

Heimer, C.A. (1988) Social structure, psychology and the estimation of risk, *Annual Review of Sociology*, 12: 491–519.

Helweg-Larsen, M. and Shepperd, J.A. (2001) The optimistic bias: moderators and measurement concerns, *Personality and Social Psychology Review*, 5: 74–95.

Horney, K. (1937) *The Neurotic Personality of Our Time*. London: Routledge and Kegan Paul.

Horney, K. (1950) *Neurosis and Human Growth: The Struggle Toward Self-Realization*. New York: W.W. Norton.

Irwin, A., Simmons, P. and Walker, G. (1999) Faulty environments and risk reasoning: the local understanding of industrial hazards, *Environment and Planning A*, 31: 1311–26.

Jallinoja, P. and Aro, A.R. (2000) Does knowledge make a difference? The association between knowledge about genes and attitude toward gene tests, *Journal of Health Communication*, 5: 29–39.

Joffe, H. (1999) *Risk and 'The Other'*. Cambridge: Cambridge University Press.

Joffe, H. (2002) Social representations and health psychology, *Social Science Information*, 41(4): 559–80.

Joffe, H. (2003) Risk: from perception to social representation, *British Journal of Social Psychology*, 42: 55–73.

Kreuter, M.W. (1999) Dealing with competing and conflicting risks in cancer communication, *Journal of the National Cancer Institute*, 25: 27–35.

Leiss, W. (1996). Three phases in the evolution of risk communication practice, *The Annals of the American Academy of Political and Social Science*, 545: 85–94.

Loftedt, R. and Frewer, L. (eds) (1998) *Risk and Modern Society*. London: Earthscan.

McKenna, F. P. (1993) It won't happen to me: unrealistic optimism or illusion of control?, *British Journal of Psychology*, 84: 39–50.

Moscovici, S. (1984) The phenomenon of social representations, in R.M. Farr and S. Moscovici (eds) *Social Representations*. Cambridge: Cambridge University Press.

O'Malley, P. (2004) *Risk, Uncertainty and Government*. London: Glasshouse Press.

Pidgeon, N., Kasperson, R.E. and Slovic, P. (eds) (2003) *The Social Amplification of Risk*. Cambridge: Cambridge University Press.

Powell, D. and Leiss, W. (1997) *Mad Cows and Mother's Milk: The Perils of Poor Risk Communication*. Montreal and Kingston: McGill-Queens University Press.

Renn, O. (1998) Three decades of risk research: accomplishments and new challenges, *Journal of Risk Research*, 1(1): 49–71.

Renn, O., Burns, W.J., Kasperson, J.X., Kasperson, R.E., and Slovic, P. (1993) The social amplification of risk: theoretical foundations and empirical applications, *Journal of Social Issues*, 48(4): 137–60.

Rosa, E.A. (2003) The logical structure of the social amplification of risk framework (SARF): metatheoretical foundations and policy implications, in N. Pidgeon, R.E. Kasperson and P. Slovic (eds) (2003) *The Social Amplification of Risk*. Cambridge: Cambridge University Press.

Rose, N. (1990) *Governing the Soul: The Shaping of the Private Self*. London: Routledge.

Rose, N. (1996) The death of the social? Refiguring the territory of government, *Economy and Society*, 25(3): 327–64.

Rose, N. (1998) *Inventing Ourselves: Psychology, Power and Personhood*. New York: Cambridge University Press.

Rose, N. (1999) *Powers of Freedom: Reframing Political Thought*. Cambridge: Cambridge University Press.

Royal Society (1992) *Risk: Analysis, Perception and Management*. London: The Royal Society.

Scholderer, J. and Frewer L. (2003) The biotechnology communication paradox: experimental evidence and the need for a new strategy, *Journal of Consumer Policy*, 26: 125–57.

Sheeran, P., Abraham, C. and Orbell, S. (1999) Psychosocial correlates of heterosexual condom use: a meta-analysis, *Psychological Bulletin*, 125: 90–132.

Sjoberg, L. (1997) Explaining risk perception: an empirical evaluation of cultural theory, *Risk, Decision and Policy*, 2: 113–30.

Sjoberg, L. (1998) Worry and risk perception, *Risk Analysis*, 18(1): 85–93.

Sjoberg, L. (2000) Factors in risk perception, *Risk Analysis*, 20(1): 1–11.

Slovic, P. (2000) *The Perception of Risk*. London: Earthscan.

Smail, D. (1984) *Illusion and Reality: The Meaning of Anxiety*. London: J.M. Dent & Sons.

Smail, D. (1998) *Taking Care: An Alternative Therapy*. London: Constable.

Smail, D. (1999) *The Origins of Unhappiness: A New Understanding of Personal Distress*. London: Constable.

Taylor, S.E. (1989) *Positive Illusions: Creative Self-Deception and the Healthy Mind*. New York: Basic Books.

Taylor, S.E. and Brown, J. (1994) 'Illusion' of mental health does not explain positive illusions, *American Psychologist*, 49(11): 972–3.

Taylor, S.E., Kemeny, M.E., Aspinall, L.G., Schneider, S.C., Rodriguez, R. and Herbert, M. (1992) Optimism, coping, psychological distress, and high-risk sexual behaviour among men at risk of AIDS, *Journal of Personality and Social Psychology*, 63: 460–73.

Taylor, S.E. and Armor, D.A. (1996) Positive illusions and coping with adversity, *Journal of Personality*, 64(4): 873–98.

Thompson, J.B. (1990) *Ideology and Modern Culture*. Cambridge: Polity Press.

Tversky, A. and Kahneman, D. (1974) Judgement under uncertainty: heuristics and biases, *Science*, 185: 1124–31.

Vogler, C. (2000) Social identity and emotion: the meeting of psychoanalysis and sociology, *The Sociological Review*, 48: 19–42.

Weinstein, N.D. (1980) Unrealistic optimism about future life events, *Journal of Personality and Social Psychology*, 69: 213–26.

Weinstein, N.D. (1982) Unrealistic optimism about susceptibility to health problems. *Journal of Behavioural Medicine*, 5(4): 441–460.

Weinstein, N.D. (1987) Unrealistic optimism about susceptibility to health problems: conclusions from a community-wide sample, *Journal of Behavioural Medicine*, 10: 481–95.

Weinstein N.D. and Lyon, J.E. (1999) Mindset, optimistic bias about personal risk and health-protective behaviour, *British Journal of Health Psychology*, 4: 289–300.

Wilkinson, I. (2001a) *Anxiety in a Risk Society*. London: Routledge.

Wilkinson, I. (2001b) Social theories of risk perception: at once indispensable and insufficient, *Current Sociology*, 49(1): 1–22.

Wilkinson, I. (2005) *Suffering: A Sociological Introduction*. Cambridge: Polity Press.

Wrong, D.H. (1961) The oversocialized conception of man in modern sociology, *American Sociological Review*, 26(2): 183–93.

## Further reading

Joffe, H. (1999) *Risk and 'The Other'*. Cambridge: Cambridge University Press.

Pidgeon, N., Kasperson, R.E. and Slovic, P. (eds) (2003) *The Social Amplification of Risk*. Cambridge: Cambridge University Press.

Rose, N. (1999) *Powers of Freedom: Reframing Political Thought*. Cambridge: Cambridge University Press.

Slovic, P. (2000) *The Perception of Risk*. London: Earthscan.

Wilkinson, I. (2001) *Anxiety in a Risk Society*. London: Routledge.

# 3   Criminology and risk

*Pat O'Malley*

## Introduction

While there is general agreement that risk has become a central issue for criminology, there is not always consistency either about what exactly this means or how it should be understood. For some, risk specifically is the use of statistically predictive techniques to minimize harms (Feeley and Simon 1994). For others, such as Rose (2000), it refers to a broader, preventative orientation including 'uncertainty' (i.e. the use of non-statistical techniques). Since many criminologists use either or both meanings, this chapter will take the more inclusive definition, but will note the distinction where this is important. Thus 'crime prevention' is usually treated as an example of 'risk' even though, as Haggerty (2003) argues, little of it involves statistically based prediction and much simply involves routines such as persuading neighbours to watch over their streetscape. Also, risk appears in a second form as 'subjective risk'. On the one hand are victim perceptions of risk, the 'fear of crime' and attempts to manage this by police and government agencies. On the other is the more problematic 'risk taking' which, while intrinsic to many idealized visions of capitalist activity and 'enterprise cultures', in criminological accounts frequently becomes pathologized as a cause of crime.

## Risk and criminal justice

In the early 1980s, two influential reports by criminologists were published, more or less simultaneously on either side of the Atlantic. Commissioned in the mid-1970s, the British 'Floud Report' (Floud 1982) and the American 'Greenwood Report' (Rand Corporation 1982) heralded a major shift in the way crime was to be imagined and governed. In somewhat divergent ways, both reports recommended that a new focus on risk should be developed in criminal justice. For some years, a groundswell of doubt had gathered momentum about the effectiveness of the whole expert-led, correctional project of penal modernism, summed up and given political prominence by Martinson's (1974) influential 'nothing works' paper. These doubts were joined with other contemporaneous discontents with penal modernism (scientific corrections) and its ignoring of victims. The Floud Report reflected a number of these concerns. Questioning expert prediction and the ability of the system to reduce crime and reform criminals, Floud recommended the development of protective sentences as a way of 'relieving someone else of substantial risk of grave harm – we are justly redistributing a burden of risk that we cannot immediately reduce'. In turn, the case for a protective sentence was not so much based on the particular offender's diagnosis, but would vary 'with the size of the population at risk from the offender concerned' (Floud 1982). In parallel with Floud's concerns, the Greenwood Report's proposal argued that statistical techniques provided the optimal route to identifying those offenders who were at high risk of re-offending, and who should therefore be incapacitated by long sentences as a risk-reducing strategy.

Despite beliefs that such policy-related mobilization of risk only appears in criminology in recent years, this is far from true. No doubt the best-known precursor was the work of the Gluecks (1946). They developed a variety of predictive instruments based on statistical data relating to offenders and their official and self-reported rates of recidivism. While the Gluecks (1946) demonstrated the predictive superiority of these techniques over professional diagnoses, and sought to have these techniques taken up by judges and parole boards, their efforts were largely unsuccessful. Prior to this, a number of prominent US criminologists had developed similar predictive scales, but only one – Burgess (1928, 1936) – had achieved even limited success when the State of Illinois appointed sociologist-actuaries to develop improved actuarial tables (Ohlin 1951; Glaser 1962). In Britain, Mannheim and Wilkins (1955) developed parallel techniques and used them to achieve significantly better predictions than the judgements of prison experts. Riding on the back of such work Wilkins, working with Gottfredson, was commissioned by the US Board of Parole to develop statistically driven predictors of parole outcomes, which formed the basis of the federal parole guidelines and were adopted by a majority of state parole boards (Glaser 1985). Nevertheless, Glaser was struck by the singular lack of effect statistical prediction models had on sentencing as opposed to parole decisions. In his view (1985: 376), this was largely attributable to the importance of two factors: the long-term but increasing pressure on judges to conform to just deserts principles, and the importance of plea-bargaining – both of which interfered with the courts' ability and willingness to accept risk-based sentencing.

In the late 1980s and early 1990s, a number of criminologists began to note the increasing role played by risk and preventative frameworks in sentencing and justice policy (see for example, Cohen 1985; Feeley and Simon 1992; O'Malley 1992). This 'new penology' was marked by a shift away from the foci of penal modernism, with its emphasis on correctional-therapeutic interventions tailored to the expert diagnosis of individuals' criminogenic needs. Instead, the emphasis was seen to be on 'the replacement of a moral or clinical description of the individual with the actuarial language of prob-abilistic calculations and statistical distributions applied to populations' (Feeley and Simon 1992: 452). In their conceptualization of this as 'actuarial justice', Feeley and Simon (1994) linked increased use of statistically based tariffs in sentencing, displacement of correctionalism by incapacitation as the goals of sentences, and a managerial emphasis on maximizing throughputs: the three elements together being regarded as optimizing 'effective control' of risky populations. Such developments reflected the particular interpretation of risk provided in the Floud and Greenwood Reports. Risk had expanded from being a technique for governing parole to include sentencing, and with that had come a refocusing of justice onto protection of the community rather than reform of the offender. In this process, social and judicial ex-pertise was marginalized in favour of risk management. Of at least equal importance, the burden of risk was to be transferred from potential victims to repeat offenders. As it developed, most notoriously into the American 'three strikes' laws, this meant that the issue of just deserts was increasingly over-ridden by a legislated tariff that was focused not on the offence immediately on hand (which might be relatively trivial), but on the 'risk' that this in-dicated. Thus whereas the problem of sentencing people for their prospective risks had long been recognized as unjust because some of them would not have re-offended, this objection was now swept aside. Formally, at least, ju-dicial resistance to risk had been overcome by legislatures mandating long sentences aimed at incapacitating repeat offenders.

More broadly, interpreters such as Rose (2000) and Bauman (2000) have seen the deployment of risk as creating a bifurcated criminal justice system in which high risk offenders are consigned to exclusionary gulags while the lower risk population is channelled into circuits of reform or guarded tol-eration. Indeed, Feeley and Simon's (1994) own analysis was consistent with this conclusion because actuarial justice's logic of risk targeted the largely black and Hispanic 'underclass' in the USA. Feeley and Simon concluded that the form of risk-based incapacitation was directed precisely at populations that had 'fallen below the threshold of deterrence': those who were outside the legitimate economy, and who in consequence were regarded as having no prospect of being reintegrated. If reform was pointless and ineffective, and deterrence would not work, they could thus be governed only through in-capacitation. As Rose (2000: 333) puts it: 'in these exclusionary circuits the role of custodial institutions is redefined. They are understood and classified not in terms of their reformatory potential, but in terms of the secure con-tainment of risk.'

Did this grim forecast eventuate? There is little doubt the development of risk-based sanctions corresponds in time with the massive increase in im-prisonment in many countries, especially the USA. It is quite possible, if not officially admitted, that much of this expansion flows from a changed attitude towards the role of prisons as merely containing risks. But as Simon and Feeley (1995) themselves later recognized, this cannot be attributed to the impact of actuarial justice, for it has not taken over as the new penology. They suggest, echoing Glaser, that resistance stemmed from an enduring attachment to volitional just deserts theories of crime, and to sentencing as a spectacle of moral denunciation – while risk management strategies are dispassionate, seemingly amoral and technical. Other research has certainly suggested that criminal justice officials played a key role in this resistance to risk techniques. Freiberg's (2000) analysis suggested that judges did not appreciate having their discretion overridden by schedules, or their commitment to the principle of proportionality of offence and punishment violated. His work indicated that the judiciary retain significant discretion even in the face of mandatory sentencing regimes. This may be achieved, for example, by judicial redefinition of the offence into a category that does not attract risk-based sanctions. In addition, Austin and his colleagues (1999) have found that resistance stems from criminal justice officials' recognition of the practical limits to implementation – for example, in the form of the finite capacity of prison systems. The result of such resistance has been uneven. Sentencing has been affected with respect to repeat sexual and violent crime. Many jurisdictions specify long sentences – or in Britain, life sentences – for such offenders in the name of risk reduction (Kemshall and Maguire 2001). Excepting the doubtful case of 'three strikes' laws – doubtful because their rationale and justification appear to have much more to do with retribution than with risk – the situation with respect to sentencing remains much as it was when Glaser puzzled over risk's marginal role 20 years ago. Now, as then, risk has been most influential in the *post*-sentencing phases. However, this does not mean that criminal justice is largely unchanged, for risk has undoubtedly encroached considerably further in these latter areas.

In risk's most striking manifestation, 'Megan's Laws', operative in a majority of states in the USA, mandate some form of continued surveillance and restrictions on released sex offenders, and often require public notification of their whereabouts. In Britain, released sex offenders are required to notify the police of their home address. Together with the probation service, police undertake a risk assessment of the offender, and where the risk is considered high enough, they may notify other organizations, individuals or even the local community. In Simon's (1998) view, this is part of a new politics of vengeance – a process of 'managing the monstrous' – in which risk has been married to an overtly moralized and repressive agenda. According to the courts, however, this does not constitute a further punishment after completion of the sentence, but rather is a practice that allows communities to be aware of the risk in their midst and to take appropriate precautions (Levi 2000). Nevertheless, in these procedures, Kemshall and Maguire (2001) note that in Britain while there are actuarial risk assessment schedules available for determining post-release conditions, these are never the sole basis upon which decisions are made. Rather, they play a key role in the initial filtering process, while final decision-making is heavily reliant on the case record approach. Rather than actuarial risk techniques simply displacing expert judgement, what is emerging are new combinations of the two, so that actuarial techniques become only one element in the risk assessment exercise. Nor is this merely an example of resistance by social workers adhering to old ways, for a 1996 Home Office Probation Circular stressed that the predictive device was 'no more than an aid to the judgement of probation officers in preparing (reports) . . . it cannot be a substitute for that judgement' (cited in Kemshall 1998: 35).

It is also clear that risk has reshaped the provision of correctional services, particularly in the form of 'risk–needs' analysis. One of the standard criticisms of correctional interventions was that they were wasteful of resources, providing all manner of services that may or may not have been effective in correction. Beginning in the late 1980s, psychological criminologists such as Andrews and Bonta (Andrews 1989; Andrews and Bonta 1989) began developing risk assessment instruments that identified the 'criminogenic needs' of offenders. These are 'needs' that are linked to the particular offender's risk factors for recidivism, treatment of which will reduce the risk of re-offending. As part of this thinking, only those risks regarded as 'manageable', that is, which on intervention will have a measurable impact, will be recognized. As Hannah-Moffatt (1999, 2005) has shown in her studies of Canadian prisons, risk–needs have reshaped the major approaches to offender management. Rose's 'secure containment of risks' is not simply associated with incapacitation but 'now involves efficient, rational calculations of need' (Hannah-Moffatt 2005: 34). In the process, however a 'slippage' has been created between risk and need, so that need itself is transformed – all manner of non-criminogenic or non-manageable problems of offenders (e.g. health and poverty) disappear from the register of 'needs'. Hannah-Moffatt argues that this bears particularly hard on women, for needs associated with children, abuse and trauma – problems affecting very many women prisoners – will be ignored if not linked to the reduction of their recidivism risks. In sum, while risk has become much more pervasive in criminal justice, it has not developed into anything resembling actuarial justice. Risk plays only a minor role in sentencing. While incapacitation may be a major rationale of imprisonment in some jurisdictions, this is not necessarily attributable to risk. Indeed, where risk has been explicitly involved in the shaping of sanctions it has been linked with expert therapeutic and correctional knowledge. In some respects, this is also what has happened in crime prevention.

## Crime prevention

While prevention had been a major rationale of police for Peel and Colquhoun, until the 1980s crime prevention was a minor aspect of policing. Most forces had a crime prevention officer, but this role usually was restricted to limited data gathering and public relations functions. The eventual development of prevention was partly an effect of insurance industry pressures (Litton 1982), and perhaps for this reason, the first area in which risk was registered in the field of prevention was with respect to situational crime prevention. This approach, directed mainly at property crime, stressed redesign of statistically high-risk 'criminogenic' environments and settings to render them less vulnerable. Advocates of situational crime prevention argued that spiralling crime rates demonstrated that attempts to control crime through criminologically informed rehabilitation had failed and that it was time to move away from this model (Geason and Wilson 1988, 1989). In a fairly aggressive self-description, the National Crime Prevention Institute (1986: 18) in America developed 'the contemporary perspective in criminology' which took as its guiding principles the idea that

> Prevention (and not rehabilitation) should be the major concern of criminologists; no one is sure how to rehabilitate offenders; punishment and/or imprisonment may be relevant in controlling certain offenders; criminal behavior can be controlled primarily through the direct alteration of the environment of potential victims; crime control programs must focus on crime before it occurs rather than afterward; and as criminal opportunity is reduced, so too will be the number of criminals.

This was not just a rethinking of crime as a preventable risk, for it was a very specific formulation of risk technique. It has been seen already that parallel developments such as risk–needs analysis put great faith in (risk-driven) rehabilitation as a preventative technology. Situational crime prevention, on the other hand, is much closer to actuarial justice in the sense that it is unconcerned with reform, and pays no attention to the biography, circumstances or character of the offender – who is regarded as a rational choice actor (Heal and Laycock 1986). Both approaches share something in common with neo-liberal governance, for this also put considerable faith in economic models of behaviour, and had a corresponding antipathy to the social sciences. This was especially the case for those social sciences that regarded crime as a social or political problem rather than a matter of individual responsibility. Accordingly, neo-liberal governments had a considerable sympathy with situational crime prevention – for it imagined the offender simply as any person faced with an opportunity (O'Malley 1992). Also, neo-liberals' governmental adoption of such business principles as loss minimization rendered crime prevention in general very attractive (Shearing and Stenning 1985). More than this, situational crime prevention was a site where a number of business and political discourses converged on the responsibility of the victim. Thus, a senior official of the Australian Insurance Council has noted 'severely restricted police resources and the sheer frequency of crime, mean that any improvement in the situation will rely heavily on property owners accepting responsibility for their own property and valuables' (Hall 1986: 243) and the then UK prime minister Margaret Thatcher blamed a large proportion of crimes on the victims' carelessness: 'we have to be careful that we ourselves don't make it easy for the criminal', she said (quoted in O'Malley 1992). Even criminologists began to take on this view, suggesting that 'the general public's apathy about self-protection arises mainly from ignorance of the means of protection, and a perception that somebody else – "the Government" or insurance companies – bears most of the cost of theft and vandalism' (Geason and Wilson 1989: 9). Not surprisingly, it was in this environment that community organizations such as *Neighbourhood Watch* attained their high watermark.

While situational crime prevention remains a major risk-oriented approach to crime prevention, its implicit victim focus has also proven one of its vulnerabilities to political critique. In the late 1980s the British Home Office advised women to avoid high-risk situations, including being alone in public at night. The response from feminist criminologists and others (e.g. Stanko 1990b) was striking, including a call for a 'feminist crime prevention strategy' and calls for a response that 'concentrated on reducing violence against women by targeting the involvement of the community to change male behaviour and attitudes, empower women in unsafe situations and change community perceptions and understandings about violence toward women' (see also Stanko 1990a; Thurgood 1991; Walklate 2002). This joined with a parallel movement already under way towards more socially oriented approaches to crime prevention that had been developing in social democratic environments. For example, the French Bonnemaison programme which incorporates much that is focused on social justice, was picked up widely in the English-speaking world, particularly in Australia where situational crime prevention was integrated quite explicitly with a government focus on social justice and was shaped accordingly with an emphasis on attending to the criminogenic factors associated with inequality (Sandon 1991). Linked with this, developmental crime prevention has succeeded in marrying risk with a more traditional, social and behavioural science form of criminology, by translating the old 'causes' of crime into 'risk factors'. Thus the key risk factors in developmental criminology are reminiscent of the 1950s 'causes' of crime. They include 'family isolation', 'inadequate parenting', 'single parents', 'attachment difficulties', 'low self-esteem', 'poor social skills', 'poor cognitive skills', and so on (National Crime Prevention 1999a: 17). By such means, the preventative and rehabilitative agendas of the former 'social' era are re-introduced. In addition, much developmental crime prevention of late has begun explicitly to identify as risk factors the kinds of social conditions identified as problematic under welfare programmes and sociological crim-inology. Thus, the Crime Prevention Council of Canada (1997: 10) argues that a comprehensive crime prevention strategy to deal with young people 'at risk' must provide 'educational, social and health services', and urges that it 'is essential that this strategy address child poverty' (1997: 11). Likewise Australia's National Crime Prevention (1999b: 13) lists 'socio- economic disadvantage', 'population density and housing conditions', 'lack of support services' and 'social or cultural discrimination' among its crime-related 'cul-tural and community factors'. The agenda, although situated within a risk discourse, gives expression to the welfare-social rationalities, and in so doing begins to hint at social justice and certainly of the kinds of socially – rather than individually – ameliorative programmes that were associated with the welfare state.

## Risk and policing

While, historically speaking, the police have eschewed crime prevention, by the late 1980s this had become much more central. On the surface, much of this engagement may be regarded as peripheral to mainstream policing, and is vulnerable to the accusation that it is largely about getting others to carry out preventative actions. Participation in crime prevention panels and campaigns, organizing Neighbourhood Watch and Shop Watch programmes, promotion of home security and community awareness practices, property marking schemes, the operation of 'police shops' (often aimed at reducing fear of crime as well as promoting security consciousness), school education programmes and so on, are typical of these. However, Bennett (1994) has pointed to the development of risk-targeted policing, in which police provide concentrated surveillance and presence at high-risk locations and times, and others (O'Malley and Mugford 1992) have pointed to the rise of drink-drive 'blitzes' and random alcohol checks as risk-focused patterns of policing. It must also be recognized that many of the 'multi-agency' developments that have a risk content incorporate the police (Hughes 1999). This has been seen already, for example, with respect to the registration, monitoring and com-munity posting programmes in relation to registered sex offenders (Hebenton and Thomas 1996).

Yet all these developments can be dismissed as comparatively minor in the face of what Ericson and his colleagues (Ericson 1994; Ericson and

Haggerty 1998) see as the fundamental restructuring and realigning of police work in 'the risk society'. Rather than fighting crime or maintaining order, Ericson (1994: 151) argues that the police officer now 'produces and distributes knowledge for the risk management activities of operatives in other institutions'. Such institutions include local government, the private security industry, the insurance industry, community organizations, and so on. In part, this security-knowledge brokering function becomes identified with police because police forces are security agencies with a historical licence to generate, receive and store such information. But equally it is because they are, for much the same reason, situated at the intersection of a huge network of security-focused social relations and agencies. A corollary of this, they argue, is that as risk consciousness generalizes throughout society, responsibility for effecting security increasingly passes from the police to these other sites and agencies, which must create and mobilize their own risk-management plans and procedures. Pushing their case still further, 'community policing' is claimed to emerge as a discourse to 'capture' this shift. In the risk society, not only does consciousness of risk shape the police, 'it accounts for the fact that our communities are based on risk communications that provide no sense of place or identity beyond institutionalised risk classifications' (Ericson and Haggerty 1998: 446).

## Subjective risk and victimization

Virtually all the analysis thus far has focused on risk as an 'objective' set of defensive procedures mobilized in order to minimize (criminal) harm. But risk's subjective side – the experience and valuation of risk – also has a vital place in criminology. Most closely linked with the defensive function of risk has been the literature on 'fear of crime' and its relationship to the 'objective' measures of risks confronting subjects. The development during the 1980s of research into subjective risk of crime and crime victimization, and policy responses to this, were linked to the same refocusing of attention onto victims and away from offenders that we have seen influence the rise of risk-based criminal justice and crime prevention. Initially, much of this work was intended to reveal the victim perspective and experience of crime that had been obscured by the rise of penal modernism. Such work, as Young (1988) suggested, has considerable democratic significance. But these victimization studies were to prove a double-edged sword. To begin with, they were appropriated – arguably developed – by government agencies and researchers eager to show that fear of crime was greatly exaggerated when contrasted with rates of victimization. As Hough and Mayhew (1983: 157) argued, such work would 'act as an antidote to public misinterpretations of crime' and 'puncture the inaccurate stereotypes of crime victims'. This was reinforced by arguments that those most fearful, for example, older women, are those least likely to be crime victims. Conversely, those most likely to experience crime victimization are those who express least fear, primarily young males. Later research has indicated that 'fear of crime' is often a conduit for the expression of many anxieties and concerns that have little to do with crime as such (Loader et al. 2000), and that willingness to admit to fear of crime is profoundly gendered (Stanko 1990a), casting quite a different light on such findings. However, the first conclusion drawn in the 1980s was that much fear of crime was irrational, and that the best policy solution would be to deal with this uncertainty and ignorance (Gottfredson 1984). There are obvious parallels here with the early psychological studies into risk perception recounted by Wilkinson in the previous chapter. By implication, it could be argued that perceptions of the 'crime problem' were exaggerated and political or personal critiques of government policy and police practice should moderate. A second – and linked – conclusion was that since statistical risks of experiencing serious crime are very low – for example, that there is less than 1 per cent probability of being a victim of assault resulting in injury in any given year – then those who do experience crime, especially repeat experiences, are in some sense contributing to their victimization. The victim, perhaps ironically, now became a new subject of risk, to be worked with and upon in order to correct ignorance, vulnerability and misunderstanding, in order that they could make informed choices and adapt their lifestyle more appropriately to 'real' risks. As crime victimization and crime prevention were woven together during the 1980s and 1990s, 'irrationality' emerged as a failure to align objective risk with behaviour. Victims, or potential victims, were assigned the responsibility of comporting themselves in such a way and in such places that attract least risk (Elias 1993). The effect of this, as many have noted was profound (Hale 1996; Stanko and Curry 1997; Walklate 1997; Stanko 2000). Crime risk readily became an individual issue rather than a collective concern to be governed by individual choice. As Kemshall will demonstrate shortly, the individualization of crime risks is associated with governmental notions of the desirable prudential citizen. Of course, this kind of 'neo-liberal' vision has been extensively challenged, not least because it deploys statistical probabilities while choosing to ignore both the fact that that probabilities draw on *collective* data, and – as Durkheim would have taken to be obvious – the implication that the phenomena of risk are irreducibly *social*. Thus, Stanko (2000: 28) has urged that the category of being individually 'at risk' masks, or translates into a moralized mathematics, the socially unequal distribution of violence, exclusion and fear produced by a society 'that has not rid itself of the persistent remnants of hierarchies founded in the historical legacies of colonialism, patriarchy, heterosexism and class'.

Among other such 'remnants', are those relating to a final set of criminological issues bearing on risk: risk taking. A fairly standard thesis in positivist criminology has been that much crime, by which is meant crime committed by young males, arises out of inappropriate or pathological risk taking in search of excitement. In one of the classic statements, Miller (1958) argued that lower-class culture is signally shaped by the routine and repetitive nature of working-class labour and life. Ignoring the probability that the same could be said of low-crime *middle*-class life, Miller suggests that this gives rise to a search for release in excitement and thrills. 'For many lower class individuals the venture into the high risk world of alcohol, sex and fighting occurs regularly once a week', an 'explosive' mixture 'frequently leading to "trouble" [that] is semi-explicitly sought by the individual' (1958: 11). In another example, Cohen's (1955) ground-breaking study of 'the delinquent subculture' stressed that much crime was not simply a response to poverty or blocked opportunities, as much orthodox criminology argued, but had to be understood as the risk-laden seeking after excitement. Pathologized as 'short-run hedonism', this too was associated with 'the social class from which the delinquents characteristically come, (Cohen 1955: 31). That is, for Cohen the problem was that while risk taking may be culturally acceptable, lower-class subcultures fail to govern this in appropriate ways, and increase the risks of offending. In subsequent years, there have been attempts to develop frameworks of risk-taking and excitement-seeking that do not pathologize such action in class or race terms. For example, using Lyng's (2005) concept of 'edgework' – voluntary risk-taking in which participants seek thrills at the 'edges' of control – a variety of offending has been examined in ways that escape the class hierarchical assumptions of traditional criminology. Drug consumption, for example, has been studied as part of a culture of 'consuming risks' in pursuit of excitement, that has become generalized in contemporary market economies (O'Malley and Mugford 1994; O'Malley 1999; Reith 2005). Also, high-level financial crime, of the type made notorious by Nick Leeson, has been analysed in terms of a culture of fiscal risk-taking that valorized what Smith (2005) refers to as 'market edgework.' But as Walklate (1997) has argued, even this way of accounting for crime remains profoundly gendered. Lyng's framework assumes a masculinity that centres power and control, and that assigns high value to these risk-taking capacities. Women, she suggests face a double bind with respect to risk taking. To take risks is at least accepted as part of hegemonic masculinity, even though it creates second-order risks of offending. For women, however, risk *avoidance* is deemed appropriate. Walklate (1997: 43) posits that this has fed into criminological research and theory:

> Women unquestionably seek pleasure, excitement, thrills and risks. How and under what circumstances this occurs, however, has been explored relatively infrequently, and when it has it has often been

pathologized. Women are, after all, the 'Other'; typically defined as being outside the discourse of risk and risk seeking.

Such exploratory work is only just beginning with work on women offenders in such fields as prostitution and drug taking (Denton 2001; Batchelor 2005) as well as outside the field of criminology proper (Lois 2005). Nevertheless, one of the implications of such work is already emerging. The more women are regarded criminologically as risk takers, as using risk as a means of generating excitements and pleasures, then the more the vision of women offenders as passive victims is challenged. Of course, there are still available crime prevention critiques of fecklessly putting themselves in the way of harm. Their risk taking may be pathologized in much the same way as male working-class risk taking. But they become active and capable in ways that little criminology, not just the criminology of risk, has hitherto taken on board (Denton 2001: 5).

## Conclusion: beyond the risk society

Risk generally has received rather a bad press among contemporary criminologists, in part because of a mistaken notion that the most negative forms of actuarial justice and Megan's Laws represent the 'real' or essential nature of risk (Hannah-Moffatt 1999; Hudson 2000). It should be clear, however, that risk can take many forms, including those – such as developmental criminology and risk–needs – that deliver much the same benefits with much the same shortcomings as the correctional and therapeutic initiatives of penal modernism. The question that emerges, therefore, is not whether criminologists should be for or against risk *per se*, let alone whether they should regard criminal justice as shaped by something as all-embracing as 'the risk society'. Such blanket responses distract analysis from risk's diversity, and appear to impose certain restricted choices or options on us, or in the vision of 'the risk society' appear to link risk into a kind of paranoid politics in which risk appears as an ideology masking a real inability to predict. Rather, the analysis in this chapter suggests that we should not be circumspect but open-minded. The key question concerns how we should discriminate among the various applications and practical configurations of risk, for risk itself is a rather abstract technology. Risk may be used to take potential offenders out of society and warehouse them or expose them to a local politics of hatred, or it may be used as a way to allocate and deliver social resources to young people in socially and economically deprived circumstances. Our options, the array of policy-making choices available within the domain of risk, are thus very varied. Indeed, as a result, in this kind of decision-making exercise I would suggest that we would look at very little that is peculiar to risk. The critical issues will not be about risk *per se* but will concern the implications of what we do for how offenders and victims are thought about and treated, and the implications for questions of social and juridical justice. In short, we return to questions of the substantive purpose and impact of criminal justice interventions, and forms of criminological analysis to which they are linked. This does not mean that risk is unimportant. Clearly this chapter indicates otherwise. Risk is part of the contemporary world that will not likely go away in the foreseeable future. It has effects that are intrinsically important, such as the fact that it singles out for some kind of intervention numbers of 'at risk' people who may never have offended. But it is an abstract technology capable of many applications. The problem for criminology and criminologists is how best to shape and deploy risk as a way of generating justice and security.

## Study questions

1  Do developments in the governance of crime fit with the idea that we have entered the era of a 'risk society' and does the idea of the risk society help us understand what is happening in criminal justice?

2  In the criminological field, risk is sometimes defined narrowly as the 'statistical probability of harm' and sometimes broadly as 'harm prevention'. Why might the distinction be important, and is it worth retaining?

3  How would you deal with the tensions between using risk to protect potential victims and safeguarding the rights of 'at risk' offenders and former offenders?

## References

Andrews, D. (1989) 'Recidivism' is predictable and can be influenced: using risk assessment to reduce recidivism, *Forum on Corrections Research*, 1(2): 78–88.

Andrews, D. and Bonta, D. (1989) *The Psychology of Criminal Conduct*. Cincinatti, OH: Andersons.

Austin, J., Clark, J., Hardyman, P. and Henry, D. (1999) The impact of 'three strikes and you're out', *Punishment and Society*, 1(1): 131–62.

Batchelor, S. (2005) 'Prove me the bam!' Victimization and agency in the lives of young women who commit violent offences, *Probation Journal*, 52(4): 358–75.

Bauman, Z. (2000) Social issues of law and order, *British Journal of Criminology*, 40(2): 205–21.

Bennett, T. (1994) Police strategies and tactics for controlling crime and disorder in England and Wales, *Studies on Crime and Crime Prevention*, 3: 146–67.

Burgess, E. (1928) Factors making for success or failure on parole, *Journal of Criminal Law and Criminology*, 19: 239–306.

Burgess, E. (1936) Protecting the public by parole and parole prediction, *Journal of Criminal Law and Criminology*, 27: 491–502.

Cohen, A. (1955) *Delinquent Boys*. Glencoe, IL: The Free Press.

Cohen, S. (1985) *Visions of Social Control*. Cambridge: Polity Press.

Crime Prevention Council of Canada (1997) *Preventing Crime by Investing in Families*. Ottawa: NCPC.

Denton, B. (2001) *Dealing: Women in the Drug Economy*. Sydney: UNSW Press.

Elias, R. (1993) *Victims Still*. London: Sage.

Ericson, R. (1994) The division of expert knowledge in policing and security, *British Journal of Sociology*, 45(2): 149–75.

Ericson, R. and Haggerty, K. (1998) *Policing the Risk Society*. Toronto: University of Toronto Press.

Feeley, M. and Simon, J. (1992) The new penology: notes on the emerging strategy of corrections and its implications, *Criminology*, 30: 449–74.

Feeley, M. and Simon, J. (1994) Actuarial justice: the emerging new criminal law, in D. Nelken (ed.) *The Futures of Criminology*. New York: Sage.

Floud, J. (1982) Dangerousness and criminal justice, *British Journal of Criminology*, 22: 213–28.

Freiberg, A. (2000) Guerillas in our midst? Judicial responses to governing the dangerous, in M. Brown and J. Pratt (eds) *Dangerous Offenders: Punishment and Social Order*. London: Routledge.

Geason, S. and Wilson, P. (1988) *Crime Prevention: Theory and Practice*. Canberra: Australian Institute of Criminology.

Geason, S. and Wilson, P. (1989) *Designing Out Crime: Crime Prevention through Environmental Design*. Canberra: Australian Institute of Criminology.

Glaser, D. (1962) Prediction tables as accounting devices for judges and parole boards, *Crime and Delinquency*, 8: 239–58.

Glaser, D. (1985) Who gets probation and parole: case study versus actuarial decision making, *Crime and Delinquency*, 31: 367–78.

Glueck, S. and Glueck, E. (1946) *After-Conduct of Discharged Offenders*. New York: Macmillan.

Gottfredson, M. (1984) *Risk of Victimisation: Findings from the 1982 British Crime Survey*. London: HMSO.

Haggerty, K. (2003) From risk to precaution: the rationalities of personal crime prevention, in R. Ericson and A. Doyle (eds) *Risk and Morality*. Toronto: University of Toronto Press.

Hale, C. (1996) Fear of crime: a review of the literature, *International Review of Victimology*, 3: 195–210.

Hall, J. (1986) Burglary 1985: the insurance industry viewpoint, in S. Mukherjee (ed.) *Burglary: A Social Reality*. Canberra: Australian Institute of Criminology.

Hannah-Moffatt, K. (1999) Moral agent or actuarial subject: risk and Canadian women's imprisonment, *Theoretical Criminology*, 3(1): 71–95.

Hannah-Moffatt, K. (2005) Criminogenic needs and the transformative risk sub-ject, *Punishment and Society*, 7(1): 29–51.

Heal, K. and Laycock, G. (1986) *Situational Crime Prevention: From Theory into Practice*. London: HMSO.

Hebenton, B. and Thomas, T. (1996) Sexual offenders in the community: reflec-tions of problems of law, community and risk management in the USA, England and Wales, *International Journal of the Sociology of Law*, 24: 427–43.

Hough, M. and Mayhew, P. (1983) *The British Crime Survey*. London: HMSO.

Hudson, B. (2000) Punishment, rights and difference, in K. Stenson and R. Sulli-van (eds) *Crime, Risk and Justice*. Exeter: Willan.

Hughes, G. (1999) *Understanding Crime Prevention: Social Control, Risk and Late Modernity*. Buckingham: Open University Press.

Kemshall, H. (1998) *Risk in Probation Practice*. Aldershot: Dartmouth.

Kemshall, H. and Maguire, M. (2001) Public protection, 'partnership' and risk penality, *Punishment and Society*, 3(2): 237–54.

King, M. (1991) The political construction of crime prevention: a contrast between the French and British experience, in K. Stenson and D. Cowell (eds) *The Politics of Crime Control*. Newbury Park, CA: Sage.

Levi, R. (2000) The mutuality of risk and community: the adjudication of com-munity notification statutes, *Economy and Society*, 29: 578–601.

Litton, R. (1982) Crime prevention and insurance, *The Howard Journal*, 21: 6–22.

Loader, I., Girling, E. and Sparks, R. (2000) After success? Anxieties of affluence in an English village, in T. Hope and R. Sparks (eds) *Crime, Risk and Insecurity*. London: Routledge.

Lois, J. (2005) Gender and emotion management in the stages of edgework, in S. Lyng (ed.) *Edgework: The Sociology of Risk Taking*. London: Routledge.

Lyng, S. (2005) *Edgework: The Sociology of Risk Taking*. London: Routledge.

Mannheim, H. and Wilkins, L. (1955) *Prediction Methods in Relation to Borstal Training*. London: HMSO.

Martinson, R. (1974) What works? Questions and answers about prison reform, *The Public Interest*, 10: 22–54.

Miller, W. (1958) Lower class culture as a generating milieu of gang delinquency, *Journal of Social Issues*, 14: 5–19.

National Crime Prevention (1999a) *Pathways to Prevention: Developmental and Early Intervention Approaches to Crime in Australia*. Canberra: Commonwealth At-torney General's Department.

National Crime Prevention (1999b) *Hanging Out: Negotiating Young People's Use of Public Space*. Canberra: Commonwealth Attorney General's Department.

National Crime Prevention Institute (1986) *Crime Prevention*. Louisville: NCPI.

Newman, O. (1973) *Defensible Space: Crime Prevention through Urban Design*. New York: Macmillan.

Ohlin, L. (1951) *Selection for Parole*. New York: Russell Sage Foundation.

O'Malley, P. (1992) Risk, power and crime prevention, *Economy and Society*, 21: 252–75.

O'Malley, P. (1999) Consuming risks: harm minimisation and the government of drug users, in R. Smandych (ed.) *Governable Places: Readings on Governmentality and Crime Control*. Aldershot: Dartmouth.

O'Malley, P. and Mugford, S. (1992) Moral technology: the political agenda of random drug testing, *Social Justice*, 18: 122–46.

O'Malley, P. and Mugford, S. (1994) Crime, excitement and modernity, in G. Barak (ed.) *Varieties of Criminology*. Westport, CT: Praeger.

Rand Corporation (1982) *Selective Incapacitation*. New York: Rand Corporation.

Reith, G. (2005) On the edge: drugs and the consumption of risk in late modernity, in S. Lyng (ed.) *Edgework: The Sociology of Risk Taking*. London: Routledge.

Rose, N. (2000) Government and control, *British Journal of Criminology*, 40(2): 321–39.

Sandon, M. (1991) *Ministerial Statement: Safety, Security and Women*. Melbourne: Parliament of Victoria.

Shearing, S. and Stenning, P. (1985) From panopticon to Disneyland: the development of discipline, in A. Doob and E. Greenspan (eds) *Perspectives in Criminal Law*. Toronto: Canada Law Book Company.

Simon, J. (1998) Managing the monstrous: sex offenders and the new penology, *Psychology, Public Policy and Law*, 4: 452–67.

Simon, J. and Feeley, M. (1995) True crime: the new penology and public discourse on crime, in T. Blomberg and S. Cohen (eds) *Law, Punishment and Social Control: Essays in Honor of Sheldon Messinger*. New York: Aldine de Gruyter.

Smith, C. (2005) Financial edgework: trading in market currents, in S. Lyng (ed.) *Edgework: The Sociology of Risk Taking*. London: Routledge.

Stanko, E. (1990a) *Everyday Violence*. London: Virago.

Stanko, E. (1990b) When precaution is normal: a feminist critique of crime prevention, in L. Gelsthorpe and A. Morris (eds) *Feminist Perspectives in Criminology*. Milton Keynes: Open University Press.

Stanko, E. (2000) Victims R Us: the life history of the 'fear of crime' and the politicization of violence, in T. Hope and R. Sparks (eds) *Crime, Risk and Insecurity*. London: Routledge.

Stanko, E. and Curry, P. (1997) Homophobic violence and the self 'at risk', *Social and Legal Studies*, 6: 513–32.

Thurgood, P. (1991) Safety, security and women, paper presented at the Crime Prevention Seminar, Ministry of Police and Emergency Services, Melbourne: 30 August.

Young, J. (1988) Risk of crime and fear of crime: a realist critique of survey-based assumptions, in M. Maguire and J. Ponting (eds) *Victims: A New Deal?* Milton Keynes: Open University Press.

Walklate, S. (1997) Risk and criminal victimization: a modernist dilemma? *British Journal of Criminology*, 37(1): 35–45.

Walklate, S. (2002) Gendering crime prevention: exploring the tensions between policy and process, in G. Hughes, E. McLaughlin and J. Muncie (eds) *Crime Prevention and Community Safety: New Directions*. London: Sage.

## Further reading

Ericson, R. and Haggerty, K. (1998) *Policing the Risk Society*. Toronto: University of Toronto Press.

Hope, T. and Sparks, R. (eds) (2000) *Crime, Risk and Insecurity*. London: Routledge.

Kemshall, H. (1998) *Risk in Probation Practice*. Aldershot: Ashgate.

O'Malley, P. (ed.) (1998) *Crime and the Risk Society*. Aldershot: Ashgate.

Stenson, K. and Sullivan, R. (2001) *Crime, Risk and Justice*. Cullompton: Willan.

# 4  Social policy and risk

## Hazel Kemshall

## Introduction

Our lives are increasingly dominated by 'risk', and it is often characterized as the major preoccupation of contemporary life (Adams 1995), resulting in what Power (2004: 10–11) has called 'the risk management of everything' with the consequent result that 'risk management is now at the centre stage of public service delivery'. However, the term 'risk' remains slippery, open to debate and subject to differing interpretations, and its usage in social policy has been variable (Kemshall 2002). This chapter will explore the evolving role of risk in social policy, with particular reference to contemporary changes in welfare provision. However, in this context, social policy is also interpreted more broadly than mere welfare, but as the strategic state organization of social provision in its many forms and its use within broader public policy (Lavalette and Pratt 1997). Following Power (2004), the very ambiguity of risk is taken as a starting point. This enables a focus on how risk is framed by social policy for attention, and how risk has been characterized as an area of concern since the initial inception of the welfare state.

The key objectives of the welfare state were: 'the pooling of risks, to protect everyone from shared vulnerability to the contingencies of industrial society, and to establish common standards in the provision of universal needs' (Jordan 1998: 100). In effect, a system that pooled common risks, and redistributed them via systems such as universal health care, welfare benefits, state pensions, and unemployment benefits. This formed the underlying principle of the social insurance approach to social policy and welfare typical of the Second World War era. Aharoni (1981) has described the welfare state as a 'no risk' society in which welfarism promised security from a range of external risks. The social engineering of the welfare state was aimed at the collective amelioration of such risks – usually defined as needs (e.g. unemployment or ill health), and the citizen was seen as the 'no fault' victim of such risks. However, it is contended by numerous commentators that since the late 1970s the state has 'retreated' from welfare, and social policy has been strategically used to reconfigure the collective provision of the state and also the relationship between citizen and state (Clarke and Newman 1997;

Lavalette and Pratt 1997; Pierson 1998; Kemshall 2002; Manning and Shaw 2000). Risk-led social policy accepts risk as a fact of late modern life, and largely unavoidable as we navigate through our life course (Giddens 1998, 2003). Protection is afforded to the individual only in very specific cases, and welfare responses are 'residual'. The prudential citizen is encouraged to manage his/her risks largely through the labour market (Kemshall 2002). This approach has re-characterized the citizen as an active risk manager, responsible for identifying and dealing with risks, constantly negotiating risk opportunities and threats throughout the life course (Giddens 1991; Beck 1992) and exercising prudential choices over lifestyle, health choices, personal insurance, private pension provision, and so forth (Castel 1991; Petersen 1996; Dwyer 2004). Freeman (1992) has labelled this a social policy of prevention serving a number of purposes, not least the management of social problems rather than their costly eradication, maintenance of the status quo and protection of vested interest, and the reconstruction of social problems as individual choices and responsibilities. A key feature of social policy in the 'risk society' is the meshing of risk, responsibility and the exercise of prudent choice. However, it is important to avoid simple contrasting characterizations and the temptation to see the development of social policy since the Second World War as fitting into neat periods of change. Research and analysis of social policy development and welfare change are a highly contested area, and debate rages as to the extent and on the nature of continuity and change (Powell and Hewitt 2002). It is useful to bear this in mind when considering the issues addressed in the next section of this chapter.

## Key research themes and current explanations

While social policy in the Anglophone countries, and most particularly in the UK and USA, has been radically transformed since the late 1970s, plotting changes in social policy and welfare provision has proved challenging (Powell and Hewitt 2002; Dwyer 2004). There are various 'grand' explanations of why change has occurred, and attributing the demise of the welfare state in particular to significant events has proved contentious (Powell and Hewitt 2002). Attributing causal explanations to complex change processes has also proved troublesome, with analysts such as Schwartz (2001) arguing that 'causal chains' are difficult to establish, and establishing the respective weight and influence of factors is challenging. Nevertheless such explanations have been attempted and, according to Powell and Hewitt, fall into four categories: economic, political, organizational and social. However, they are keen to conclude that no one explanation can capture the complexity of recent social policy and welfare change. With some adaptation these four themes will now be reviewed.

## Economic factors and structural change

The growing and unsustainable economic costs of welfare provision and the restrictive impact this was deemed to have on the expansion of the private sector have been seen as significant factors (Langan 1998). A long-term political strategy begun under Thatcherism and continued under New Labour has been the increased selectivity of welfare and the reduction of dependency (Giddens 1998, 2001; Field 2000; Dean 2003; Dwyer 2004). New Labour social policy has been described as a redistribution of opportunity – primarily the opportunity to work – and a move away from a redistribution of wealth *per se* (Lister 2000). Equal opportunity is not the same as equality of outcome (Jordan 1998, 2000). Economic and social policy have been meshed, and an effective social policy is one that serves the needs of the economy, particularly in reducing dependency, keeping citizens active in the marketplace, and in securing a flexible and responsive labour force: 'the Government's aim is to rebuild the welfare state around work' (DSS 1998: 23). A clear distinction is made between the responsible citizen and the 'irresponsible' and 'feckless'. The irresponsible are either excluded or are compelled back to work (Driver and Martell 2000; Levitas 1998).

These transformations are located in a broader 'sea-change' characterized by the demise of traditional capitalist Fordist states concerned with mass industrial production and mass consumption supported by a Keynesian welfare state (Jessop 1993, 1994, 2000). For Jessop (1993: 14), Fordist states are characterized by social cohesion and a mode of social regulation that supports and legitimizes capital production and consumption. Fordist states have been challenged by the 'rise of new technologies', 'growing internationalisation', and 'the regionalisation of global and national economies' (Jessop 1993: 25). Flexibility of production and low labour costs are seen as central to maintaining a competitive edge against the emerging economies of the newly industrialized countries. Jessop has argued that this has resulted in 'a structural transformation and fundamental strategic reorientation of the capitalist state' (1993: 24) characterized by:

- flexibility of labour market and production;
- technological innovation;
- economic regulation based upon an enterprise culture and the reward of flexible technological skills rather than collective bargaining;
- leaner organisational forms designed to deliver flexible supply systems.

(Jessop 1993, reproduced in Kemshall 2002: 17)

While pure economic determinism is disputed (Schwartz 2001; Powell and Hewitt 2002), policy responses to industrial decline, globalization and rapid technological change can be discerned (Mishra 1999). This is particularly evident in New Labour's emphasis upon the supply side – creating an active, well-educated and flexible labour force in the UK (Blair and Schroeder 1999; Hutton 1999). However, there is no inexorable logic to residual social policy. Policy is a matter of political choice, and as Powell and Hewitt put it: 'globalisation serves as a convenient rationalisation for neo-liberal policies' (2002: 94). However, a key outcome of the economic framing of social policy is the reframing of need as individual failing rather than as a product of social causes, and collective responsibility is reframed as an individual one. In effect, this re-inscribes needs as risks and justifies increased selectivity and targeting in social policy responses (Kemshall 2002).

## Political choices and the value framing of risk

The political and ideological wish to reduce state intervention and individual dependency on the welfare state, and the reduction in the power of the welfare state and the public sector, particularly as a site of opposition to New Right governments have also been cited (Deakin 1987; Clarke et al. 1994; Clarke and Newman 1997; Lavelette and Pratt 1997; Kemshall 2002). The extent of New Labour's change or continuity with the New Right has been much debated; however, some key themes can be identified. The most pertinent are the continuation of selectivity and targeting in welfare provision, and the emphasis upon the reduction of dependency. The 'Thatcher years' and the programme of the New Right eroded the notion of social insurance and in many respects reconfigured needs as the result of personal misfortune and the failure to manage risk appropriately (Rose 1996b; Kemshall 2002). New Labour's 'Third Way' has not returned to an agenda of alleviating individual need, but has stressed a programme of social investment and opportunity creation – a 'something for something' society rather than a dependent society in which the work ethic is at the centre of the welfare state (Blair 1997; Jordan 1998). Rights – particularly to welfare – are linked to the duties of citizenship and welfare entitlement is conditional (Blair 1998; Dwyer 2004). The Third Way in effect introduced a political discourse of selectivity while appearing to preserve the welfare state – an emphasis upon a 'hand up not a hand out' (Blair 1998), and as Franklin shows in Chapter 9, entitlement is limited by notions of duty and obligation. In this discourse, risk and responsibility were meshed, resulting in what Jordan (2000) has called 'tough love' – a welfarism of non-dependency, and the replacement of a safety net with a 'trampoline' (Leonard 1997).

### Organizational factors and the modernization agenda: restructuring welfare

The modernization agenda has been seen as influential, particularly the overhaul of the NHS, education, and the personal social services (Clarke and Newman 1997). The key factors here are seen as privatization and market-ization; partnership; and managerialism (Clarke and Newman 1997; Clarke et al. 2000; Kemshall 2002). Mooney (1997) has noted the rise of the market and the mixed economy of welfare as a strategic tool in the reconfiguration of health and the personal social services. Hugman (1998) has documented the commodification of welfare provision particularly in respect of the elderly, and the pursuit of efficiency, effectiveness and value for money in an effort to reduce public spending. The impact upon the structure of the welfare state and the delivery of key services has been well documented (Deakin 1987; Kemshall 2002; Powell and Hewitt 2002). In welfare delivery and organiza-tion, the key outcome was a 'new managerialism' stressing evaluation, ac-countability and increased regulation of the activities of the workforce (Clarke and Newman 1997). For Power, risk has become the new audit tool used to hold the public sector workforce to account and is deployed as a key mechanism for 'challenging the quality of public services in the absence of real markets' (Power 2004: 19). This opened up the public sector to 'value for money' assessments, and the three 'E's' of effectiveness, efficiency and economy. Cost rather than need became a key driver in social policy pro-vision, and risk became a key mechanism for rationing and allocating ser-vices. In these processes, risk is characterized as either exposure to risk, that is, *vulnerability*, for example, children at risk, or vulnerable adults; or as posing a risk that is *dangerous*, for example, mentally disordered offenders. This echoes the discussion of risk management in relation to offenders presented by O'Malley in Chapter 3. The risk inscription is the key criterion for eligibility to the service (Langan 1998; Kemshall 2002).

In broader social policy terms, the modernization agenda has justified targeting and selectivity, and has reconfigured need to enable increased ex-clusion from provision (Kemshall 2002). It has also extended the notion of provider beyond the state, to communities, families, networks, voluntary sector and private providers. This is not merely a matter of introducing market processes to social policy provision, it has also resulted in a dis-placement of responsibility from the state to individuals for care provision (Dean 2003). This has been most noticeable in the personal social services where services were already partially selective and targeted, and is less de-veloped in areas such as education and health care where the principles of universalism are still accepted by the public and are less open to state re-duction (Taylor-Gooby et al. 1999; Taylor-Gooby 2001).

## Social changes and social theories

'Risk society' and the issues of governance in postmodern neo-liberal societies have been seen as crucial to recent social policy changes although the extent to which risk has been a key driver is contested (Culpitt 1999; Kemshall 2002). In brief, the contention is that the state has increasingly devolved responsibility for the management of risks – for example, ill health, unemployment – onto the individual and that social responsibility has been eroded (Rose 1996a). This reduces the costs to the state, but, just as importantly, reduces dependency and moral hazard (Parker 1982), and encourages a more flexible and risk-taking attitude to the navigation of the life course and the changes that will inevitably take place (Giddens 1991, 1998). The 'active' rather than the 'passive' citizen is seen as desirable, both morally and economically, particularly in an era of rapid social and technological change. This 're-sponsibilization' as it is dubbed, has also been associated with neo-liberal modes of governance – that is regulation of conduct – described by Rose (1996b) as 'government at the molecular level' in which conduct is regulated less by overt state power and more by moral expectation. The responsible citizen knows what is expected and does it. These expectations are conveyed through a social policy infused with notions of responsibility – for one's own health, pension planning, employment skill updating, lifelong learning, and so forth (Petersen 1997; Rose 1996a, 2000). As Rose puts it, such prudential-ism requires the citizen to adopt a calculating attitude towards most if not all of her/his decisions, whether these be decisions over healthy eating options or the installation of burglar alarms. Thus, the individual, not society, becomes the primary site of risk management, and the 'good' citizen is the responsible and prudential one (Rose 1996a, 1996b). Prudence is not a new concept, and has been emphasized at least since Victorian times in the distinction between the 'deserving' and 'non-deserving' poor. However, what is new here is the 'construction of active citizenship in an active society' (Rose 1996b: 60) and that this underpins contemporary forms regardless of political spectrum or political ideology. The contention is that social policy is no longer about the alleviation of individual needs or about the pursuit of a collective good. Rather, it is about the prevention of risk and the displace-ment of risk management responsibilities onto the 'entrepreneurial self' who must exercise informed choice and self-care to avoid risks (Castel 1991; Petersen 1996, 1997). This approach to social policy analysis is most often associated with the theorizing of Foucault and the role of welfarist disciplinary techniques (Foucault 1973; Donzelot 1980; Dean 1989). In such analyses social policy is characterized as 'soft policing' (Rodger 2000), a mechanism for regulating and normalizing deviant populations. Late – or post – modernity is seen as posing significant difficulties for traditional forms of regulation and integration (Burchell et al. 1991) and advanced liberal characterizations of the state and the role of social policy within it owe much to postmodern considerations (Carter 1998). Such analyses are most often associated with the work of Leonard (1997) who has outlined a postmodern programme of welfare. In brief, globalization and the uncertainties of postmodernity characterized by diversity and pluralism are seen as problematic for government (Harris 1999). Advanced liberal forms of responsibilized social policy have been characterized as a response to the indeterminacy and deregulation of the risk society. Diversity and pluralism threaten social solidarity and overt state control is eschewed on the grounds of cost and public acceptability (Turner 1997). Displacement of responsibility to the morally reconstituted free will of the individual is seen as more effective and efficient (Miller and Rose 1990). However, whether the social is really dead (Rose 1996a) is a contested point, and social policy at present is probably more easily characterized as a mixture of modern social insurance and individual prudentialism (Kelly and Charlton 1995).

## Major research and theoretical contributions: where are we now?

### Differing characterizations of risk and security

Within these differing explanations of social policy development since the late 1970s it is possible to identify both significant continuities between New Right and New Labour (Powell and Hewitt 2002), but also significant discontinuities as postmodern welfare begins to take shape (Leonard 1997; Harris 1999). However, one clear unifying theme is risk and the differing approaches taken towards it by social policy in this period (Kemshall 2002). Interestingly, different characterizations of risk are taken. Negative characterizations see risk as a threat or hazard, and see the challenge for social policy as the requirement to provide citizens with protection, safety and security from external risks – usually characterized as outside the individual's control – arising from globalization, expanding markets and rapid economic change (Hall 1998; Jordan 1998). Positive characterizations of risk, most associated with the work of Giddens and the 'Third Way', see risk as innovation, opportunity and responsibility, what Giddens (1998: 63) has called 'the positive side of risk' and the 'active exploration of risk environments.' He sees 'a positive engagement with risk as a necessary component of social and economic mobilisation' (Giddens 1998: 63). In this characterization of risk, the challenge for social policy is to promote 'productive risk taking' (Giddens 1998) and to facilitate constructive risk taking throughout the life course (Dwyer 2004). These are also questions about how much security the state should afford the citizen, and the appropriate balance between risk and security.

## Is it really risky?

Grand theoretical claims about a risk-led social policy require empirical support – if the contentions are correct, then it should be possible to see risk played out in material forms of service provision in various arenas (Kemshall 2002). As Harris and McDonald (2000) argue, the case for wholesale shifts in welfare need to be subject to empirical tests prior to any grand claims for transition. However, if key areas of welfare and social policy are examined, then the shift is less clear-cut. The 'needs-based' discourse of the welfare state has in practice been subject to numerous social, economic and political processes in its construction and use (Langan 1998; Kemshall 2002) and social policy has long been concerned with risks, for example, protection from disease, accidental injury and unemployment (Simon 1987). The origins of the Beveridge welfare state are in collective concerns with these latter risks.

There is now a growing body of empirical research on the role of risk in social policy and welfare provision. For example, Alaszewski et al. (1998) on health, Kemshall (2002) on welfare, Parton et al. (1997) on child protection and Culpitt (1999) on the role of risk in social policy. There is consensus from these in-depth case studies that risk has replaced need as the key organizing principle of welfare provision, and that needs are re-inscribed either as 'vulnerability', that is exposure to risk – 'at risk' children, the 'vulnerable elderly' – or as posing a risk to others such as mentally disordered persons, or risky youth. In the health arena, the situation is more contestable. Certainly the NHS has been exposed to modernization and to advances of privatization and marketization. It is also possible to identify a preoccupation with risk in the discourse of the 'New Public Health' (Petersen 1996, 1997; Harrison 2002) and to discern increased responsibilization for risks – healthy eating, exercise, and so on – with an obligation on the responsible citizen to manage their own health well (Petersen and Lupton 1996).

Grand theories of risk have also tended to characterize risk as largely negative (Kemshall 2003) although it is a matter of dispute as to whether the contemporary discourse of risk in social policy and welfare is entirely negative (Titterton 2005). In the areas of mental health provision and care of the elderly in particular, there is much evidence to support a positive framing of risk, focusing on the empowerment of vulnerable people to take risks, make choices and exercise personal autonomy. In this context, risk is associated with the 'right to self-determination' and the management of risk is presented as the balance between risks and rights (Norman 1980; Titterton 2005). This is mirrored in policy documents throughout the 1990s seeking to balance the autonomy and independence of older persons with their appropriate care, particularly in residential settings (Centre for Policy on Ageing 1996, 1999), paralleled by similar concerns for mental health service users (Counsel and Care 1992, 1993; Davis 1996). These positive framings of risk, and arguments for a more explicit balance between rights and risks in social policy are due primarily to two major imperatives: the challenge and advocacy of user groups and recent human rights legislation, particularly on rights to liberty, privacy and family life. Titterton (2005), for example, speculates that restraint on the rights of vulnerable people to take risks may be actionable under the European Convention on Human Rights. Similar concerns have been raised about overly restrictive practices in criminal justice (Kemshall 2003), resulting in broader debates about the appropriate balance between risks and rights (Hudson 2003) and autonomy and safety (Langan 1999).

## Conclusion: beyond the risk society

Rodger (2000: 3) has described the key principle of the 'new moral economy of welfare' as the 'privatisation of responsibility'. This suggests a wholesale shift to an individualized and responsibilized risk-based welfare and a social policy characterized by concerns to redefine citizenship as proactive and to replace 'moral hazard' with the work ethic (Kemshall 2002). However, this presumes that the development of social policy is preordained and that it is driven by an 'inexorable logic of risk' (O'Malley 2001). Parallel work in penal policy indicates that this is not necessarily the case, and that policy choices on the management of risk are never morally neutral but always carry some value-laden imperative (O'Malley 2001, 2004; Kemshall 2003). A key task for research is to unpick these underlying moral rationalities. In essence, this suggests further work on risk framing: how risks are defined and framed by policy-makers and why, and how some risks gain saliency while others do not (Sparks 2001). Social theories of risk, particularly in the area of penal policy and environmental risks, have made a significant contribution to analysis of this type. Within this framing of risk the focus is not individual risk decision-making, but on how some risks are chosen for attention while others are not – for example, the attention to 'stranger-danger' in child sexual abuse and the relative neglect of sexual abusing within families (Kitzinger 2004). Such work pays attention to the symbolic and cultural meanings carried by risk (Douglas 1992) and the political rationalities and strategies that underpin them (Sparks 2001). As Lupton and O'Malley have demonstrated, risk technologies can be deployed differently in different contexts and organizational settings. This suggests that comparative work, particularly across countries, could be useful in mapping the differing future possibilities of welfare and social provision in advanced liberal societies. Emerging work comparing differing Anglophone countries, and also countries in Western Europe indicate that there are different responses to the effects of globalization and high costs of welfare. Castles and Pierson (1996) have compared Australia, the UK and New Zealand and conclude that social policy developments remain quite diverse. It is also contended that Scandinavian countries have resisted the worst excesses of neo-liberalism and still have a strong commitment to social democracy and welfarism (Moses et al. 2000; Swank 2000; Powell and Hewitt 2002). A further area of research is likely to be the interaction of political institutions, politicians and risk. This has been a growing research area for environmental, health and scientific risks and focuses on risk decision-making within the context of political institutions, and the interaction of such institutions with the public (European Commission 2004). The important focus is on how risks are perceived by politicians and policy-makers. Research in this area is also concerned to identify the most effective processes for communicating risks and subsequent risk management strategies to the public in order to gain and maintain public support for the risk management choices taken (European Commission 2004). Research of this type will require collaboration between economists, political scientists, sociologists, social policy analysts, and social psychologists.

While such research is more common in public policy, less work of this type has taken place in the social policy arena – although there is research on whether 'politics matters' in the restructuring of welfare (Powell and Hewitt 2002). Debates about social policy provision have tended to take place within the 'bidding wars' of electoral politics, or framed as issues of higher or lower taxation. Pensions may be the arena in which such debate could flourish as the issue between collective and individual provision becomes sharper, and private/occupational coverage fails to provide adequate cover (Brindle 1996; Hargreaves and Christie 1998). Despite massive expansion in pension provision, poverty in old age remains a perennial issue (Johnson 1998), and pension funds cannot keep pace with the number of prospective pensioners and lengthening life expectancy. Initial pension provision was based upon a collective insurance scheme (Beveridge 1942) and this is an area of provision where the risk (old age) is inevitable, faced by all, and traditionally seen as requiring a collective not individual response. As the population ages, and the employed workforce shrinks in comparison, collective rather than individual decisions about the management of this risk will be required. This question of the management of pension provision is picked up again by McMylor in Chapter 11.

Such considerations also raise research questions about how people perceive risks and how they expect them to be managed. Taylor-Gooby (1985, 1991, 2000) has extensively researched public views on welfare provision, and has found that support for the welfare state remains strong and that there is little public acceptance for the individual management of many risks (Taylor-Gooby 2000). There is some distinction about types of provision, with higher levels of support for mass services such as the NHS that most people expect to use at some point in their lives, and welfare benefits where distinctions between the 'deserving' and 'non-deserving' poor are regularly made – for example, in debates about the provision made to asylum seekers. Universal services appear to be acceptable if the public perceive a general and highly probable risk, such as ill health or old age, but residual services appear to require ever increasing levels of justification, in which the perception of a 'no fault' risk is crucial. Residual services with little universal support are prey to criticism and ultimate removal. In so far as politicians might find responsibilization attractive, the public may have a more selective attitude about what provision it is used for and to whom it is applied. This indicates that more research is required on public acceptability and perception of risks in the social policy area and the extent to which they are related to changes in the spread and general experience of risks. This would suggest a move from research commentary on the restructuring of welfare towards a greater emphasis upon public acceptability of risks and social policies designed to ameliorate them.

## Study questions

1 What is the evidence that social policy and welfare are now led by risk rather than by need?
2 How would you assess the strengths and weaknesses of the case that contemporary social policy is a key mechanism in the responsibilization of citizens?
3 What do you think are the most important factors in public acceptability of welfare provision?

## References

Adams, J. (1995) *Risk*. London: UCL Press.
Aharoni, Y. (1981) *The No-Risk Society*. Chatham, NJ: Chatham House.
Alaszewski, A., Harrison, J. and Manthorpe, J. (1998) *Risk, Health and Welfare*. Buckingham: Open University Press.
Beck, U. (1992) *The Risk Society: Towards a New Modernity*. London: Sage.
Beveridge, W. (1942) *Social Insurance and Allied Services*. Cmnd 6404. London: HMSO.
Blair, T. (1997) Durham Speech, 22nd December. Viewable at http://www.labour.org.uk
Blair, T. (1998) *The Third Way*. London: Fabian Society.
Blair, T. and Schroeder, G. (1999) *Europe: The Third Way/Die Neue Mitte*. London: Labour Party.
Brindle, D. (1996) NHS to sell private care plans, *The Guardian*, 25 March.
Burchell, G., Gordon, C. and Miller, P. (eds) (1991) *The Foucault Effect: Studies in Governmentality*. London: Harvester Wheatsheaf.

Carter, J. (ed.) (1998) *Postmodernity and the Fragmentation of Welfare.* London: Routledge.

Castel, R. (1991) From dangerousness to risk, in G. Burchell, C. Gordon and P. Miller (eds) *The Foucault Effect: Studies in Governmentality.* London: Harvester Wheatsheaf.

Castles, F. and Pierson, C. (1996) A new convergence? Recent policy developments in the United Kingdom, Australia and New Zealand, *Policy and Politics,* 24(3): 233–45.

Centre for Policy on Ageing (1996) *A Better Home Life: A Code of Good Practice for Residential and Nursing Home Care.* London: Centre for Policy on Ageing.

Centre for Policy on Ageing (1999) *National Required Standards for Residential and Nursing Home Care.* London: Centre for Policy on Ageing.

Clarke, J., Cochrane, L. and McLaughlin, E. (eds) (1994) *Managing Social Policy.* London: Sage.

Clarke, J., Gewirtz, S. and McLaughlin, E. (eds) (2000) *New Labour, New Managerialism.* London: Sage.

Clarke, J. and Newman, J. (1997) *The Managerial State.* London: Sage.

Counsel and Care (1992) *What If They Hurt Themselves?* London: Counsel and Care.

Counsel and Care (1993) *The Right to Take Risks.* London: Counsel and Care.

Culpitt, I. (1999) *Social Policy and Risk.* London: Sage.

Davis, A. (1996) Risk work and mental health, in H. Kemshall and J. Pritchard (eds) *Good Practice in Risk Assessment and Risk Management.* London: Jessica Kingsley Publishers.

Deakin, N. (1987) *The Politics of Welfare.* London: Methuen and Co.

Dean, H. (1989) Disciplinary partitioning and the privatisation of social security, *Critical Social Policy,* 24: 74–82.

Dean, H. (2003) The Third Way and social welfare: the myth of post-emotionalism, *Social Policy and Administration,* 37(7): 695–708.

Department of Social Security (1998) *New Ambitions for Our Country.* London: The Stationery Office.

Donzelot, J. (1980) *The Policing of Families.* London: Hutchinson.

Douglas, M. (1992) *Risk and Blame.* London: Routledge.

Driver, S. and Martell, L. (2000) Left, right and third way, *Policy and Politics,* 28(2): 147–61.

Dwyer, P. (2004) Creeping conditionality in the UK: from welfare rights to conditional entitlements? *Canadian Journal of Sociology,* 29(2): 265–87.

European Commission (2004) *Towards Inclusive Risk Governance: TRUSTNET 2.* Brussels: European Commission.

Field, F. (2000) Interview on *World at One,* BBC Radio 4, 27 September.

Foucault, M. (1973) *The Birth of the Clinic: An Archaeology of Medical Perceptions.* London: Tavistock.

Freeman, R. (1992) The idea of prevention: a critical review, in S. Scott, G. Williams, S. Platt and H. Thomas (eds) *Private Risks and Public Dangers.* Aldershot: Avebury.

Giddens, A. (1991) *Modernity and Self-identity: Self and Society in the Late Modern Age.* Cambridge: Polity Press.

Giddens, A. (1998) *The Third Way: The Renewal of Social Democracy.* Oxford: Polity Press.

Giddens, A. (2001) *The Global Third Way Debate.* Cambridge: Polity Press.

Giddens, A. (2003) *Runaway World: How Globalization Is Reshaping Our Lives.* London: Routledge.

Hall, S. (1998) The Great Moving Nowhere Show, *Marxism Today*, November/December: 9–14.

Hargreaves, I. and Christie, I. (1998) Re-thinking retirement, in I. Hargreaves and I. Christie (eds) *Tomorrow's Politics: The Third Way and Beyond.* London: Demos.

Harris, J. and McDonald, C. (2000) Post-Fordism, the welfare state and the personal social services: a comparison of Australia and Britain, *British Journal of Social Work*, 30: 51–70.

Harris, P. (1999) Public welfare and liberal governance, in A. Petersen, J. Barns, J. Dudley and P. Harris (eds) *Poststructuralism, Citizenship and Social Policy.* London: Routledge.

Harrison, D. (2002) Health promotion and politics, in R. Bunton and G. Macdonald (eds) *Health Promotion: Disciplines, Diversity and Developments.* London: Routledge.

Hudson, B. (2003) *Justice in the Risk Society.* London: Sage.

Hugman, R. (1998) *Social Welfare and Social Value: The Role of the Caring Professions.* Basingstoke: Macmillan.

Hutton, W. (1999) *The Stakeholder Society: Writings on Economics and Politics.* Cambridge: Polity Press.

Jessop, B. (1993) Towards a Schumpeterian welfare state? Preliminary remarks on post-Fordist political economy, *Studies in Political Economy*, 40: 7–39.

Jessop, B. (1994) The transition to a post-Fordist and Schumpeterian welfare state, in R. Burrows and B. Loader (eds) *Towards a Post-Fordist Welfare State?* London: Routledge.

Jessop, B. (2000) From the KWNS to the SWPR, in G. Lewis, S. Gerwitz and J. Clarke (eds) *Rethinking Social Policy.* London: Sage/Open University.

Johnson, P. (1998) Parallel histories of retirement in modern Britain, in P. Johnson and P. Thane (eds) *Old Age from Antiquity to Post-modernity.* London: Routledge.

Jordan, B. (1998) *The New Politics of Welfare.* London: Sage.

Jordan, B. (2000) *Social Work and the Third Way: Tough Love as Social Policy.* London: Sage.

Kelly, M. and Charlton, B. (1995) The modern and the post-modern in health promotion, in R. Bunton, S. Nettleton and R. Burrows (eds) *The Sociology of Health Promotion.* London: Routledge.

Kemshall, H. (2002) *Risk, Social Policy and Welfare.* Buckingham: Open University Press.

Kemshall, H. (2003) *Understanding Risk in Criminal Justice.* Buckingham: Open University Press.

Kitzinger, J. (2004) *Framing Abuse: Media Influence and Public Understanding of Sexual Violence against Children*. London: Pluto Press.

Langan, J. (1998) *Welfare: Needs, Rights and Risks*. London: Open University Press/ Routledge.

Langan, J. (1999) Assessing risk in mental health, in P. Parsloe (ed.) *Risk Assessment in Social Care and Social Work*. London: Jessica Kingsley Publishers.

Lavalette, M. and Pratt, A. (eds) (1997) *Social Policy: A Conceptual and Theoretical Introduction*. London: Sage.

Leonard, P. (1997) *Postmodern Welfare*. London: Sage.

Levitas, R. (1998) *The Inclusive Society?* Basingstoke: Macmillan.

Lister, R. (2000) To RIO via the Third Way, *Renewal*, 8(4): 9–20.

Lupton, D. (1999) *Risk*. London: Routledge.

Manning, N. and Shaw, I. (eds) (2000) *New Risks: New Welfare*. Oxford: Blackwell.

Miller, P. and Rose, N. (1990) Governing economic life, *Economy and Society*, 19: 1–13.

Mishra, R. (1999) *Globalisation and the Welfare State*. Cheltenham: Edward Elgar.

Mooney, G. (1997) Quasi-markets and the mixed economy of welfare, in M. Lavalette and A. Pratt (eds) *Social Policy: A Conceptual and Theoretical Introduction*. London: Sage.

Moses, J., Geyer, R. and Ingebritsen, C. (2000) Introduction, in R. Geyer, C. Ingebritsen and J. Moses (eds) *Globalisation, Europeanisation and the End of Scandinavian Social Democracy?* Basingstoke: Macmillan.

Norman, A. (1980) *Rights and Risks*. London: Routledge.

O'Malley, P. (2001) Risk, crime and prudentialism revisited, in K. Stenson and R. Sullivan (eds) *Crime, Risk and Justice: The Politics of Crime Control in Liberal Democracies*. Cullompton: Willan.

O'Malley, P. (2004) The uncertain promise of risk, *Australian and New Zealand Journal of Criminology*, 37(3): 323–43.

Parker, H. (1982) *The Moral Hazard of Social Insurance*. Research Monograph 37. London: Institute of Economic Affairs.

Parton, N., Thorpe, D. and Wattam, C. (1997) *Child Protection: Risk and the Moral Order*. Basingstoke: Macmillan.

Petersen, A. (1996) Risk and the regulated self: the discourse of health promotion as politics of uncertainty, *Australian and New Zealand Journal of Sociology*, 32(1): 44–57.

Petersen, A. (1997) Risk, governance and the new public health, in A. Petersen and R. Bunton (eds) *Foucault, Health and Medicine*. London: Routledge.

Petersen, A. and Lupton, D. (1996) *The New Public Health: Health and Self in the Age of Risk*. London: Sage.

Pierson, C. (1998) *Beyond the Welfare State*. Cambridge: Polity Press.

Powell, M. and Hewitt, M. (2002) *Welfare State and Welfare Change*. Buckingham: Open University Press.

Power, M. (1994) *The Audit Explosion*. London: Demos.

Power, M. (2004) *The Risk Management of Everything: Rethinking the Politics of Uncertainty*. London: Demos.

Rodger, J. (2000) *From a Welfare State to a Welfare Society: The Changing Context of Social Policy in a Postmodern Era*. London: Macmillan.

Rose, N. (1996a) The death of the social? Refiguring the territory of government. *Economy and Society*, 25(3): 327–56.

Rose, N. (1996b) Governing 'advanced' liberal democracies, in A. Barry, T. Osborne, and N. Rose (eds) *Foucault and Political Reason: Liberalism, Neo-liberalism and Rationalities of Government*. London: UCL Press.

Rose, N. (2000) Government and control, *British Journal of Criminology*, 40: 321–39.

Simon, J. (1987) The Emergence of a Risk Society: Insurance, Law and the state, *Socialist Review*, 95: 61–89.

Schwartz, H. (2001) Round up the usual suspects! In P. Pierson (ed.) *The Politics of the Welfare State*. Oxford: Oxford University Press.

Sparks, R. (2001) Degrees of estrangement: the cultural theory of risk and comparative penology, *Theoretical Criminology*, 5(2): 159–76.

Swank, D. (2000) Political institutions and welfare state restructuring, in P. Pierson (ed.) *The New Politics of the Welfare State*. Oxford: Oxford University Press.

Taylor-Gooby, P. (1985) *Public Opinion, Ideology and State Welfare*. London: Routledge and Kegan Paul.

Taylor-Gooby, P. (1991) *Social Change, Social Welfare and Social Science*. Hemel Hempstead: Harvester Wheatsheaf.

Taylor-Gooby, P. (2000) *Risk, Trust and Welfare*. Basingstoke: Macmillan.

Taylor-Gooby, P. (2001) Risk, contingency and the Third Way: evidence from the BHPS and qualitative studies, *Social Policy and Administration*, 35(2): 195–211.

Taylor-Gooby, P., Dean, P., Munro, M. and Parker, G. (1999) Risk and the welfare state, *British Journal of Sociology*, 50(2): 177–94.

Titterton, M. (2005) *Risk and Risk Taking in Health and Social Welfare*. London: Jessica Kingsley Publishers.

Turner, B. (1997) Foreword: from governmentality to risk, some reflections on Foucault's contributions to medical sociology, in A. Petersen and R. Bunton (eds) *Foucault, Health and Medicine*. London: Routledge.

## Further reading

Kemshall, H. (2002) *Risk, Social Policy and Welfare*. Buckingham: Open University Press.

Manning, N. and Shaw, I. (eds) *New Risks: New Welfare*. Oxford: Blackwell.

Powell, M. and Hewitt, M. (2002) *Welfare State and Welfare Change*. Buckingham: Open University Press.

Rodger, J. (2000) *From a Welfare State to a Welfare Society: The Changing Context of Social Policy in a Postmodern Era*. Basingstoke: Macmillan.

Taylor-Gooby, P. (2000) *Risk, Trust and Welfare*. Basingstoke: Macmillan.

# PART II
## EMBRACING THE RISK
## AGENDA

# 5 Health and risk

## Rob Flynn

## Introduction

As previous chapters have shown, we increasingly live in societies saturated with apparent risk and uncertainty. Perhaps nowhere is this more evident than in the case of health and illness. The mass media continuously report a multitude of new risks and increased propensity among some groups to engage in – or have higher levels of exposure to – 'risky' behaviour. Simultaneously, those same media regularly feature new scientific discoveries and medical applications providing innovative treatments for known conditions, as well as entirely new possibilities affecting people's life-chances – for example in reproductive medicine. The unanticipated and negative effects of drug treatments and clinical procedures have long been the focus for critique of medical professionals (Illich 1977). Medical errors – or 'adverse incidents' – have caused higher levels of public anxiety, stimulated an industry for lawyers and insurance companies based on claims against medical negligence, and led to the emergence of a vast array of bureaucratic systems of regulation (Flynn 2004; Harrison 2004). New techniques and types of medication are usually required to undergo extensive clinical trials and scrutiny to minimize harm to patients. Sometimes there is a lengthy period before problems are identified, and then contentious disputes about causality and responsibility. Health is thus intrinsically and inevitably associated with risk. This inherent feature of health (as risk) is not solely about individuals' chances of survival, well-being and longevity; it also entails institutional levels of risk as they affect demographic structures and the overall functioning of social systems. As late modern societies have developed, health has also become increasingly commodified and politicized: the state, business – including the pharmaceutical industry and for-profit healthcare institutions – healthcare professionals and consumers/clients/patients are necessarily engaged in a competition for scarce resources and conflicts over the degree to which healthcare should be the province of the private market or public sector. This also affects whether, and how, health risks are recognized, categorized and acted upon.

Other contributors have already discussed the pervasiveness and ubiquity of risk in connection with Beck's (1992a) analysis of contemporary society. It is evident that health and illness concurrently manifest both the multi-dimensional character of risk and its multiplication (as Beck suggested). At the time of writing, for example, the British press carried stories about the following:

- differentials between social class groups and geographical areas in the risk of cancer and inequalities in the provision of treatment;
- the withdrawal by the British Medicines and Healthcare Products Regulatory Agency of a long-established painkiller (co-proxamol) because of links with increased risk of accidental deaths and suicides;
- fears of a pandemic caused by 'Asian bird flu';
- the accidental despatch by an American agency of vials containing a lethal virus to over 3,700 laboratories across the world;
- possible risks of contamination caused by unlicensed importation of genetically modified (GM) rice into the UK food chain;
- the British Medical Association complaining that government targets for treatment in hospital accident and emergency departments was putting seriously ill people 'at risk';
- the possibility that 'New Variant CJD' may be linked to contamination of some baby foods from 1970;
- widespread incidence of an infectious 'superbug' – MRSA – in NHS hospitals, and its link with rising levels of hospital-acquired infections;
- the publication of patients' death rates by hospital surgeons, showing considerable and unexplained variation;
- chemical substances (phthalates) in plastics entering pregnant women's bloodstream and harming the development of male foetuses;
- rising levels of obesity in the population and increased risks of diabetes.

The list could continue almost indefinitely, but the point is to illustrate the almost limitless agenda surrounding health risks. Most people are now familiar with public debate about HIV/AIDS, some may have heard about Creutzfeld-Jakob disease and some others are concerned about scares over the measles, mumps and rubella vaccination, prompted by fears of a hypothetical – but unproven – connection with autism in children (Bellaby 2003, 2005; Petts and Niemeyer 2004). Health risks associated with some patterns of food consumption, obesity and lack of exercise have prompted a varied response in popular culture, industry and government. Among certain sections of the population, this has resulted in an increased preoccupation with body image, diet and exercise, coinciding with the growth of the health and fitness industries, and public health campaigns to promote healthier lifestyles. Alcohol and tobacco consumption have become public issues provoking controversies over health risks and also – to some extent, in Britain – almost a kind of 'moral panic'. So-called 'binge drinking' among young people is frequently vilified and some medical professionals have questioned whether smokers should enjoy full rights to NHS treatment for their smoking-related – 'self-inflicted' – illnesses. Risks in health may not always be associated with random events, mere chance or passive victims; sometimes their very existence is seen – or rather, culturally defined (as in the early stages of recognition of HIV/AIDS) – as voluntarily chosen and a product of moral (ir)responsibility.

Health risks are seemingly all-embracing and ever-extending. But this reflects the paradox that Beck, among others, previously noted: historically there have been massive absolute improvements in general public health and overall reductions in mortality rates in the past half-century, yet variations in morbidity and mortality persist between social classes, ethnic groups and genders, and new previously undiagnosed illnesses and conditions have emerged. People in general may now be less vulnerable to certain types of infection, they may enjoy greater life expectancy, and standards of healthcare have risen – while at the same time exposure to environmental pollution and other causes of ill-health may have increased, and new illnesses have emerged – for example, 'ME', myalgic encephalomyelitis or chronic fatigue syndrome. This forces us to consider fundamental theoretical questions about how 'real' these health risks are, and how far they are subject to variable degrees of social construction.

This chapter, then, first discusses alternative conceptualizations of health and illness. It then briefly considers some of the most salient aspects of risk as they affect health. The contrast between social constructionist approaches and realist approaches as they apply to health and illness is outlined, and some examples given. Finally, the chapter will propose that a 'weak' constructionist standpoint can be combined with a critical realist framework to obtain a more cogent and grounded explanation of risks in health.

## Concepts of health and illness

From a common-sense point of view, we may all believe that we know what health and illness consist in, but there are numerous examples of social and cross-cultural variation in how health/illness is conceptualized. In modern Western societies, the evolution of medical science based on anatomy, biology, physiology and related sciences, has come to dominate most people's routine understanding of disease. Many writers have remarked on the conventional dichotomy between 'disease' as a manifestation of some abnormality or pathology, and 'illness' as a culturally and subjectively defined experience. The biomedical model assumes that disease and illnesses are caused by some organic dysfunction in the body; genetic factors and/or bacterial or viral infections may be identified as important factors in specific instances. As Annandale (1998) noted, the biomedical model assumes that diseases have a specific aetiology – particular sets of biological causes. It also assumes that health is essentially a 'natural' phenomenon intrinsic to people's bodies. It further assumes that medical science can produce rational, objective and value-free knowledge about disease and its treatment. Bury (2004) also notes that this model argues that illness results in identifiable physical symptoms, and that disease itself causes harmful changes in bodily functions and physiology.

The critique of this model originated largely (but not exclusively) in medical sociology – which itself transformed into 'the sociology of health and illness', to signal its distance from the orthodox biomedical paradigm (Armstrong 2000). Various writers, from different perspectives, have pointed out that some causes of diseases were environmental and others were related to stages of economic growth and the distribution of wealth – implying that illnesses *per se* could not be wholly explained in terms of individual pathological physiology, and that broader socio-economic and political factors needed to be investigated. Others, for example those focusing on mental illness, showed how ideas about madness were historically and culturally contingent. Studies of the evolution of medical knowledge demonstrated important shifts in the ways in which illnesses are defined and also showed that medical professionals have interests and values associated with their claims to expertise, which in turn influence their accounts of disease and its treatment (see Freidson 1986, 1994; Annandale et al. 2004). Various studies indicated that people with apparently similar conditions and symptoms expressed different subjective beliefs and feelings about their illness, its intensity or severity. Studies of 'lay beliefs' about health have also shown that concepts of health vary between individuals, between social groups, and across cultures, and that people may hold multiple accounts of any specific illness (Nettleton 1995). Annandale (1998) emphasized that people's ideas about health include a wide range of different meanings, and they experience differing degrees of discomfort and disability. Consequently, 'health and illness are not polar opposites ... health, like illness ... needs to be approached from the reference point of the individual concerned' (Annandale 1998: 262). Yet because the meanings of health do vary, 'it is notoriously difficult to access concepts of health rather than illness' (Annandale 1998: 262). Similarly, Nettleton (1995) has noted that some attempts have been made to move beyond the dichotomous model of health/illness – where the medical model of health sees it as the absence of disease – to a more positive concept, such as the World Health Organization's definition of health – a complete state of physical, mental and social well-being. Bryan Turner (1987, 1995) commented on the necessity to move beyond conventional distinctions between disease as biological malfunctions, illness as subjective awareness of disorder, and sickness as defined in terms of an appropriate social *role*. Turner rejected the body/mind dualism, and promoted a 'sociology of the body' to examine the entire complex of *embodiment*. Significantly, Turner (2000: 9) has argued that 'there is little consensus about what constitutes "health" and "illness", which are, and remain, essentially contested concepts'. He also emphasized that concepts of health and illness are highly contested because they involve disputes about ultimately *moral* questions, intimately connected with norms and values about normality and suffering, purity and danger, praise and blame.

The interdependency physical and cultural/social dimensions of health and illness has been increasingly recognized. Annandale et al. (2004) point out that the conventional distinction between biological and social models of health is now outmoded: these are regarded as inextricably linked. Illness (or 'ill health', *sic*) is acknowledged to be conditioned and patterned by social factors and processes (Albrecht et al. 2000), and disease is predominantly seen as having multiple, interacting causes (Nettleton 1995; Turner 2000). Nevertheless, despite this sociological critique, and increasing public interest in alternative or complementary medicine, some commentators regard the biomedical paradigm as still dominant in public discourses about health. For example, Bury (2004) has identified the accelerating pace of innovation linked with modern advances in pharmacology, immunology and the new genetics as prompting a resurgence in medicalized models of health. What this signifies is that the meanings of health and illness are themselves context-dependent and are socially produced and mediated. The history of medicine illustrates the changing concepts of diseases, their causes and their treatment. Medical sociology has established the importance of 'lay beliefs' as well as the varying impact of professional power on clinical concepts of disease and forms of treatment. As Turner (1987) forcefully argued, any general sociological explanation of health and illness must deal with three inter-related dimensions or levels of analysis: the subjective experience of illness, the social construction of disease categories, and the societal organization of healthcare systems. Risk, in its many forms, permeates each of these dimensions of health.

## Concepts of risk as applied to health

As previous chapters have discussed, Ulrich Beck (1992a) argued that in late modern society we encounter new types and unprecedented magnitudes of risk. Modernization itself has created new dangers and risks: these have been 'manufactured' and produced by industrial and technological processes – and arguably by lifestyles – rather than occurring as random or natural events. Many of these risks are globalized and threaten animal and human life;

matters of life and death have become subjected to new forms and levels of risk and without spatial and temporal limits. Historically, Beck notes, famines, plagues and natural disasters all had widespread impact and may have created an 'equivalent' degree of harm when compared with contemporary hazards. But while pre-industrial hazards – 'no matter how large and devastating' – were 'strokes of fate' (Beck 1992b: 98), modern societies' risks are generated by their economic and industrial systems and technological decisions. For instance, industrial pollution may be connected with certain respiratory illnesses, and some new pharmacological treatments may result in unanticipated side effects and unintended damage in the long term to patients' health. As Siegrist (2000: 101) observes: 'a health-damaging social environment includes poor housing, air pollution, heavy traffic and associated risk of accident, inappropriate sanitation, and noxious workplaces'. The risks to health are thus intrinsic to, and exacerbated by, the process of modernization. But how can risks in – or of – health be analysed?

An immediate difficulty is the lack of precision in defining 'risk', as colleagues in other chapters have noted. Gabe (1995) highlighted the prevalent use of risk in health contexts as referring to the likelihood of exposure to a hazard, and/or negative outcomes of treatment. He stressed the growing importance and scale of a new industry of risk assessment and risk management in the health field. It is demonstrated most clearly in public health discourse (particularly about environmental risks) but also in relation to individuals' behaviours and lifestyles. Furedi (1997) noted that risk is a term used in many different ways in different contexts, and that no definition is comprehensive. He suggests that risk refers to 'the probability of damage, injury, death or other misfortune associated with a hazard. Hazards are generally defined to mean a threat to people and what they value' (Furedi 1997: 17). Alaszewski (1998) noted the ambiguity surrounding the term 'risk' in relation to health, but emphasized its usual association with the possibility of negative, undesirable or unintended consequences of some action or process. Bellaby (2001) among others has also stressed its origins in actuarial, statistical and scientific estimates of probability of harm from hazards. Boyne (2003: 109) commented that the 'core components' of most definitions of risk are 'an estimation of the probability of an adverse future event and the estimation of the magnitude of the foreseeable consequences should it happen'. Gabe et al.'s (2004) basic definition of risk also implies involving exposure to a given danger or hazard.

While it can be assumed that individuals have always been anxious about hazards and threats to their health, the emergence of state concern about public health is historically relatively recent. Foucault documented the rise of the clinical gaze and development of 'governmentality' and surveillance as part of a new system of disciplinary power from the eighteenth century (see Foucault 1991; Petersen 1997; Turner 1997; Dean 1999). More recently,

Lupton (1994) has described the evolution of public health discourse in which people's bodies were seen as dangerous sources of disease, posing risks not only to themselves but also to wider society. She showed how modern epidemiology and the public health movement converged upon the identification of people 'at risk' and the measurement of associated 'risk factors'. Individuals were increasingly seen as responsible for their own health, and measures were promoted to encourage the avoidance of risk. 'Excess' alcohol and tobacco consumption, coronary heart disease, diabetes, lung cancer, obesity were all seen as illnesses resulting from individuals' risky behaviour. They in turn posed risks not only to the patients but also collectively to the wider social structure. As Sanders discusses in the following chapter, certain categories of the population, assessed against epidemiological indicators, have come to be labelled as 'risk groups' – or, groups 'at risk' – engaging in 'risk behaviours'. This has been most apparent in the treatment of sexual health and also illicit drug use, and is reflected in public policy to influence people's 'lifestyles' (see Nettleton 1995). Bunton (1998) has used a Foucauldian approach to argue that risk analysis in neo-liberal societies is integral with governmentality. In this context, risks to health are monitored at the population level, public health systems endeavour to reduce those risks, but this is accomplished through individuals taking greater personal responsibility for managing the risks to their own bodies and selves.

Lupton (1999) has also shown that while in contemporary society risk has become associated with danger and with undesirable and negative effects on people's life chances, the concept has also become conflated with uncertainty. Beck (1996) argued that in the 'risk society', risks arise from the active transformation of uncertainty and hazards into decisions. He identified chemical, ecological, genetic and nuclear risks as comprising the most fundamentally challenging problems: as they are not limited in time or space, they cannot be reduced to conventional explanations of blame or liability, and they cannot be insured against. These hazards are frequently invisible, uncertain and unaccountable. As Barbara Adam (1998) pointed out, new chemical processes, air and water pollution, ozone depletion, nuclear radiation, or new diseases tend to be 'unbounded' and invisible until they materialize in problems and symptoms which are only recognized long after their initiation and in ways in which their causality is largely indeterminate.

Paradoxically, it is this very uncertainty that has been confronted by medical science and clinical risk assessment, and has spawned new subdisciplines (such as epidemiology and public health) with their own academic and technical literatures, professional organizations and policies (see Gabe 1995; Turner 1995; Higgs 1998; Levinson 1998; Nettleton 2004). Bury (1998: 11) observed that the rational calculation of risk in health has become an 'almost obsessive preoccupation', and modern healthcare systems are routinely engaged in surveillance and 'screening' to identify, manage and control health risks. One important aspect of this concern with assessing risks – and more widely with medical professionals ensuring 'patient compliance' with expert diagnosis and treatment – is the frequently observed difference between professional and lay knowledge. In health policy and practice, it has been a long-standing assumption by medical professionals that patients' understandings of their own conditions and treatment are limited, incorrect or simply absent. Health promotion and public health programmes, as well as medical training in the NHS, have been oriented to remedying what is widely regarded as a knowledge deficit among sections of the population, or a failure to follow professional advice (see Baggott 2000). Thus, the so-called 'New Public Health' movement 'goes beyond an understanding of human biology and recognises the importance of those social aspects of health problems which are caused by "lifestyles"' (Watterson 2003: 3). Health risks have become increasingly seen as comprising *more* than genetic, physiological and environmental factors. People's behaviour and lifestyle have become acknowledged as problematic, and as direct and indirect causes of illness – for example, in the correlation between smoking and lung cancer, and 'unsafe' sexual practices and HIV/AIDS (Blaxter 1990; Baggott 2004).

However, many medical sociologists have pointed out that lay knowledge, or 'popular epidemiology', rather than being seen as irrational or invalid, should be investigated and acknowledged as a necessary element in people's understanding of the experience of health and illness and how it affects their actions (Calnan 1987; Kelleher et al. 1994; Popay and Williams 1994, 1996). Numerous studies have shown that people's health beliefs may not conform with orthodox epidemiological and scientific assessments of risk, but there has been controversy about whether (and how much) credence should be attached to this 'lay knowledge' (Prior 2003). During the 1960s, cognitive psychological approaches to risk perception produced the 'health beliefs' model. This suggested that people's health behaviour was explained by their beliefs about how serious a threat a risk was, and how far individuals reacted to external 'triggers' (Gabe 1995). Among other critics, Bloor (1995) showed (in his study of HIV-related risk behaviour) the limitations of this health beliefs model – because of its assumptions of calculative rationality, its stress on human agency, and its underestimation of cultural context. Nevertheless, psychological, or more precisely 'psycho-social' factors, are still regarded as important variables in the explanation of health risk. For example, it is well established that psycho-social risks associated with stress (e.g. divorce, unemployment) are correlated with increased chances of poor health (Gabe et al. 2004). What remains unclear is how, in specific contexts, different individuals' and groups' beliefs and values determine their actions, and how those actions might vary in relation to different forms of health risk. The fundamental question that then arises is whether it is valid to conceptualize health risks as objectively real, or as socially constructed.

## Social constructionism and realism in analysing health risks

The debate about social constructionism and realism encompasses all of the social sciences and reflects long-standing philosophical disputes about the nature of knowledge and perception, and the nature of explanation, which cannot be discussed here (see Archer 1998; Williams 1998). The specific issue in connection with health risks is how much significance can be given to objectively *real* hazards and causes of illness, as compared with cultural and historical variations in medical knowledge about illnesses and treatments, and also variations in people's (socially constructed) awareness, definitions and experiences of health and illness. Much of this debate has been prompted by the post-structuralist and especially the Foucauldian critique of conventional 'modernist' thought. In relation to medicine and the body, Foucauldian analysis stresses the historically contingent character of knowledge, and its 'disciplinary' functions. The implication is that medical and scientific knowledge(s) are bound or shaped by their cultural and social context, and that as discourses and practices they are intrinsically connected with power and surveillance (Lupton 1994). As O'Malley pointed out earlier, risk assessment can never be wholly neutral and objective as it must be influenced by prevailing morals and values, and by different social interests.

Mary Douglas's (1992) cultural/symbolic approach can be classified as a strong social constructionist view. Douglas argues that risk is usually associated with blame and moral questions about responsibility. Risks, in this context, must always be explained in terms of different cultural values associated with the positioning of social groups along dimensions of 'grid' and 'group'. Thus, in Douglas's approach, what is regarded as a risk is culturally determined and relative to specific types of social group. As Green (1997) showed in her study of accidents, there are contradictory discourses about accidents and risk. In official mortality statistics, accidents are among the leading causes of death. But Green argued that there is no natural (objective) category of events that are 'accidents'. This is not to deny that the effects of such events are not evidently real or damaging. Instead, Green stresses, some 'misfortunes' are regarded as more dangerous, and some are defined and treated as accidents, while others are not. More generally, Lupton (1999) has argued that in a social constructionist approach, risks are not seen as realities 'out there' but comprise an assemblage of beliefs, meanings and understandings about phenomena. Consequently, risk assessment – and perception – are always filtered through the prism of current belief systems and cultural practices.

The argument that risks are products of cultural meanings and social processes does not sit easily with conventional positivist and realist epistemology. It certainly does not seem compatible with the biomedical model of health and illness. Many commentators have pointed out that in Beck's account of the risk society, there is a strong emphasis on the objective reality of risks – particularly an increase in environmental risks – but there are nonetheless ambiguities in Beck's discussion (see Lupton 1999; Wilkinson 2001; Mythen 2004). There is, according to Mythen (2004), a tension in Beck's writings between 'natural objectivism' and 'cultural relativism'. Beck implies that risks are real and have been manufactured in quantitatively and qualitatively new ways in late modern society. This view of risk, Mythen argues, constitutes a realist position, but Beck himself also accepts a 'weak' form of social constructionism. In a review of the risk society debate, Beck (2000) emphasized that the choice between a constructivist or realist approach was not an either/or choice. He favoured a pragmatic decision, arguing: 'I am both a realist and a constructivist, using realism and constructivism as far as these meta-narratives are useful for understanding the complex and ambivalent nature of risk' (Beck 2000: 212). Once again, Beck stressed that hazards are often invisible and untraceable, beyond everyday perceptions but nevertheless real – their reality becomes evident from their impact, but that may not be immediately apparent. Risks, then, for Beck, are simultaneously real *and* constituted by social perception; risks have a hybrid character.

This intermediate position has become more widely accepted. Lupton (1999) distinguished between 'strong' and weak' versions of both realism and social constructionism, suggesting that Beck's original arguments reflected a weak form of social constructionism. This claims that real dangers and hazards exist, but may be conceptualized and acted upon in different ways by different groups and societies. In a large-scale qualitative empirical study, Tulloch and Lupton (2003) showed how 'risk knowledges' are highly contextualized, contingent and contested. In their case studies of risk perceptions, they showed how interviewees held different concepts of risks, and that individuals reflexively related risks to their age, gender, stage in the life-course, occupation, sexual identity, and so on. Some respondents stressed the changing nature of their perceptions of risk, and also alluded to the positive aspects of risk taking.

In a study of risk taking among motorcyclists, Bellaby and Lawrenson (2001) noted that while statistically the chance of serious accidents among motorcyclists was eight times that of car drivers, the motorcyclists regarded risks as positive, or not specifically caused by the motorcyclists, or as avoidable. In their study, Bellaby and Lawrenson (2001: 381–2) argued that while the deaths and injuries were real, to understand the beliefs of the motorcyclists, a weak constructionist approach could be combined with a realist perspective: 'motorcyclists' deaths and injuries on the roads *are* real, whatever construction is placed on them'. They go on to argue that risks of accidents and injuries to the body can be both real and culturally constructed, and that cultural constructs can be real in their consequences – cultures of risk have a material ('real') base.

When applying these arguments more generally to health and illness, Lupton (1994) acknowledged that a modified social constructionist approach was valuable. She argued that the reality of disease or illnesses or bodily experiences was not being disputed, but that it was necessary to recognize that both medical knowledge and lay experience were socially mediated. She disavowed a wholly relativist position, stressing that pain and death are evidently biological realities, while at the same time noting that their meaning varies culturally. Similarly, Turner (2000) was critical of 'strong' social constructivist accounts of medicine: clinical categories of disease are not entirely socially constructed, and even though people's beliefs about illness may change over time, the clinical condition does not. Turner argues strongly that it is not contradictory to accept that there is a clinical reality (disease) *and* that associated concepts of illness – both professional and lay – may change and be influenced by cultural values: 'to say that fever is socially produced is not to say that is a "fiction", or that it does not exist ... however, the signs and symptoms of a fever in a clinical setting are mediated through and by the experiences and training of physicians' (Turner 2000: 21). Other medical sociologists have also stressed that strong social constructivism and its postmodernist variants are unconvincing. Bury (1986, 1998) has pointed out that people's suffering of disability and pain is implicitly neglected by some forms of social constructivism; he is also critical of the inherent relativism of this approach, arguing that medical knowledge and treatments have advanced and have made real improvements to people's experiences of illness (Nettleton 1995; Annandale 1998). There is then a broad consensus that there is a set of health risks which is simultaneously real but also subject to differential understandings and cultural variations in its conceptualization, among both medical professional and lay people. One example is highly relevant at this point. For many years in capitalist industrial societies it was recognized that standardized mortality rates and other indicators of morbidity correlate strongly with socio-economic status. While historically there have been absolute improvements in health and illness, relative disparities between social classes remain significant. The 'social class gradient' in health was famously highlighted in Britain in 1980 by the Black Report (Townsend and Davidson 1982). This led to controversial political debate and academic research on the causes of social class inequalities in health, concentrating on 'material' and 'structural' factors as compared with 'behavioural' or 'cultural' factors (Whitehead 1988). Numerous studies have investigated the interrelationships between poverty, poor housing and environmental pollution, for example, as potentially damaging the life-chances of lower socio-economic groups. Other studies have focused upon the higher than average incidence of smoking, higher alcohol consumption and higher levels of obesity among lower socio-economic groups; the inference is frequently made that these display some active choice or preference among those groups to take unnecessary risks with their health. However, Wilkinson (1996), among others, pointed out that when comparing whole societies, class variations in health can be related to the overall distribution of income and wealth. Generally, the extent of health inequalities is lower in more egalitarian societies. The implication is that the structure and organization of the economy and society are highly influential in affecting social cohesion, and that this in itself indirectly affects the incidence of social class inequalities in health.

Most recently, other analysts have argued that health inequalities are related to a variety of risk factors, including stress, and that these are connected not only with environmental hazards but occupational security and wider forms of social capital. Most writers acknowledge the 'multi-factorial' nature of explanations of social class variations in health – including biological, cognitive and psychosocial variables (Blaxter 2000). Nonetheless, it is evident that not only are the social class inequalities in health real, but their causes are also real. Obviously people may interpret their circumstances differently, and evaluate the risks differently, and may make different *constrained* choices about how to behave – about what foods to eat, whether to smoke or take exercise – and they may act upon information and expert advice differentially. All these activities are influenced by the prevailing attitudes to and cultural norms about what constitutes sickness and how it can be treated. However, exposure to environmental hazards and risks of occupational diseases, risks of accident and injury in the workplace and in the home, exposure to infection caused by damp and overcrowded housing, and exposure to a multitude of financial and social 'stress factors', are not reducible to social constructions. As Siegrist (2000: 101) has noted, different social groups are exposed to 'specific health-detrimental risks in their social environment ... individuals may have acquired different resources to cope with these health risks, and processes of resource acquisition are ... socially patterned'. Siegrist argues convincingly that middle-range theories are required to link individual susceptibility to illness to socio-structural and biological causes.

This example usefully illustrates the need to combine theories and concepts at different levels of abstraction, but in addition it also indicates the value of a realist, or more precisely 'critical realist', approach to health risks. Layder (1993) cogently argued for middle-range theory and research employing a realist epistemology, which incorporates analysis at the macro (structural and institutional) levels as well as the micro (behaviour and interaction) levels. He advocated that we address questions about different 'domains' – the setting and context, 'situated activity' and the self – while emphasizing that these are both empirical phenomena and theoretical abstractions. Layder argues:

> The broadly realist position ... insists that social reality is not simply composed of people's meanings, experiences and subjective understandings, but that it is in large part constituted by systemic features that are relatively impersonal, inert and which represent the standing conditions confronting people in their everyday lives.
>
> (1998: 95)

He notes that societal structures – for example, markets and bureaucracies – do have inherent properties of control and power that shape – but need not wholly determine – social action and change.

A similar critical realist argument has been made by Sayer (2000). Realism provides an alternative to positivist empiricism, and relativism; it is a means of 'combining a modified naturalism with a recognition of the necessity of interpretive understanding in social life' (Sayer 2000: 2). Critical realists, Sayer argues (following Bhaskar 1975) attempt to identify causal processes and differentiate between the real, the actual and the empirical. The real is whatever exists (natural or social) comprising 'the realm of objects, their structures and powers' (Sayer 2000: 10), whether or not it is an empirical object (i.e. directly observed or observable) for people, and whether or not people have an adequate understanding of it. These real objects have causal powers or capacities to behave in specific ways, or passive susceptibility to change. The 'actual' refers to 'what happens if and when those powers are activated, to what they do and what eventuates when they do' (Sayer 2000: 12). 'The empirical' is the domain of individual and social experience, but it is contingent whether this experience is of 'the actual' or 'the real'. Realist explanations seek to establish causal mechanisms and identify whether they have been activated and in what circumstances. They recognize that social phenomena are meaningful to individuals, and that such meaning is part of the process of social construction – but such meanings and constructions are connected with material circumstances and practical contexts. Again, as Sayer (2000: 19) observes: 'Much of what happens does not depend on or correspond to actors' understandings; there are unintended consequences and unacknowledged conditions and things can happen to people regardless of their understandings.' What is *critical* about this approach is that it assumes the possibility of alternative conditions. It asks what must and what might happen, and it is critical of existing structures and processes – critical realism aspires to offer a potentially emancipatory analysis associated with normative choices. Social scientific explanations based on critical realism are distinctively different from – and critical of – lay accounts and actions, and they indicate how realities might be different under different conditions. Scambler (2002) has extended this approach to the specific questions surrounding health, and has combined it with a Habermasian framework. For Scambler (2002: 43), 'natural and social worlds alike are not composed merely of events (the actual) and experiences (the empirical) but also of underlying generative mechanisms (the real) that exist, independently of whether they are detected, and govern or facilitate events'.

Consequently people's health experiences in contemporary capitalist society – as part of their interpretive and symbolic 'lifeworlds' in Habermas's terms – are necessarily shaped by class relations *and* through govern-mentality. Thus, political economy and 'system rationalisation' influence professional discourses on disease, as well as individuals' experiences and narratives of ill health. They also affect the power relationships between different social groups, and so, following Scambler, require a critical sociology which develops the capacity for 'deliberative democracy' and the possible empowerment of different communities within civil society. By this is meant, crudely, an open debate in the public sphere of alternative conceptualizations of disease and treatment and their causes, as well as questioning of the ma-terial conditions in which they emerge, and potential alternative policies and practices. Critical realism necessarily engages with the possibilities for social change, and thus has direct relevance in debates about risks in health.

## Conclusion: beyond the risk society

This chapter has outlined some of the conceptual and theoretical arguments about risks in health. It has been argued that the very concepts of health and illness are themselves contested and socially constructed. However, it has also been argued that diseases and their experiences are real, and their causation is complex and multi-factorial. People's health beliefs and cultural practices, and professional medical discourses, are obviously 'socially constructed', but that in itself does *not* provide a comprehensive explanation of their illnesses, or of the chances of contracting them. Health and illness are constituted within a real material context and parameters which are biological (genetic), physiological and environmental. Exposure to hazards – and relative risk – is variable, and influenced by many different factors. These include real struc-tural features of the political economy – such as the organization of industrial production and technology, the nature of work and occupational hazards for example – which have differential impact on different social groups. At the population level, while overall longevity is increasing and mortality rates in general are improving, it is known that, for example, one in three people in Britain will develop cancer during their lives, and the age-standardized in-cidence of cancer increased between 1971 and 2002 (Office of National Sta-tistics, 2005). Similarly, death rates from coronary heart disease (CHD) have been falling historically, but are still officially regarded as too high; moreover, systematic studies of the evidence indicate that changes in so-called 'risk factors' (e.g. reduced smoking, cholesterol levels, obesity) have a greater impact on CHD than medical intervention *per se* (NHS Health Development Agency 2004).

The position adopted here supports a critical realist analysis, but it also acknowledges the importance of a 'soft' or 'weak' form of social constructionism in so far as it enables us to appreciate the cultural and historical variation in lay and professional categorization of disease and treatment. At different times, and for different groups, the relative salience of specific conditions and symptoms will vary, and be subject to contestation and negotiation. It may also be subject to different forms of representation; the putative risks are the partial result of lay beliefs, professional discourses and media amplification. But that too indicates the relevance of a critical realist approach involving 'deliberative' debate, setting out alternative explanations and rationally considering alternative priorities for treatment. If we consider some of the health issues likely to confront the public and policy-makers in the next decades, it is evident that decisions on priorities for resource allocation are inherently associated with competing definitions and estimates of risk. The probable long-term effects of an increasingly ageing population are reasonably well known, but what is difficult to predict is how far different social groups' assessments of the need for changes in lifestyle or new levels of healthcare investment will be influenced by competing accounts of health risks. New types of treatment may become available for Alzheimer's disease, for example, but is its increased incidence a health risk the general population will simply accept, or will they demand action to reduce it? Some illnesses, especially mental illness, do not achieve a high public profile or significant level of public investment – is this entirely explained by their relative prevalence or perceived risk? Rapid advances in biotechnology and the new genetics potentially offer the prospect of revolutionary treatment – and replacement – of diseased organs and tissue. But the cost–benefit trade-offs (quantified as 'QALYs' – quality adjusted life years) for these and different forms of innovative surgery (transplantation) are also necessarily connected with different attitudes to risk and the competing demands of different 'claims-making' interest groups. The more pronounced these dilemmas about alternative risks become, the more probable that questioning of clinical effectiveness and its regulation will also intensify. Elements of risk in health – for lay people and medical professionals – are inescapable, but their importance, outcomes, and the capacity for intervention and change, can all be the focus of deliberative debate.

## Study questions

1   What factors influence whether health risks are categorized as requiring public intervention?

2    Who determines what is 'risky' behaviour or lifestyle?
3    How important are health risks compared with risks in other sectors of social life?


# References

Adam, B. (1998) *Timescapes of Modernity*. London: Routledge.

Alaszewski, A. (1998) Risk in modern society, in A. Alaszewski, L. Harrison and J. Manthorpe (eds) *Risk, Health and Welfare*. Buckingham: Open University Press.

Albrecht, G., Fitzpatrick, R. and Scrimshaw, S. (eds) (2000) *The Handbook of Social Studies in Medicine*. London: Sage.

Annandale, E. (1998) *The Sociology of Health and Medicine*. Cambridge: Polity Press.

Annandale, E., Elston, M.A. and Prior, L. (2004) Medical work, medical knowledge and health care: themes and perspectives, in E. Annandale, M.A. Elston and L. Prior (eds) *Medical Work, Medical Knowledge and Health Care*. Oxford: Blackwell.

Archer, M.S. (1998) Social theory and the analysis of society, in T. May and M. Williams (eds) *Knowing the Social World*. Buckingham: Open University Press.

Armstrong, D. (2000) Social theorizing about health and illness, in G. Albrecht, R. Fitzpatrick and S. Scrimshaw (eds) *The Handbook of Social Studies in Medicine*. London: Sage.

Baggott, R. (2000) *Public Health: Policy and Politics*. Basingstoke: Palgrave Macmillan.

Baggott, R. (2004) *Health and Health Care in Britain*. Basingstoke: Palgrave Macmillan.

Beck, U. (1992a) *Risk Society*. London: Sage.

Beck, U. (1992b) From industrial society to risk society, *Theory, Culture & Society*, 9: 97–123.

Beck, U. (1996) Risk society and the provident state, in S. Lash, B. Szerszynski and B. Wynne (eds) *Risk, Environment and Modernity*. London: Sage.

Beck, U. (2000) Risk society revisited, in B. Adam, U. Beck and J. van Loon (eds) *The Risk Society and Beyond*. London: Sage.

Bellaby, P. (2001) Evidence and risk, in A. Edwards and G. Elwyn (eds) *Evidence-Based Patient Choice*. Oxford: Oxford University Press.

Bellaby, P. (2003) Communication and miscommunication of risk: understanding UK parents' attitudes to combined MMR vaccination, *British Medical Journal*, 327: 725–8.

Bellaby, P. (2005) Has the UK government lost the battle over MMR? *British Medical Journal*, 330: 552–3.

Bellaby, P. and Lawrenson, D. (2001) Approaches to the risk of riding motorcycles, *Sociological Review*, 49(3): 368–88.

Bhaskar, R. (1975) *A Realist Theory of Science*. Leeds: Leeds Books.

Blaxter, M. (1990) *Health and Lifestyles*. London: Routledge.

Blaxter, M. (2000) Medical sociology at the start of the new millennium, *Social Science and Medicine*, 51(8): 1139–42.

Bloor, M. (1995) A user's guide to contrasting theories of HIV-related risk behaviour, in J. Gabe (ed.) *Medicine, Health and Risk*. Oxford: Blackwell.

Boyne, R. (2003) *Risk*. Buckingham: Open University Press.

Bunton, R. (1998) Inequalities in late modern health care, in A. Petersen and C. Waddell (eds) *Health Matters: A Sociology of Illness, Prevention and Care*. Buckingham: Open University Press.

Bury, M. (1986) Social constructionism and the development of medical sociology, *Sociology of Health and Illness*, 8(2): 137–69.

Bury, M. (1998) Postmodernism and health, in G. Scambler and P. Higgs (eds) *Modernity, Health and Medicine*. London: Routledge.

Bury, M. (2004) Medical model, in J. Gabe, M. Bury and M.A. Elston (eds) *Key Concepts in Medical Sociology*. London: Sage.

Calnan, M. (1987) *Health and Illness: The Lay Perspective*. London: Tavistock.

Dean, M. (1999) *Governmentality*. London: Sage.

Douglas, M. (1992) *Risk and Blame*. London: Routledge.

Flynn, R. (2004) Soft bureaucracy, governmentality and clinical governance, in A. Gray and S. Harrison (eds) *Governing Medicine*. Maidenhead: Open University Press.

Foucault, M. (1991) Governmentality, in G. Burchell, C. Gordon and P. Miller (eds) *The Foucault Effect*. London: Harvester Wheatsheaf.

Freidson, E. (1986) *Professional Powers*. Chicago: University of Chicago Press.

Freidson, E. (1994) *Professionalism Reborn*. Cambridge: Polity Press.

Furedi, F. (1997) *Culture of Fear*. London: Cassell.

Gabe, J. (1995) Health, medicine and risk – the need for a sociological approach, in J. Gabe (ed.) *Medicine, Health and Risk*. Oxford: Blackwell.

Gabe, J. (2004) Risk, in J. Gabe, M. Bury and M.A. Elston (eds) *Key Concepts in Medical Sociology*. London: Sage.

Green, J. (1997) *Risk and Misfortune: A Social Construction of Accidents*. London: UCL Press.

Harrison, S. (2004) Governing medicine, in A. Gray and S. Harrison, (eds) *Governing Medicine*. Maidenhead: Open University Press.

Higgs, P. (1998) Risk, governmentality and the reconceptualization of citizenship, in G. Scambler and P. Higgs (eds) *Modernity, Medicine and Health*. London: Routledge.

Illich, I. (1977) *Limits to Medicine: Medical Nemesis*. Harmondsworth: Penguin Books.

Kelleher, D., Gabe, J. and Williams, G. (1994) Understanding medical dominance in the modern world, in J. Gabe, D. Kelleher and G. Williams (eds) *Challenging Medicine*. London: Routledge.

Layder, D. (1993) *New Strategies in Social Research*. Cambridge: Polity Press.

Layder, D. (1998) The reality of social domains, in T. May and M. Williams (eds) *Knowing the Social World*. Buckingham: Open University Press.

Levinson, R. (1998) Issues at the interface of medical sociology and public health, in G. Scambler and P. Higgs (eds) *Modernity, Medicine and Health*. London: Routledge.

Lupton, D. (1994) *Medicine as Culture*. London: Sage.

Lupton, D. (1999) *Risk*. London: Routledge.

Mythen, G. (2004) *Ulrich Beck: A Critical Introduction to the Risk Society*. London: Pluto Press.

Nettleton, S. (1995) *The Sociology of Health and Illness*. Cambridge: Polity Press.

Nettleton, S. (2004) Surveillance and health promotion, in J. Gabe et al. (eds) *Key Concepts in Medical Sociology*. London: Sage.

NHS Health Development Agency (2004) Relative contributions of changes in risk factors and treatment to the reduction in coronary heart disease mortality, Briefing Paper by M.P. Kelly and S. Capewell, London: Health Development Agency.

Office of National Statistics (2005) National Statistics Online: Health, Cancer and Cancer Survival: http://www.statistics.gov.uk [accessed 1 June 2005].

Petersen, A. (1997) Risk, governance and the new public health, in A. Petersen and R. Bunton (eds) *Foucault, Health and Medicine*. London: Routledge.

Petts, J. and Niemeyer, S. (2004) Health risk communication and amplification: learning from the MMR vaccination controversy, *Health, Risk and Society*, 6(1): 7–23.

Popay, J. and Williams, G. (1994) Introduction, in J. Popay and G. Williams (eds) *Researching the People's Health*. London: Routledge.

Popay, J. and Williams, G. (1996) Public health research and lay knowledge, *Social Science and Medicine*. 42: 759–68.

Prior, L. (2003) Belief, knowledge and expertise, *Sociology of Health and Illness*, 25: 41–57.

Sayer, A. (2000) *Realism and Social Science*. London: Sage.

Scambler, G. (2002) *Health and Social Change: A Critical Theory*. Buckingham: Open University Press.

Siegrist, J. (2000) The social causation of health and illness, in G. Albrecht et al. (eds) *The Handbook of Social Studies in Health and Medicine*. London: Sage.

Townsend, P. and Davidson, N. (1982) *Inequalities in Health*. London: Penguin.

Tulloch, J. and Lupton, D. (2003) *Risk and Everyday Life*. London: Sage.

Turner, B.S. (1987) *Medical Power and Social Knowledge*. London: Sage.

Turner, B.S. (1995) *Medical Power and Social Knowledge*, 2nd edn. London: Sage.

Turner, B.S. (2000) The history of the changing concepts of health and illness, in G. Albrecht et al. (eds) *The Handbook of Social Studies in Health and Medicine*. London: Sage.

Watterson, A. (2003) Introduction, in A. Watterson (ed.) *Public Health in Practice*. Basingstoke: Palgrave Macmillan.

Whitehead, M. (1988) *The Health Divide*. London: Penguin.

Wilkinson, I. (2001) Social theories of risk perception, *Current Sociology*, 49(1): 1–22.

Wilkinson, R. (1996) *Unhealthy Societies*. London: Routledge.

Williams, M. (1998) The social world as knowable, in T. May and M. Williams (eds) *Knowing the Social World*. Buckingham: Open University Press.

## Further reading

Annandale, E. (1998) *The Sociology of Health and Medicine*. Cambridge: Polity Press.

Annandale E., Elston, M.A. and Prior, L. (2004) *Medical Work, Medical Knowledge and Health Care*. Oxford: Blackwell.

Bury, M. and Gabe, J. (2004) *The Sociology of Health and Illness*. London: Routledge.

Gabe, J., Bury, M. and Elston, M.A. (2004) *Key Concepts in Medical Sociology*. London: Sage.

Scambler, G. (2002) *Health and Social Change*. Buckingham: Open University Press.

# 6 Sexuality and risk

## Teela Sanders

## Introduction

This chapter will review how the historical and current literature in the studies of sexuality can be applied to the concept of risk that has been re-defined in recent years. The first part of this chapter will present a brief theoretical overview of how risk has been understood by sociologists and how we can apply this understanding to the construction of sexual practices and identities. This review will highlight the historical tradition that has labelled certain expressions of sexuality morally degenerative, pathological and the signal of a decaying society. I describe how the discourse of risk is applied to certain sexual behaviours and identities as a control mechanism to regulate those considered as 'Other'. Following on from these traditions, I assess the current state of the theoretical debates around risk and sexuality. Here I rely on two examples: HIV/AIDS and female sex workers. Through these prominent examples of risk discourse, I demonstrate how the sexual body that appears to transgress that which is considered 'normal', produces anxiety, fear and a threat to the social order. Using my own empirical findings (Sanders 2005a), I argue that risk in prostitution is not the same for all women, but instead is an interplay between individual biography, material resources and external structures, such as police enforcement. In addition, I also demonstrate that the popular perceptions of sexual health risk in prostitution need to be considered among other types of occupational hazards that sex workers place on a 'continuum of risk'. Next, I briefly set out the counter-theories in relation to risk taking and risk avoidance that is gendered in nature, highlighting the dynamics between pleasure seeking, identity formation and relationships. Finally, to summarize, I evaluate the contributions that theory has made to our understanding of sexuality and risk, offering some critiques of dominant risk theories. It is not the aim of this chapter to assess the relative merits of the competing claims but instead to assess the theoretical contributions and empirical basis on which we can understand sexuality and risk.

# Risk and sexuality: merging theories

Although explicit theoretical approaches that combine the concepts of sexuality and risk are absent in the literature, the theorizing that has been done around 'risk' in modernity can offer insights into the social and cultural processes that construct sexuality. Douglas (1992) explains how the concept of risk no longer refers to a scientific calculation of probability but instead the term 'risk' refers to danger, or as Lupton (1999: 8) explains, 'risk is now generally used to relate only to negative or undesirable outcomes'. Although historically, the sexual body has always been targeted by ideas of danger, sinfulness and immorality, the re-conceptualization of risk away from the cognitive scientific interpretation of probability towards an individualized understanding of risk has returned the focus of risk to sexuality and the body. Through the sociological concept of risk, boundaries are drawn around what types of sexualities are undesirable and therefore what is natural, acceptable and 'normal' (Harding 1998: 36).

Before exploring the complexities and consequences of the relationship between the sociological concept of risk and that of sexuality, it is important to iron out some basics concepts and theoretical approaches. When discussing the work of the risk theorists, the term 'discourse' is often used to refer to 'a bounded body of knowledge and associated practices, a particular identifiable way of giving meaning to reality via words or imagery' (Lupton 1999: 15). This chapter will combine an analysis of both the discourses of risk and the discourses of sexuality to provide insight into the cultural and social nature of these two phenomena.

The socio-cultural perspectives on risk provide a framework in our investigations of the relationship between risk and sexuality. The cultural/symbolic theory of risk promoted by Douglas (1992) describes how definitions and interpretations of risk are used to establish and sustain conceptual boundaries of acceptability, concentrating specifically on the human body as a site for symbolic discourses of risk. Also, the theory of 'governmentality' developed by Foucault (1991) is also useful to understand how sexuality is regulated and controlled through risk discourse. Here, risk is explored in the context of surveillance, discipline, and the regulation of groups and their behaviour that in turn perpetuates a certain set of norms. Within these socio-cultural interpretations of risk, broader theoretical approaches of structuralism, post-structuralism and phenomenology are useful to categorize ideas. The work of Douglas (1992) speaks from a structuralist standpoint that attempts to uncover the cultural hierarchies that are prominent in defining what is risky behaviour. As an anthropologist originally concerned with pollution, purity and danger in societies, Douglas explores the socio-cultural reasons for adopting risk as a mechanism to separate out the self and the

Other. Explaining how the discourses of risk adopt a function to maintain cohesion, norms and values in society, this group of 'functional structuralists' argues that ideas about risk are applied to certain sexual practices and identities of sexuality in order to minimize deviant, non-normative identities and secure a heterosexual society.

The post-structuralist theorists come mainly from the Foucauldian camp that locates power relations at the centre of any investigation of risk. More interested in shifting discourses and meanings of risk than rigid social structures, the post-structuralists focus on the type of knowledge that is circulated about different sexual identities and practices. This theoretical approach explores the power relations that determine what is risky and the boundaries of acceptable sexual activity. Foucault (1979: 77) propounded that the very act of identifying certain groups as 'risky' is a mechanism of regulation and control. The process of defining the group as 'risky' translates to 'mechanisms of power that frame the everyday lives of individuals' (1979: 77). For instance, in the wake of an AIDS epidemic, groups who were considered at 'high risk' of infection because of their sexual lifestyles were targeted by HIV screening and monitoring programmes. In this example, public health campaigns were directly used as a regulatory tool of the state (medical institutions and 'expertise' are a main agent of social control), methods of surveillance and the control of specific behaviours to regulate a 'dangerous' form of sexuality.

In contrast, phenomenologists concentrate on the 'situated meanings' that are attached to behaviours and identities that are considered 'risky'. The focus here is on the lived experience of how individuals experience the world, emphasizing the need to understand the micro context of risk in everyday life. Phenomenologists studying sexuality and the implications of risk would rely on in-depth qualitative methods and data to tap into the experiences of groups that are marginalized because of their sexual orientation or practices – for example, sex workers, sado-masochists, transsexuals, lesbians, people living with AIDS. The task here would be to give voice to how individuals and groups, as social actors, interact with the world in order to respond to wider discourses of risk.

The cultural construction of sexuality defines certain sexual activities and groups as 'risky' through a process of assessing behaviours that are considered against a 'natural' benchmark or 'biological imperative' (Weeks 2003: 4). As Scott and Jackson (2000: 168) describe, the social ordering of sexuality privileges heterosexuality and marginalizes lesbian and gay sexualities. This social ordering is constructed through strict sexual scripts that define what sexual acts are considered normal and those that are considered perverted and obscure. Discourses of anxiety, vulnerability and uncertainty have long been associated with certain types of sexual behaviour that are considered dangerous and so should be avoided if a rational, civilized life and society are to continue. This can be demonstrated with the dominant narratives of how the missionary position is the favoured form of heterosexual intercourse in the West, ignoring the culturally specific construction of what is regarded as normal sexual engagement (Scott and Jackson 2000: 171). As part of the civilizing process, discourses from across the disciplines promote categories of sexual unacceptability. For example, public health discourses have promoted moral judgements against non-normative groups and behaviours such as women involved in commercial sex, teenage mothers, same-sex relationships, and promiscuity. As a result, these activities have been targeted by methods of regulation and control that serve to marginalize unwanted behaviours and reinforce the dominant sexual ideology that privileges monogamous heterosexuality, preferably within marriage. The discourses of risk play a prominent role in the methods of regulation that work to separate out those who are different. As Lupton (1995: 80) argues, 'discourse of risk becomes a political strategy' that 'serve[s] to identify Self and Other, to apportion blame upon stigmatised minorities' (1995: 91). These regulatory processes will be examined and critiqued in relation to the discovery of and reaction to HIV/AIDS and women who engage in sex work.

## HIV/AIDS: the 'gay plague'

One of the most recent and familiar examples of the sexuality/risk discourse is related to the discovery of HIV/AIDS in the USA in the 1980s. Initially known as the 'gay plague', this infection was associated with imagery of 'dirt, disorder and decay' and was connected specifically to male gay communities (Weeks 2003: 102). HIV/AIDS was considered a new danger but was associated with the traditional notion of moral laxity and depravity of non-normative groups. Led by the powers of clinical expertise and medical knowledge that originally termed the disease GRID (Gay-Related Immune Deficiency), Weeks (1991: 117) reports how it was not until 1982 that there was a shift in the scientific understanding of the disease, renaming it AIDS (Acquired Immune Deficiency Syndrome). Alongside the medical explanations, the moral entrepreneurs of the New Right used AIDS to justify their crusade against homosexuality and its supposed threat to nuclear family life and ultimate cement of Western society. Here, AIDS was cast as a punishment for sinful behaviour and 'nature's retribution for sexual misdemeanours' (Weeks 1991: 102). Gay men were blamed and even considered deserving of a deadly illness because of their sexual habits and were placed in sharp contrast to the 'innocent victims' who contracted the disease through blood transfusions or babies who were infected in the womb.

The anxiety around AIDS initially took the form of scapegoating gay men. Sexual practices such as anal intercourse and sexual habits such as multiple partners were associated exclusively with male homosexuality. Interpreted as moral judgements, these sexual and social features were used to blame this group of people for the contraction and spread of the disease. From this point of the debate, supported by the strong arm of the media, the argument moved from 'the idea that homosexuals *caused* "the plague" ... to the idea that homosexuality itself was a plague' (Weeks 2003: 103). The risk discourse surrounding HIV/AIDS blamed people who practised male same-sex relationships, when the reality was that, at a global level, the majority of those infected were heterosexual.

Douglas (1992) makes the links between the political application of the concept of risk with the blame that is placed on one group in society. Links between how the body is controlled and how wider groups in society are controlled are evident through this example of the treatment of those infected with HIV or who are considered to practise 'risky' sexual behaviour. Certain types of behaviours are cast as socially polluting and discourses of disapproval and decay are constructed which are closely tied to moral codes. The anxiety around HIV/AIDS also spread to drug taking, permissive sexual lifestyles and promiscuity, as well as specific ethnic groups such as black Africans. The scaremongering around this disease brought shame and stigma with it, and consequently certain sexualities were categorized as dangerous. Weeks (2003: 105) describes how the regulation of sexuality takes place through powerful discourses of dangerousness, where certain types of sexual acts are coloured with 'risk', that in turn determine who is afforded sexual citizenship and who is excluded. Through the moral panic that surrounded HIV/AIDS, social anxiety was directed towards the gay community, which led to an increase in public homophobia, violence and harassment (Weeks 2003: 102). Only since the 1990s have public health and safe sex campaigns constructed the heterosexual population as 'at risk' of HIV/AIDS (Lupton 1995). Yet this process of the 'universalization' of risk is still questionable as heterosexuality is considered a 'low risk' compared with the 'high risk' of the homosexual lifestyle (Adkins 2001: 45). As Adkins documents, this 'hierarchization of risk' and sexuality is played out by the demand that certain groups are more rigorously screened and tested for HIV than others. This highlights how the narratives surrounding sexually transmitted diseases justifies the surveillance of certain groups through regulatory processes such as health checks.

Interestingly, the discourse of risk in the moral panic over HIV/AIDS reaction was not applied proportionately to all non-heterosexual communities. Richardson (2000) documents the representation of lesbians throughout the history of the HIV epidemic, noting the changing risk status afforded to this group of women. Initially in the 1980s, lesbians were also categorized as a 'high risk' group, probable carriers of the disease and were included in the popular media discourse of AIDS. At this point, lesbians were associated with sexual deviancy because of their non-normative sexual activities, and hence considered to be the Other in contrast to heterosexual women in the same way that gay men were set up in opposition to the 'normality' of heterosexual masculinity. Richardson describes how during the mid-1980s there was a shift in the sexual status afforded lesbians as over time they were considered to be safe. This shift took place as a result of the 'de-gaying of the discourse around AIDS because of medical, political and social recognition of global infection in predominantly heterosexual communities' (Richardson 2000: 141). The change in status that left lesbians outside the risk discourses was also because of the conceptualization of risk in behavioural terms. Gay men were targeted not because of their same-sex affiliations but instead their sexuality was reduced down to the practice of anal sex – something that lesbians were not associated with. As Miller (1997: 99–101) describes, there have long been strong cultural codes that associate the anus in sex as transgressing bodily functions, rendering anal intercourse disgusting and contaminating. Such sexual behaviours placed homosexual men at the extreme end of the 'risk' spectrum.

The social, political and medical reactions to HIV/AIDS and its consequences of stigma, blame and exclusion are not a new phenomenon. Alongside moral and religious agendas, the scientific expertise of medical knowledge has historically linked sexuality and disease (Levine 2003). Fuelling a moral panic, or indeed a 'sex panic', the general parameters of these links between sexuality and disease remain stable while the target group for the risk categorization alters throughout time. The HIV/AIDS discourse documents this exact shift away from prostitute women in the nineteenth century who were blamed for the spread of syphilis (Corbin 1990), to be replaced with gay men in the latter end of the twentieth century. The discourses connected to prostitution demonstrate the continuity of relating female sexuality and risk.

## Sex work, risk and reality

Like HIV/AIDS, the case of female sex work has long been an example of the discourses that combine risk and sexuality. Political and scientific discourses to perpetuate stigmatizing and exclusionary narratives of sexual practices have been continually applied to women involved in commercial sex (Day 2000). Walkowitz (1980) describes how historically female sex workers have been represented as responsible for the spread of infections. For instance, this group of women were blamed for the syphilis epidemic in the nineteenth century, resulting in female promiscuity being strongly associated with the spread of disease. Strongly advocated by the medical profession, this discourse was reinforced by a legal framework (three Contagious Diseases Acts in the

1860s) that enabled the police and medical profession to force women to undergo a health inspection and, if found positive, could be detained against their will in a Lock hospital (Self 2003). The discourse of associating promiscuity with risk is a particularly gendered narrative because in heterosexual men, high levels of sexual interaction are considered biologically natural to the point of being celebrated and encouraged in modern Western popular culture. However, the continual prejudicial treatment of female sex workers demonstrates how women who express sexual agency are defined as deviant, transgressive and contaminated. Women who work as sex workers, by contrast to other women in the community, appear to be risk taking, placing them outside acceptable conceptions of femininity. The ideas associated with prostitution and risk are that women put their own health, and that of the public, at risk by engaging in unprotected sex with a multiple number of men. Take the commonly held assumption that women involved in prostitution are a 'high risk group' for carrying and spreading sexual infections. The recent Home Office (2004: 67) review *Paying the Price: A Consultation Paper on Prostitution* took on board this stereotypical mantle that continues to associate prostitution with disease and decay, ignoring up-to-date medical evidence of low levels of infection among sex workers (Ward et al. 2004) and high rates of condom use unless in coerced or violent situations. The rhetoric directed towards sex workers by the media and government policy is an example of the misinformation about who practises 'risky' behaviour, setting up distinct (false) binaries of those who practise safe sexual activities and those who do not.

Below, I use the case of female sex work, relying on my own empirical investigations in the UK (Sanders 2005b), to examine some basic misconceptions about the taking and avoidance of the gendered nature of risk. First, I challenge the notions that risk is the same for all sex workers. Second, I suggest that there is a spectrum or 'continuum of risk' that affects the professional and personal lives of sex workers. Sex workers experience different types of risks that are contrary to the public and state perception that emphasizes sexual health as the main element of risk in relation to prostitution.

### The individual nature of risk

Prostitution has been described as a risky practice because of the exposure to sexual health infections (Bloor 1995), coercive and non-compliant clients (Scambler and Scambler 1997), as well as high levels of violence (Church et al. 2001). Although the types of risks that sex workers face has, to some extent, been addressed by the literature, the risks to health, well-being and social status experienced through prostitution are not the same for all sex workers. Recent empirical work has established that women who work from indoor premises encounter less violence than women who work on the street because of the relative control they exercise over working and environmental conditions (Whittaker and Hart 1996; Raphael and Shapiro 2004; Brents and Hausbeck 2005; Sanders 2005a). On the other hand, in the UK the criminalization of street prostitution dramatically increases the risks that sex workers encounter. Kantola and Squires (2004) note the dominant discourses of public nuisance directed towards both female sex workers and men who 'kerb crawl' that has led to an increase in legislation in the UK. Elsewhere (Sanders 2004a), I have agued that the high visibility of the police, increased numbers of arrests for soliciting and the recent flux of Anti-Social Behaviour Orders given to street sex workers reduces the strategies that women use to keep themselves safe (see also Jones and Sager 2001).

Using empirical work with migrant and trafficked sex workers in Europe, Wallman (2001: 83) identifies how the experiences of danger and risk are not the same for all sex workers. Through narratives of migrant and trafficked sex workers, Wallman identifies the range of global threats, 'the mess of options', power structures, knowledge, networks and the effects of local and national policy that affects individuals' propensity to take or avoid risks in prostitution. The differences in the propensity for risk taking and risk aversion can be understood through the model of risk promoted by Adams (1985) who argues that the persistence of risky behaviours can be understood through the metaphor of a 'risk thermostat'. The setting of the thermostat varies for each individual and therefore behaviours fluctuate depending upon what an individual considers above or below their personal risk threshold. As Wallman (2001: 77) summarizes: 'Weighing-ups before a risk is taken are explained less by the options available than by the need to adjust risk levels to match the thermostat.'

Adams (1985) developed a model of personal risk taking where individuals assess risks based on four levels of cultural filters or perceptions of risk. These four interpretations of risk can be translated into four types of people. First, the egalitarian, who is averse to risk taking and will take precautions at all times. Second, the individualist, who is optimistic about low levels of risk and will assume an absence of risk unless there is an obvious indicator otherwise. This filtering of risk instead concentrates on the rewards that risk taking brings. Third, the fatalist, will approach each risk as it is presented. Fourth, the hierarchist, detests uncertainty and will rely on expert knowledge to maximize information about risk and minimize the actualities. This typology of filters that determine perceptions of and interactions with risk can be applied to how sex workers manage the risks of violence and harm in their everyday negotiations of the sex work environment and male clients. The egalitarian avoids environments such as the street or escorting that are inherently dangerous but will instead decide to work in the safety of collective brothels or saunas. In addition, their working routines will be guided by precautions at all stages. The individualist will generally consider prostitution as non-risky unless obvious danger from sexual health or a violent client is presented. Instead the emphasis for this type of sex worker is to concentrate on maximizing financial profit while minimizing the time needed to make the money. This could justify why a minority of women may engage in risky sexual practices – such as sex without a condom – for higher remuneration. The fatalist sex worker will be well aware of the risky nature of sex work, especially on the street, but will not use precautionary tactics to prevent this danger. Instead, remedial actions will be taken if attacked, for instance. In contrast, the hierarchist will be well informed through health professionals and advice from peers, relying on expert knowledge to minimize their risks by creating mechanisms to reduce risk taking. This model of individual risk perception and risk decision-making stands in contrast to some of the more traditional notions of risk taking. Wallman (2001: 55) criticizes the tidiness of the popular analytical perspectives of risk for leaving out the 'messier realities of life' where decisions about risk and risk behaviours are made. Equally, it must be challenged whether sex workers are passive receptors of risk. As Day (2000: 34) summarizes from several years of observations with sex workers who attend a London health clinic: '"Risk" becomes a marker of sex workers' attempts to recover some agency through the transformation of risk into safety, civil rights and career development.'

The probability of encountering risks is determined not only by varying dispositions to risk taking and risk avoidance but also by competing preferences. Sex workers I interviewed were engaged in constantly juggling three preferences: (1) the desire to stay physically safe; (2) the desire to maintain their sanity; and (3) the desire to earn money. When analysing the risk behaviour of groups that are considered to perform transgressive sexual activities it is a combination of individual risk behaviour and the social and cultural environment that determines the outcome. Rhodes (1997: 216) suggests risk behaviour is not simply the outcome of 'individual choices', it is the outcome of 'negotiated actions'. Considering that the police have periodically used the possession of condoms as evidence that a woman is soliciting for business on the street, structured power relations determine these negotiated actions, highlighting direct mechanisms used to control unwanted behaviours.

Having established that the levels of risk are not the same for sex workers depending on their environmental setting, material resources, external structures and the individual propensity to take risks, it is important to reconceptualize exactly what is referred to when risk is associated with prostitution.

## A continuum of risk

To some extent, the literature on prostitution suggests that sexual health is the most prominent risk faced by sex workers, followed by issues associated with drug use and violence from clients. However, evidence suggests that in prostitution there are several different issues that affect the risk perception for individual sex workers, the objective calculation of risk and the propensity to take risk. Further, the popular perception that sex workers are carriers of disease or in some way a danger to public health must be challenged. Risk avoidance is written into the everyday routines and practices of sex workers as they learn from peers and professionals how to stay safe. Ironically, from my own ethnography of the indoor sex markets, sex workers considered their health to be the easiest risk to manage, especially given the specialist sexual health medical services that are readily available for this group of women. The consistent use of condoms was written into the sex work activities and risk occurred on the rare occasion that a condom slipped off or was forcibly removed.

From my findings, I argue that sex workers 'construct a continuum of risk which prioritises certain types of dangers depending on the perceived consequences and the likelihood of the risk happening' (Sanders 2004b: 557). The risk that received the most attention in the form of planning strategies was that of the psychological and emotional toil of selling sex as work. Sex workers created strategies to protect their own sense of identity by constructing a 'manufactured identity' specifically for work (see Sanders 2005b), as well as strategically using the condom as a psychological barrier in addition to its health preventative function (see Sanders 2002). In addition to the emotional labour associated with selling commercial sex, the fear of being discovered working in prostitution by a loved one was prioritized on the continuum of risk. This fear meant that many sex workers operated a double life and engaged in a series of cover stories, job aliases, lies and deception (see Sanders 2005a). Yet, although this was the main risk for many sex workers, there was a minority that were open about their status as a sex worker to people in their personal lives. Hence, for this group, there was no need to lie or deceive as their own individual biography meant that being discovered was not a risk. Despite the claim by Beck and Beck-Gernsheim (1995) that women in late modernity are now expressing more agency in careers and relationships and are no longer constrained by the prescriptions of womanhood, the options to perform agency are thwarted for women such as sex workers who appear to practise some forms of regressive sexuality, that is continually linked to deviance and criminality. In the case of female sex workers, 'risk and risk management are a complex interplay between individual biography, responses to risk and external structures and dynamics' (Sanders 2005a: 43).

## The gendered nature of risk taking and risk avoidance

More recent theorists have examined the counter-discourse in relation to risk taking and risk avoidance that is gendered in nature and often associated with sexual behaviour. Thrill-seeking sexual behaviour is an expected feature of socialization that young males are encouraged to adopt through promiscuity, explicit sexual aggressiveness and non-commitment to sexual partners. In contrast, the active risk-taking role enjoyed as pleasure by some women – for example, through dress, dancing, drinking, drug taking – is categorized as dangerous, vulnerable and stepping outside the boundaries of femininity. For both sexes, sexual risk taking is pursued as a pleasurable opportunity to perform gender and express sexuality publicly, yet female sexual risk taking is considered unacceptable, immoral and irresponsible. Hawkes (1996: 36) notes that the gendered nature of pleasure is not only ordered with the primacy of heterosexuality but within this there is a continued ambivalence around women's sexuality. Even in recent times where women's sexuality is accepted as equal to men's, the male sexual fantasy, desires and identities shape sexual expectations in private and public. This is most notable through the eroticization of the high street through the mainstreaming of erotic dancing and nudity in lap dancing clubs. The gendered nature of risk has been theorized in relation to the specific hazards that women face. Chan and Rigakos (2002) describe how the nature of risk is different for various social groups and that women's taking and avoidance of risk are inherently gendered:

> What constitutes risky behaviour is filtered through a masculine lens that conditions what we identify and define as 'risky'. Moreover, when women do take exceptional risks, the tendency is to conflate women's exceptional risk taking with 'amorality' as in the case of promiscuity.
>
> (Chan and Rigakos 2002: 743)

Even the definitions of and the constructions around risk are from a masculine perspective. No agency is afforded those who are considered to take risks. For instance, Rhodes and Cusick (2000) interviewed HIV positive people who have unprotected sex with their primary partners and found that the lived experience of what could be considered highly risky sexual practices was defended through discourses of 'relationship safety', 'trust' and 'intimacy'.

Walklate (1997: 44) suggests there is a gendered conceptualization of risk that encourages a preoccupation with risk avoidance and calls for an 'explanation of risk as a gendered concept subjectively experienced'. The gendered meanings of risk are formulated alongside the concept of risk avoidance associated closely with assumptions of femininity: 'Dominant notions of femininity tend to represent the careful avoidance of danger ... they are more often portrayed as the passive victims of risk than as active risk takers' (Lupton 1999: 161). These dominant discourses construct those women who appear to take risks through drug taking, dancing and sexual expression, for instance, as wild and wayward rather than actively making decisions about pleasure seeking and identity building. The complexity of the relationship between risky behaviours and pleasure seeking unfolds through the work of Hutton (2004) who researched women's participation in the contemporary club scene. The use of ecstasy and engagement in the club scene was not considered by female respondents to be related to risky behaviour but was instead a vehicle to create positive femininity and expressions of sexuality. Hutton (2004: 226) found that, contrary to media images of 'drugged and dangerous', females involved in the underground clubbing scene preferred this space as an alternative, safer environment compared with the sexual harassment and predatory nature of the mainstream night-time economy. Female clubbers were, however, still considered to be stepping outside the boundaries of femininity and as a result subject to stereotype, scapegoating and regulation. Women who do not seem to 'toe the line' have been targeted with blame and expected to be responsible for their own vulnerability. The work of feminist criminologist Stanko (1997) has established that crime prevention advice and public understanding of women's vulnerable status result in a powerful set of 'safety discourses'. Yet these 'safety discourses' that accompany any discussion of women's safety in public concentrate on women's failure to take appropriate actions to prevent risks and danger. Stanko (1996: 51) goes on to state that it is widely considered that those women who do not follow the rules of responsibility – for example, wearing clothes that cover up the body, not walking alone at night – are either 'asking for it' or are outside the realms of public protection. Sex workers are a group of sexual minorities who are considered to willingly place themselves outside these 'safety discourses' and therefore to invite danger and trouble by not sticking to the gendered expectations of behaviour.

Risk theorists Beck (1992) and Giddens (1991) describe late modernity as an era where individuals have accepted personal responsibility for avoiding risk and, to achieve this, readily engage with and assess the advice given by 'experts' in the field. Risk is therefore considered in terms of a lifestyle choice, placing the responsibility for taking or avoiding risk with the individual. However, these macro-sociological approaches have been criticized for making generalizations and failing to take account of the subjective and unequal experience of risk depending on gender, sexuality, ethnicity and social class. Using the case of female sex workers, it is evident that risk behaviour is not simply about lifestyle choice but an outcome of environmental conditions, external structures, material resources as well as individual decision-making and biography. The research of Rhodes and Cusick (2000) with HIV positive people illustrates that decision-making around risk is not always a calculated outcome but is influenced by emotions, desires, relationships and identities. Yet at the same time the process of reflexivity also suggests that individuals make rational calculations between various risk scenarios, types of advice and voices of reason (Lupton 1999: 108). Local and situated knowledge is referred to when deciding on appropriate action and behaviour, rather than relying on the supposed wisdom of expert knowledge. Here, the place of sexual subcultures becomes functionary to develop alternative sources of knowledge in opposition to the dominant discourses of risky, dangerous and problematic sexual behaviour. A 'discourse of diversity' has developed where groups that have been marginalized because of their sexual identity have formed sub-cultures and social communities (Weeks 2003: 76). Groups of transvestites, transsexuals, sex workers, bisexuals and fetishists to name but a few are joining together to demand rights to self-expression, sexual citizenship and a legitimate place in society. In his study of how the identities of people living with HIV/AIDS in Britain are formed and shaped, Heaphy (1996) shows how medical and dominant knowledge of the disease is not accepted outright. Instead, the meanings of HIV/AIDS are negotiated, mediated through the gay press and self-help groups, so that people play an active role in creating their own identities. Similarly, sex workers in the UK are among those excluded from mainstream labour rights who are joining together through unions and collaborative initiatives to advocate for their right to be treated as workers (see Lopes 2005; Sanders 2005a: 174).

The model of individual risk that is promoted by Adams (1985) suggests that risk behaviour is a result of a mixture of rational decision-making, in-dividual propensity towards risk and the socio-cultural context. In addition, the theoretical contribution of the anthropologist Douglas highlights the need to consider the material resources and cultural context in which a be-haviour is labelled either risky or safe. This cultural context is also a political context, remembering that the discourses of risk are mobilized as a political strategy. Despite Beck's (1992) claim that the functions of risk in late mod-ernity reduce the need to construct an Other that can be compared to the self, this chapter has reviewed how certain sexual expressions, identities and be-haviours are still constructed as deviant, unnatural and marginalized for their 'risky' properties. The institutionalization of heterosexuality (Scott and Jackson 2000) and the quest to maintain this as the 'natural' and dominant form of sexuality and uphold the status quo of 'ordinary' family life, require that alternative sexual identities are cast as Other, and are actively excluded and marginalized. Despite the politics of sexual liberation influencing mod-ern sexual relations and a significant shift in attitudes towards sex and re-lationships (Jackson and Scott 2004), discourses of risk, danger and immorality continue to shape how sexuality is regulated. Institutional re-sponses through policy, practice and discourse have sanctioned strategies of exclusion and control that stigmatize and shift blame onto individuals through processes of criminalization and authoritarian rhetoric. A new reading of risk is needed that takes into account active choice and conscious efforts to construct identity. Unlike the risk theorists such as Beck who view femininity and risk only as a negative or located in the domestic sphere, risk demands to be theorized not only as harmful or imposed, but as an aspect of agency and pleasure seeking.

## Conclusion: beyond the risk society

Contributions in this chapter have been taken from across the intellectual disciplines, demonstrating how, both historically and more recently, 'risk' has been canonized as an organizing principle to understand and regulate the sexual body. The symbolic centrality of sexuality and the sexual body in medical, legal, social and political narrative is at the heart of risk discourse, risk assessment and policies to prevent and manage behaviour in late modernity. Building on from the core body of literature that examines the relationship between risk and sexuality, more work needs to be done in order to make links between contemporary risk theories and the issues relating to sexuality, sexual identities and the body. There needs to be a springboard forward into interdisciplinary arenas of collaborative investigation and research that looks critically at risk discourses.

One example of an area that has been under-researched is that of the social policy context where risk and sexuality meet. For instance, the policies and practices that draw on some of the more traditional morality discourses continue to shape health care, policing and public policy today. These are living examples of how discourses synthesize to create real outcomes for individual groups in society who are outside the mainstream. A phenomenological approach could tap into the voices of those who experience the policies in their everyday life. Within the domestic sphere there are groups that continually hit the headlines because of the dynamics associated with sexuality and risk – teenage mothers and young people's sexual behaviour, for instance. Yet it is also outside the domestic sphere that exploration of risk is needed among people who are involved in either risk-taking or risk-avoidance decision-making. Risk taking in the public sphere, such as the night-time economy, connects the disciplines of criminology, sociology and social policy as a route into finding out why and how risk taking and pleasure seeking are embedded in some aspects of contemporary youth culture.

While there is plenty of space for interdisciplinary exploration of the manifestations of risk and sexuality, at the forefront of risk studies must be the understanding that risk is not equally applied across all groups in society. The case studies identified in this chapter illuminate the inequalities in relation to sexuality and sexual behaviour in the light of HIV/AIDS and sex work. Most notably, more in-depth investigations into gender, ethnicity, disability, age, social class, rural and urban residence and religious affiliation in relation to risk taking and avoidance should form part of a new research agenda. Studied at a micro level, the dynamics between risk and social divisions can provide further understanding of the place of risk in the formation and maintenance of relationships. These wider social inequities that feed into the understanding sociologists have of risk could also re-awaken the complexities of who is afforded sexual citizenship while other groups are denied such freedoms. At the same time, the issue of agency in making decisions relating to sexual behaviour and identities could make links between existing theories of risk and new empirical findings. Categories of risk and what constitutes risky sexual behaviour or identities are continually shifting with the tides of political influence. With these changes there must also be a re-focus of research agendas to critically expose the policy frameworks and discourses that create knowledge about who is risky and who is safe. Even though there is a recognition and tolerance of sexual diversity in society, the rhetoric of risky sexuality continues to tarnish those who appear to be outside the norm resulting in a strong demarcation of acceptable sexuality and that which is considered perverse, wrong and dangerous.

## Study questions

1   What is the role of the socio-cultural theories in understanding sexuality and risk?
2   What are the consequences for individuals and groups who are considered to practise dangerous sexual activities?
3   Which different types of sexual behaviours provoke moral panics in the mass media and why?

## References

Adams, J. (1985) *Risk and Freedom: The Record of Road Safety Legislation.* London: TPP.
Adkins, L. (2001) Risk culture, self-reflexivity and the making of sexual hierarchies, *Body and Society*, 7(1): 35–55.
Beck, U. (1992) *Risk Society: Towards a New Modernity.* London: Sage.
Beck, U. and Beck-Gernsheim, E. (1995) *The Normal Chaos of Love.* Cambridge: Polity Press.
Bloor, M. (1995) *The Sociology of HIV Transmission.* London: Sage.
Brents, B. and Hausbeck, K. (2005) Violence and legalized brothel prostitution in

Nevada: examining safety, risk and prostitution policy, *Journal of Interpersonal Violence* 20(3): 270–95.

Chan, W. and Rigakos, G. (2002) Risk, crime and gender, *British Journal of Criminology*, 42(3): 743–61.

Church, S., Henderson, M., Barnard, M. and Hart, G. (2001) Violence by clients towards female prostitutes in different work settings: questionnaire survey, *British Medical Journal*, 322: 524–5.

Corbin, A. (1990) *Women for Hire: Prostitution and Sexuality in France after 1850*. Cambridge, MA: Harvard University Press.

Day, S. (2000) The politics of risk amongst London prostitutes, in P. Caplan (ed.) *Risk Revisited*. London: Pluto Press.

Douglas, M. (1992) *Risk and Danger: Essays in Cultural Theory*. London: Routledge.

Foucault, M. (1979) *The History of Sexuality*, vol 1. London: Allen Lane.

Foucault, M. (1991) Governmentality, in G. Burchell, C. Gordon and P. Miller (eds) *The Foucault Effect: Studies in Governmentality*. Hemel Hempstead: Harvester Wheatsheaf.

Giddens, A. (1991) *Modernity and Self-Identity: Self and Society in the Late Modern Age*. Cambridge: Polity.

Harding, J. (1998) *Sex Acts: Practices of Femininity and Masculinity*. London: Sage.

Hawkes, G. (1996) *A Sociology of Sex and Sexuality*. Buckingham: Open University Press.

Heaphy, B. (1996) Medicalisation and identity formation: identity and strategy in the context of AIDS and HIV, in J. Weeks and J. Holland (eds) *Sexual Cultures: Communities, Values and Intimacy*. Basingstoke: Macmillan.

Home Office (2004) *Paying the Price: A Consultation Paper on Prostitution*. London: HMSO.

Hutton, F. (2004) Up for it, mad for it? Women, drug use and participation in club scenes, *Health, Risk and Society*, 6(3): 223–37.

Jackson, S. and Scott, S. (2004) Sexual antinomies in late modernity, *Sexualities*, 7(2): 233–48.

Jones, H. and Sager, T. (2001) Crime and Disorder Act 1998: prostitution and the Anti-Social Behaviour Order, *Criminal Law Review*, November Edition: 873–85.

Kantola, J. and Squires, J. (2004) Discourses surrounding prostitution policies in the UK, *European Journal of Women's Studies*, 11(1): 77–101.

Levine, P. (2003) *Prostitution, Race and Politics. Policing Venereal Disease in the British Empire*. London: Routledge.

Lopes, A. (2005) Sex Workers and the labour movement in the UK, in R. Campbell and M. O'Neill (eds) *Sex Work Now*. Cullompton: Willan.

Lupton, D. (1995) *The Imperative of Health: Public Health and the Regulated Body*. London: Sage.

Lupton, D. (1999) *Risk and Sociocultural Theory: New Directions and Perspectives*. Cambridge: Cambridge University Press.

Miller, W.I. (1997) *Anatomy of Disgust*. Cambridge, MA: Harvard University Press.

Raphael, J. and Shapiro, D. (2004) Violence in indoor and outdoor prostitution venues, *Violence Against Women*, 10(12): 126–39.

Rhodes, T. (1997) Risk theory in epidemic times: sex, drugs and the social organisation of 'risk behaviour', *Sociology of Health and Illness*, 19(2): 208–27.

Rhodes, T. and Cusick. L (2000) Love and intimacy in relationship risk management: HIV positive people and their sexual partners, *Sociology of Health and Illness* 22(1): 1–26.

Richardson, D. (2000) Sexuality, identity and risk, in D. Richardson (ed.) *Rethinking Sexuality*. London: Sage.

Sanders, T. (2002) The condom as psychological barrier: female sex workers and emotional management, *Feminism and Psychology*, 12(4): 561–6.

Sanders, T. (2004a) A continuum of risk? The management of health, physical and emotional risks by female sex workers, *Sociology of Health and Illness*, 26(5): 1–18.

Sanders, T. (2004b) The risks of street prostitution: punters, police and protesters, *Urban Studies*, 41(8): 1703–17.

Sanders, T. (2005a) *Sex Work: A Risky Business*. Cullompton: Willan.

Sanders, T. (2005b) It's just acting: sex workers' strategies for capitalising on sexuality, *Gender, Work and Organization*, 12: 319–42.

Scambler, G. and Scambler, A. (1997) *Rethinking Prostitution*. London: Routledge.

Scott, S. and Jackson, S. (2000) Sexuality, in G. Payne (ed.) *Social Divisions*. London: Macmillan.

Self, H. (2003) *Prostitution, Women and Misuse of the Law*. London: Frank Cass.

Stanko, E. (1996) Warnings to women: police advice and women's safety in Britain, *Violence Against Women*, 2(1): 5–24.

Stanko, E. (1997) Safety talk: conceptualizing women's risk assessment as a 'technology of the soul', *Theoretical Criminology*, 1(4): 479–99.

Walklate, S. (1997) Risk and criminal victimisation: a modernist dilemma? *British Journal of Criminology*, 37(1): 35–46.

Walkowitz, J. (1980) *Prostitution and Victorian Society: Women, Class, and the State*. Cambridge: Cambridge University Press.

Wallman, S. (2001) Global threats, local options, personal risk: dimensions of migrant sex work in Europe, *Health, Risk and Society*, 3(1): 75–88.

Ward, H., Day, S., Green, K. and Weber, J. (2004) Declining prevalence of STI in the London sex industry 1985–2002, *Sexually Transmitted Infections*, 80(3): 374–6.

Weeks, J. (1991) *Against Nature: Essays on History, Sexuality and Identity*. London: River Oram Press.

Weeks, J. (2003) *Sexuality*. London: Routledge.

Whittaker, D. and Hart, G. (1996) Research note: managing risks: the social organisation of indoor sex work, *Sociology of Health and Illness*, 18(3): 399–413.

## Further reading

Day, S. (2000) The politics of risk among London prostitutes, in P. Caplan (ed.) *Risk Revisited*. London: Pluto Press.

Richardson, D. (2000) Sexuality, identity and risk, in D. Richardson (ed.) *Rethinking Sexuality*. London: Sage.

Sanders, T. (2005) *Sex Work: A Risky Business*. Cullompton: Willan.

Scott, S. and Jackson, S. (2000) Sexuality, in G. Payne (ed.) *Social Divisions*. London: Macmillan.

Weeks, J. (2003) *Sexuality*. London: Routledge.

# 7 Media and risk

## Alison Anderson

## Introduction

In recent decades, a number of media 'scares' have focused upon new, potentially far-reaching risks, which have a global impact. Such risks include those associated with terrorism and also those linked with the development of new technologies including biotechnologies (such as the genetic modification of food and crops), nanotechnologies (the design and production of extremely small devices, materials and systems on the scale of a nanometer through the manipulation of individual atoms and molecules), cyber risks, as well as recent disasters that some claim may have been exacerbated by global climate change (such as the Asian tsunami in 2004 and Hurricane Katrina in 2005). The September 11th 2001 attacks on the US World Trade Center threw into sharp relief unsettling questions about the changing role of global media in communicating contemporary risks. This and other recent crises have brought to the fore key questions concerning objectivity, censorship, democracy and citizenship and generated a growing interest among scholars in the increasingly important role that new as well as old media have come to play in mediating risks (Anderson 2003). It is therefore important to look historically at the field of risk reporting, to identify major themes and issues of relevance to contemporary debates, and to consider likely trends for future analysis.

The chapter argues that recent approaches point to a more complex understanding of risk reporting and reflect broader social changes, both in the nature of 'risk' and the structure and workings of the media. Analysis of media reporting of risk must be placed in the wider context of the growing concentration and globalization of news media ownership, and the increasingly 'promotional culture' which we inhabit; highlighted by the rapid rise of the public relations industry in recent years and claims-makers that employ increasingly sophisticated media strategies to communicate their messages far and wide. Relatively little attention has so far been paid to new media within the literature on risk, yet the Internet is increasingly becoming a key source of information in North America and Europe, especially among young people (see Internet World Statistics 2005). Real-time images can now be transmitted globally, increasing their intensity and potential power to dominate news agendas. Also, with the growing number of people taking photographs using their mobile phones, news professionals are becoming more reliant upon the public to provide pictures at the scene of disasters. Mobile phone images of the London bombings on 7 July 2005 appeared on the Internet within hours of the terror attacks and the BBC received 50 such pictures within an hour of the first bomb being set off (Douglas 2005). While news items about risk offer a complex range of meanings that may be interpreted in various ways by audiences, the ease with which images may be manipulated increases the likelihood that distinctions between 'reality' and 'representation' become blurred. Precisely how such shifts are impacting upon the field of risk reporting needs to be the focus of future critical debate.

The chapter will begin by identifying key theoretical and methodological considerations. It will then examine how this field of enquiry has evolved since the 1970s and consider a range of case studies of risk events and how they have been reported. The discussion will provide an overview of the production, content and reception of risk reporting, highlighting major research themes and assessing future research possibilities. The discussion will focus mainly on the news media since, to date, most research has concentrated upon factual rather than fictional media.

## Key conceptual and methodological concerns

As has been made clear in preceding chapters, the category of 'risk' is extremely broad and incorporates a diverse range of issues. Accordingly, researchers interested in examining the relationship between risk and the media have first had to grapple with the difficult conceptual issue of how to define 'risk' (Kitzinger 1999; Allan et al. 2005). In recent decades there appears to have been an increased news media interest in risk and a significant growth in scholarly articles on media and risk (Kitzinger 1999; Mythen 2004; Gurabardhi et al. 2005). However, risk reporting straddles a number of different areas (consumer issues, environmental affairs, war reporting, health coverage, and science and technology issues, to name but a few) and does not neatly map onto traditional journalistic beats. Deciding whether a particular news item is about 'risk' involves making a number of subjective judgements. The process through which researchers limit the focus of a study is crucial and likely to have important implications for their findings. Researchers investigating media representations of multiple 'hazards' are inevitably selective in their choice of topic areas. For example, Singer and Endreny (1987) conducted a study of media reporting of hazards based upon a sample of TV, press and magazine coverage that focused upon a range of different hazards resulting in 1,276 items. The classification scheme included 'natural hazards', 'materials hazards', 'energy hazards' but excluded hazards associated with terrorism, crime and suicide (see Kitzinger, 1999: 58).

Despite the relatively recent popularity of the concept of 'risk', studies of the media construction of hazards, disasters and social problems have a lengthy history. Anthropological and psychological studies during the 1970s and 1980s focused upon how particular social problems came to be defined as risks (Douglas and Wildavsky 1982) and on the nature of risk perception (Slovic 1987). Yet within cultural theory surprisingly little sustained attention has been devoted to the role of the media in the symbolic representation of competing rationality claims (Wilkinson 1999). Within the field of risk perception, scholars have tended to focus upon examining media content; the assumption being that risk controversies arise from distorted and inaccurate accounts of the 'facts' (Dunwoody and Peters 1992). The traditional approach treated risk reporting unproblematically in terms of how far it represented an accurate reflection of expert opinion. Typically, the problem was seen as arising from an 'information vacuum' between scientific experts and lay publics. However, the 'information deficit' model has come under mounting criticism and new concerns have increasingly focused upon citizen involvement and moving public engagement 'upstream' (Schanne and Meier 1992; Wilsdon and Willis 2004). This debate reflects differing underlying philosophical positions on the ideal role of the media in reporting risk and whether objectivity is thought to be possible or even desirable (Lichtenberg and MacClean 1991; Anderson 1997). Media coverage of risk is the product of social and cultural processes and constructs particular versions of reality that do not simply mirror a single truth. Assessing the extent to which media reporting of risks is 'accurate' and 'balanced' is extremely complex and far from straightforward. Yet those who accuse the media of routine sensationalism tend to assume that sources of official information on risk operate purely on a scientific basis. As Kitzinger (1999: 62) argues: 'The important questions are not to do with whether the media "play up" or "play down" risk but *which* risks attract attention, *how, when, why* and *under what conditions?*' Moreover, risk perception studies often uncritically viewed opinion polls and telephone surveys as reliable measures of the strength of public anxieties about risks. While these may provide an insight into general levels of public awareness about issues appearing in media agendas, they do not reveal the complex ways in which individuals make sense of media messages (Anderson 1997). However, as Wilkinson (1999) observes, there is evidence of a movement among risk communication scholars towards a greater engagement with mainstream media studies research and a growing appreciation of the complexities and uncertainties of media influence.

In the UK, the classic work of Cohen during the 1970s focused on the impact and influence of press coverage of crime, introducing the concepts of 'moral panics' and 'deviance amplification' (Cohen 1972). In addition, numerous case studies have examined news media reporting of areas such as the environment, war, terrorism, health and politics – all of which may be seen as falling broadly into the field of 'risk' studies (Anderson 1997; Kitzinger 1999; Allan 2002). The majority of studies have focused upon print news media rather than electronic news media. Most studies of risk focus upon a particular incident or risk topic but some have examined a range of diverse issues (Kitzinger and Reilly 1997; Murdock et al. 2003). The sheer breadth of topics alone makes meaningful comparisons between studies difficult. Moreover, this is compounded by scholars' use of different time-scales, sampling frames that include different media, as well as different methods of analysing media content. There are also wide variations in the degree to which rigorous methods of media analysis are applied and levels of engagement with media studies theory (Kitzinger 1999). Media are complexly differentiated and governed by different constraints therefore any generalizations about 'risk' and the 'media' have to be made with considerable caution. Also, findings tend to be specific to particular issues and socio-political contexts (Renn 1991).

Bearing these limitations in mind, what have content analysis studies revealed about broad patterns in media reporting of risk? They suggest, not surprisingly perhaps, that coverage of risks is highly selective and the media do not simply reflect 'reality'. It is not necessarily the most serious risks that attract the greatest attention. Coverage tends to be event-centred and thrives upon unexpected, dramatic disasters or unusual risks (see Anderson 1997; Kitzinger 1999). Risks that result in the death or serious illness of large numbers of people at once – such as nuclear accidents – are more likely to attract coverage than those which have a longer cumulative impact over time – such as those relating to smoking or asbestos exposure (Singer and Endreny 1987; Greenberg et al. 1989). There is also a tendency for media reporting to simplify and individualize complex scientific debates by aligning news sources in a manner which accentuates their differing positions, placing them 'for' versus 'against' (see Williams et al. 2003; Anderson et al. 2005b). The 'human interest' factor is often an important ingredient in news stories on risk (Hansen 1993; Kitzinger and Reilly 1997; Williams et al. 2003). However, a number of studies suggest that the tone of risk reporting generally tends to be reassuring rather than alarming (Schanne and Meier 1992; Petts et al. 2003). Indeed, the accusation that media coverage is sensationalist is itself likely to be a product of selective memory (Kitzinger 1999).

There is a tendency for some risk practitioners to make the naïve assumption that the media will automatically cover risk issues but, as Eldridge and Reilly (2003: 139) point out, the news media are poorly adapted for sustaining high profile ongoing coverage of long-term risks, particularly where there is considerable scientific uncertainty and official sources remain largely silent. The news media do not generally like dealing with scientific uncertainty (see Friedman et al. 1999). Indeed, there is a fundamental conflict between the tendency of scientists to qualify statements and the journalistic attraction to conclusive or controversial new findings. Moreover, the concept of 'risk' deals with speculation about what may happen a long way into the future and is in conflict with news schedules that emphasize the here and now. Unless potential risks are actually manifesting themselves in some concrete way, then they are likely simply to be ignored. In other cases, rumours proliferate in the media about the supposed risks linked with new technologies; a case in point being periodic panics over the potential health implications of mobile phones (Burgess 2004). Researchers, therefore, make a number of implicit assumptions about theoretical and methodological issues that inform empirical studies of risk. The next section briefly traces the history of the field of risk reporting before moving on to examine the explanatory potential of more recent approaches.

## Early approaches to researching risk and the media

Some of the earliest approaches to researching risk and the media originated in the disaster studies and risk communication fields. In the 1980s, researchers drew many insights from anthropological fieldwork and cultural theory in developing accounts of the social construction of risk perception (Douglas and Wildavsky 1982). At the same time a host of studies examined the role of the media in constructing social problems and Hilgartner and Bosk's 'public arenas model' became particularly influential in the USA (Hilgartner and Bosk 1988; Anderson 1997). Perhaps one of the most significant developments was the Social Amplification of Risk Framework (SARF) that was created in 1988. This model was developed by North American scholars with the aim of providing an integrative theoretical framework for a fragmented range of risk perspectives in the growing field of risk communication and risk perception (see Kasperson et al. 1988; Renn et al. 1992; Pidgeon et al. 2003). The new framework attempted to bring together insights from a diverse range of approaches in studies focusing on psychological, cultural, media and organizational dimensions of risk. According to Pidgeon et al. (2003: 2):

> [the SARF] aims to examine broadly, and in social and historical context, how risk and risk events interact with psychological, social, institutional and cultural processes in ways that amplify or attenuate risk perceptions and concerns, and thereby shape risk behaviour, influence institutional processes, and effect risk consequences.

Accordingly, the framework sought to explain why certain risk events, defined by experts as relatively non-threatening, come to attract considerable socio-political attention (amplification), and other risk events, defined as posing a greater objective threat, attract relatively little attention (attenuation). This had certain parallels with the earlier Deviance Amplification Model, which became a popular way of accounting for the impact of media in reporting risk events among European researchers. It was during the 1970s that Stanley Cohen first introduced the concepts of 'moral panics' and 'deviance amplification' (Cohen 1972), subsequently to be applied in Hall et al.'s (1978) classic study of press reporting of mugging in the 1970s. While SARF increasingly formed the basis for a growing number of empirical studies in the risk communication field, important developments were taking place within media studies that served to challenge earlier radical research traditions. In the 1980s, a new revisionist movement emerged in media and cultural studies which highlighted ambiguities and inconsistencies in media texts, seeing them as open to multiple, or 'polysemic', interpretations (Fiske 1989). Scholars such as David Morley (1980) emphasized the active, creative negotiation of media messages by audience members according to their social and discourse positions. While many of its proponents overstated the novelty of this approach – earlier work had paved the way for a greater recognition of the complexities of textual meanings – it marked an important advance within media studies (Curran 2002). Ethnographic studies demonstrated how the reception of media messages involves more complex, uncertain and dynamic processes than previously thought (see Ang 1985, 1991).

Revisionist writings also had a significant impact upon the study of media organizations as radical research traditions came under attack (Curran 2002). In the late 1970s Hall and colleagues (Hall et al. 1978) published a classic study, *Policing the Crisis*, which argued that official sources or 'primary definers' (such as government ministers and the courts) gain advantaged access to the media. The media were seen as 'secondary definers' through their role in transmitting the views of the powerful. While still influential, the 'primary definers' model has been extensively qualified over recent decades. Schlesinger (1990) argued that the model was relatively static, media-centric and overly simplistic. It underestimated the extent of competition that occurs between sources. It ignored the complexities of source–media relations such as conflict and division among powerful news sources themselves and how media access shifts over time reflecting broader changes within society. Moreover in focusing upon the processes through which official sources gain news access, it glossed over how marginal sources gain coverage. In subsequent years a range of empirical studies added weight to such critical observations, including studies in the field of crime, law and justice (Schlesinger and Tumber 1994), health (Miller and Williams 1993), and the environment (Anderson 1991, 1993, 1997; Hansen 1993). This led to a new emphasis upon viewing media arenas as battlefields for political influence (Wolfsfeld 1997). As Wilkinson notes:

> Risk controversies in the media should not be understood as a re-
> flection of the issues which concern the majority of the population,
> but rather as a product of the battles between a select range of news
> sources to define the public representation of problems so that they
> express the political and economic interests of an institutionally
> privileged elite.
>
> (1999: 22)

By the early 1990s, Ulrich Beck's theorizing on the nature of late modern
society had gained particular prominence in Europe (Beck 1992, 1995). In *Risk
Society* – first published in 1986 – and in a string of subsequent publications,
he accorded the media a key role in the formation of public understandings of
risk. He argues that in risk society the media can act both as a vehicle whereby
experts relay institutional information to publics and, paradoxically, as a
channel for reflexivity and public critique. Beck's work has had the most far-
reaching impact upon the academy and beyond, in terms of theorizing about
risk, and yet, as we shall see in the next section, it has undergone perhaps the
most sustained critique of all the approaches sketched thus far.

## Current approaches and critiques of earlier models

In recent years a number of scholars have drawn attention to the lack of
sustained, rigorous analysis of the role of the media in reporting risk, this
despite the fact that the media have been seen to fulfil a central role in risk
communication (Anderson 1997; Kitzinger and Reilly 1997; Kitzinger 1999;
Cottle 2000; Tulloch and Lupton 2001; Eldridge and Reilly, 2003: 139; Mythen 2004). In particular, Beck's account of the media to date has been critiqued as oversimplified, unevenly developed and in places contradictory
(Cottle 1998: 25; Mythen, 2004: 76). In publications such as *Risk Society*
(1992) and *Ecological Politics in an Age of Risk* (1995), Beck, like many risk
communication practitioners, shows a lack of awareness of mainstream media
theory (see Wilkinson 1999; Murdock et al. 2003; Mythen 2004). Deliberately
written in a provocative style, these publications have clearly succeeded in
stimulating widespread debate. However, he makes bold claims about the
influence of the media without empirical substantiation, and treats the media
as monolithic (Anderson, 1993: 51; 1997: 188). Research in media and cultural studies has demonstrated that the news media are differentiated, occupying their own particular market niches, and governed by a variety of
economic and political constraints (Anderson 1997; Hargreaves et al. 2003).
Representations of risk issues differ according to different media formats that
are governed by different restrictions and practices. For example, risk reporting in mass circulation UK newspapers tends to focus more on the

'human interest' angle and the experiences of ordinary people than does the elite press (Murdock et al. 2003) and television formats tend to favour risk items that are visually appealing (Anderson 1997). Moreover, recent work highlights the need to distinguish between how media cover different risks, since some risks have greater cultural resonance than others (Kitzinger 1999). There are also significant cross-cultural variations, yet Beck pays little attention to national and political cultures and contexts (Cottle 1998: 17–18). The media-centric focus of Beck's analysis shifts attention away from considering processes of news production and is: 'conspicuously silent ... on the institutional field in which "relations of definitions" compete for public recognition and legitimation' (Cottle 1998: 18). Accordingly, there is a need for rigorous empirical analysis of source–media relations and theorization that adequately captures the complexity of media involvement in framing risk (Anderson 1997; Cottle 1998). Recent work points to a more complex understanding of the relationship between news sources and media framing of risks (see Anderson 1997, 2003; Kitzinger and Reilly 1997; Miller and Riechert 2000; Manning 2001; Kitzinger et al. 2003). While numerous studies have indicated that official sources tend to dominate risk coverage, particularly where a major crisis is concerned (see Stallings 1990; Schanne and Meier 1992; Anderson 1997; Kitzinger 1999; Williams et al. 2003), elite access is not automatically guaranteed. News entry for both official and non-dominant sources is dependent on numerous contingencies (internal and external to the media). Research shows that marginal groups can gain news access (e.g. Anderson 1997; Manning 2001). However, gaining access to the media and achieving coverage is only half the battle. How news sources' claims are framed, and whether they are treated as credible and legitimate, are of critical importance. As Ryan (1991: 53) argues, 'the real battle is over whose interpretation, whose framing of reality, gets the floor'. The growth of the public relations (PR) industry is particularly significant in this regard, as news sources make increasing use of PR practitioners to parcel up their claims (see Davis 2000; Miller and Dinan 2000; Cottle 2003). Nevertheless, the contest to gain favourable media coverage is not a level playing field since official sources tend to have greater financial resources and stocks of cultural capital (Anderson 1997).

While the behind-the-scenes struggles among news sources competing for media attention has often been overlooked, within the risk field a number of scholars have traced processes of news-making through interviews with journalists and sources, examination of press releases and policy documents, or through observational methods (see Hansen 1993; Anderson 1997; Kitzinger and Reilly 1997). Such studies suggest that although non-dominant sources may lack the status, finance and PR personnel advantages enjoyed by official sources, they are often able to respond to media demands much more quickly because they are not held back by cumbersome bureaucratic procedures and political restrictions (Anderson 1997; Kitzinger 1999). Also, in the face of silence among 'official sources', journalists may more actively seek out the views of alternative sources (Anderson 1997; Kitzinger and Reilly 1997).

Risk reporting tends to be heavily focused around policy events. As Kitzinger notes, if little is happening on the policy front, then an issue is likely to have relatively little visibility on media agendas (see Kitzinger 1999). This can be seen in the case of Bovine Spongiform Encephalopathy (BSE) and genetics and, more recently, with debates concerning stem cells and nanotechnologies (Kitzinger and Reilly 1997; Nisbet and Lewenstein 2002; Nisbet et al. 2003; Williams et al. 2003; Anderson et al. 2005b). Patterns of risk reporting reflect shifting socio-political contexts (Kitzinger 1999; Anderson et al. 2005b). In the case of BSE, media coverage peaked in 1990 and again in 1996, but during the five intervening years, interest ebbed away (Miller 1999). A study by Eldridge and Reilly (2003) suggests that socio-political events, especially at the European level, were fundamental to understanding the original rise in interest in the story. News media attention began to fade away once it appeared that the issues had been resolved at a political level, though there was still a considerable amount of scientific uncertainty. An issue is also less likely to gain sustained media coverage where there is a level of consensus among news sources as to how it should be symbolically packaged (Miller and Reilly 1994; Wilkinson 1999). However, risk theorists have largely failed to engage with developments in the study of news production and media organizations. While Beck (1992) accords the media a central role in 'risk society', he overlooks the less visible processes of news production. As Cottle observes:

> Important source processes of claims-making and their institutional allegiances and institutional interdependencies – whether between the mass media, politics, science and the law – have been largely ignored insofar as the operations and interactions of the mass media are concerned, leading to a sociologically blunt (and a-historical) description of the surrounding 'risk' field and its media involvement.
> (1998: 25)

Similarly, the Social Amplification of Risk Framework (SARF) has tended to provide a media-centric account of news-media framings. Where news sources are considered within this framework, this tends to be underpinned by pluralist assumptions that news sources are competing on the same terms rather than possessing differing degrees of cultural capital. As Murdock et al. (2003: 162) point out: 'Work conducted within the SARF framework tends to concentrate on the amounts of coverage given to different issues and actors rather than the terms on which this publicity is secured.' Murdock et al. provide a more nuanced account of the interaction between journalists and their sources, emphasizing that control over the media is as much about the power to silence and suppress issues as it is to publicize them. They propose an alternative model that adapts Bourdieu's (1998) concept of 'fields of action'. For Murdock et al., risk is seen as a field of contest where claims-makers are engaged in continual definitional struggles, requiring a multifaceted analysis of the factors influencing the effectiveness of media strategies over time.

The work of Beck and SARF theorists also highlights the need to develop more analytical precision and refinement in conceptualizing media effects. In particular, there needs to be greater recognition of the difficulties of demonstrating the precise relationship between how changes in public opinion are related to the prominence of particular risks in media coverage. SARF assumes a linear flow of messages, based upon an outmoded transmission model of media effects. Both the deviance amplification model and SARF are founded on the notion that the problems stem from the distortion of expert knowledge while being transmitted to publics which leads to exaggerated or false perceptions (Hill 2001; Hornig, 2005). Instead Murdock et al. (2003: 161) see risk as a field of contest where claims-makers compete with one another to frame issues and seek to influence public opinion. As Petts et al. reason:

> SARF at best provides a highly simplistic understanding of the role and influence of the media in the amplification and attenuation of risk. At worst it could serve merely to aggravate tensions between risk experts and managers and lay publics through its failure to provide a coherent and full understanding of the impact and operations of these plural and symbolic information systems and their relationships with their consumers.
>
> (2001: x)

While individuals do not passively absorb media messages, and may negotiate meanings in complex ways, the media may potentially play an important role in shaping how risk issues become framed (McCallum et al. 1991; Hornig 1993; Miller and Reilly 1994; Philo 1999; Williams et al. 2003; Lupton 2004). Media reporting of risk may be interpreted in different ways by audiences, depending upon a range of factors including their cultural capital and extent of prior knowledge and personal experience. Yet, there are also difficulties with taking the idea of the 'active' audience too far. As Philo argues:

> It would be quite wrong to see audiences as simply absorbing media messages ... but it is also wrong to see viewers and readers as effortlessly active, creating their own meanings in each encounter with the text. Our work suggests the media can be a powerful influence on

what the audience believes and what is thought to be legitimate or desirable.

(1999: 287)

Moreover, knowledge and attitudes towards risk issues are often influenced by family, work colleagues, friends and health professionals and mediated by a range of factors including social class, age, gender and ethnicity (see Mythen 2004; Petts and Niemeyer 2004; Thirlaway and Heggs 2005). Media reporting is but one factor among many, including first-hand personal experience, which may influence risk perceptions. There is considerable variation in the degree to which people depend upon media for particular risk issues. For example, Petts et al. (2003) found that people did not depend heavily on media information for air pollution issues but they did for the millennium bug and train accidents. There has been a tendency in the past for risk researchers to neglect to examine a full range of potential information sources that publics are exposed to and assume blanket media effects. For example, a study by Mazur (1981), like much of the earlier work in the field, assumes a direct relationship between patterns of media coverage and public opinion on technological issues. As Gutteling (2005) observes, this study has largely been uncritically accepted and yet it is called into question by more recent research which points to the interaction of a range of variables – highlighting the sheer methodological difficulties involved in attempting to establish clear-cut links. As the concluding section argues, a sensitivity to the complex and dynamic range of factors involved in the reception of risk reporting needs to form the basis of future work across the risk communication field.

## Conclusion: beyond the risk society

To briefly summarize, to date, much of the empirical research that has been conducted within the field has concentrated upon media analysis but has not necessarily been informed by developments in mainstream media studies. As a number of scholars have acknowledged, there are considerable variations in the quality and rigour of work produced (Kitzinger 1999; Wilkinson 1999). Because research has tended to be restricted by traditional disciplinary boundaries, it has not always been able to benefit from the insights gained from a wider perspective and has remained very fragmented. However, there are signs of a growing recognition of the potential value of drawing upon a number of different approaches (Pidgeon et al. 2003). Indeed, cross-disciplinary work has begun to highlight the complexities of examining media constructions of risk and their context-specific impact upon public attitudes and behaviour over time.

There is a need for greater understanding of how news sources seek to influence media coverage and the factors affecting their success or failure to secure favourable representation (Anderson 1997, 2002). Accordingly, news production is an area that is likely to be an important avenue of future research. Previous research suggests that journalists tend to rely upon official, pre-packaged sources and staged events (Goodell 1986; Hansen 1994; Conrad 1999; Petersen 2001). Scientists are becoming increasingly sophisticated in packaging their work and more conscious of their public image (Nelkin 1995; Dunwoody 1999; Anderson et al. 2005a). Pressure groups campaigning around risk issues are often employing fine-tuned media strategies, increasingly investing considerable resources in utilizing new media technologies (see Anderson 1997, 2003). Further work is needed to systematically examine the kinds of rhetorical strategies that are used by claims-makers in their efforts to frame issues within the news media. In doing so, there is a need to move beyond a media-centric approach to consider the complexities and contingencies of social processes and the wider play of social power. Studies are already under way in the nanotechnologies field that are specifically focusing upon source–media relations (see http://www.research.plymouth.ac.uk/nanotechnology).

Another area that remains ripe for development is the role of the media in influencing attitudes and behaviour. Empirical research in the risk field has tended to focus more upon media content than upon reception, and few researchers have explored in-depth how people respond to media information about risk (Hornig 1993). While SARF theorists tend to assume that it is possible to arrive at some general predictions about processes of risk communication, other researchers are less optimistic given the complexities of the factors discussed above (Eldridge and Reilly 2003). Although SARF has highlighted important research questions, the approach taken has tended to be reactive and narrowly policy focused. Many studies adopting this framework assess public attitudes through questionnaire surveys (Frewer et al. 2002). In addition to such work, more qualitative studies are needed, involving methods such as in-depth interviews and focus groups, which provide a richer examination of the interaction between media messages and meanings than that elicited via standard questionnaire surveys (see Murdock et al. 2003).

Within the increasingly international, multi-digital, interactive and fragmented media environment, there is a growing need to examine how competing rationality claims are framed by different media, given that they are complexly differentiated and governed by different economic, political and organizational constraints (see Anderson 1997; Cottle 2000; Petts et al. 2003; Murdock et al. 2003). Thus far, relatively little research in this field has focused upon television, largely due to practical constraints, and most work has concentrated upon factual rather than fictional media (see Hargreaves and Ferguson 2000; Murdock et al. 2003). Future studies are likely to reflect changes in media consumption including the declining influence of the newspaper press and the growing use of the Internet and mobile phones, particularly among young people (Schneider and Foot 2004; Pauwels 2005; Schoenbach et al. 2005). Advances in technology should enable researchers to more easily study information flows between the newspaper press, digital television, and the Internet as they become more integrated.

There have been relatively few sophisticated comparative studies of media reporting of risk across countries. Large-scale international studies, such as Bauer and Gaskell (2002) provide a useful quantitative overview of the media coverage of particular risks, but rarely provide an in-depth insight into the factors explaining patterns and trends over time. In order to complement these types of studies what is needed are more in-depth, ethnographic, case studies that trace the production, content and reception of particular risk issues over time. A key task for research is to focus on visual images, since few studies have examined this aspect of risk reporting. Past research suggests that emotive images of risk, such as dying seals, can become powerful icons (Anderson 1997; Boyne 2003). Indeed, recent work by Petts et al. (2001) highlights the potent use of visual images in the popular press. It also demonstrates the importance of resonance and anchoring, at the level of everyday experience, if a risk issue is to strike a chord with publics. Moreover, there is an increasing reliance upon citizen journalism, often through mobile phone technology and portable digital camcorders (Bell 2005; Hudson, 2005). This, together with the rapid rise of the PR industry and the increasing sophistication of claims-makers targeting the media, raises a number of pressing issues for risk reporting. How such developments are changing journalistic practices, and its broader implications for democracy, needs to be the focus of future critical enquiry.

## Study questions

1  What bearing do media representations of risk have on people's everyday anxieties and behaviour?
2  How can an examination of news production processes illuminate news media framing of risk?
3  What are the most important factors explaining which risks attract most media attention?

## References

Allan, S. (2002) *Media, Risk and Science*. Buckingham: Open University Press.
Allan, S., Anderson, A. and Petersen, A. (2005) Reporting risk: science journalism and the prospect of human cloning, in S. Watson and A. Moran (eds) *Risk, Trust and Uncertainty*. London: Palgrave, 165–80.

Anderson, A. (1991) Source strategies and the communication of environmental affairs, *Media, Culture and Society*, 13(4): 459–76.

Anderson, A. (1993) The production of environmental news: a study of source–media relations, unpublished PhD thesis, University of Greenwich.

Anderson, A. (1997) *Media, Culture and the Environment*. London: UCL.

Anderson, A. (2002) In search of the holy grail: media discourse and the new human genetics, *New Genetics and Society*, 21(3): 327–37.

Anderson, A. (2003) Environmental activism and news sources, in S. Cottle (ed.) *News, Public Relations and Power*. London: Sage.

Anderson, A., Allan, S., Petersen, A. and Wilkinson, C. (2005b) The framing of nanotechnologies in the British newspaper press, *Science Communication*, 27(2): 200–20.

Anderson, A., Petersen, A. and David, M. (2005a) Communication or spin? Source–media relations in science journalism, in S. Allan (ed.) *Journalism: Critical Issues*. Buckingham: Open University Press.

Ang, I. (1985) *Watching Dallas: Soap Opera and the Melodramatic Imagination*. London: Methuen.

Ang, I. (1991) *Desperately Seeking the Audience*. London: Routledge.

Bauer, M.W. and Gaskell, G. (eds) (2002) *Biotechnology: The Making of a Global Controversy*. Cambridge: Cambridge University Press.

Beck, U. (1992) *Risk Society: Towards a New Modernity*. London: Sage.

Beck, U. (1995) *Ecological Politics in an Age of Risk*. Cambridge: Polity Press.

Bell, E. (2005) Opinion: London's citizen reporters prove their worth with their coverage of bombing, *The Guardian*, 11 July.

Bourdieu, P. (1998) *On Television and Journalism*. London: Pluto Press.

Boyne, R. (2003) *Risk*. Buckingham: Open University Press.

Burgess, A. (2004) *Cellular Phones, Public Fears and a Culture of Precaution*. New York: Cambridge University Press.

Cohen, S. (1972) *Folk Devils and Moral Panics: The Creation of Mods and Rockers*. London: MacGibbon and Kee.

Conrad, P. (1999) Uses of expertise: sources, quotes, and voice in the reporting of genetics in the news, *Public Understanding of Science*, 8: 285–302.

Cottle, S. (1998) Ulrich Beck, 'risk society' and the media: a catastrophic view?, *European Journal of Communication*, 13(1): 5–32.

Cottle, S. (2000) TV news, lay voices and the visualisation of environmental risks, in S. Allan, B. Adam and C. Carter (eds) *Environmental Risks and the Media*. London: Routledge, 29–44.

Cottle, S. (ed.) (2003) *News, Public Relations and Power*. London: Sage.

Curran, J. (2002) *Media and Power*. London: Routledge.

Davis, A. (2000) Public relations, news productions and changing patterns of source access in the British national media, *Media, Culture and Society*, 22(1): 39–59.

Douglas, M. and Wildavsky, A. (1982) *Risk and Culture: An Essay in the Selection of*

*Technological and Environmental Dangers*. Berkeley, CA: University of California Press.

Douglas, T. (2005) Shaping the media with mobiles, *BBC News*, 4 August. http://news.bbc.co.uk/1/hi/uk/4745767.stm.

Dunwoody, S. (1999) Scientists, journalists, and the meaning of uncertainty, in S. Friedman, S. Dunwoody and C. L. Rogers (eds) *Communicating Uncertainty: Media Coverage of New and Controversial Science*. New York: Lawrence Erlbaum.

Dunwoody, S. and Peters, H.P. (1992) Mass media coverage of technological and environmental risks: a survey of research in the United States and Germany, *Public Understanding of Science*, 1(2): 199–230.

Eldridge, J. and Reilly, J. (2003) Risk and relativity: BSE and the British media, in N. Pidgeon, R.E. Kasperson and P. Slovic (eds) *The Social Amplification of Risk*. Cambridge: Cambridge University Press.

Fiske, J. (1989) *Understanding Popular Culture*. Boston: Unwin Hyman.

Frewer, L., Miles, S. and Marsh, R. (2002) The media and genetically modified foods: evidence in support of social amplification of risk, *Risk Analysis*, 22(4): 701–11.

Friedman, S., Dunwoody, S. and Rogers, C.L. (eds) (1999) *Communicating Uncertainty: Media Coverage of New and Controversial Science*. New York: Lawrence Erlbaum.

Goodell, R. (1986) How to kill a controversy: the case of recombinant DNA, in S. Friedman, S. Dunwoody and C.L. Rogers (eds) *Scientists and Journalists: Reporting Science as News*. New York: Free Press.

Greenberg, M.R., Sachsman, D.B., Sandman, P.M. and Salome, K.L. (1989) Network evening news coverage of environmental risk, *Risk Analysis*, 9(1): 119–26.

Gurabardhi, Z., Gutteling, J.M. and Kuttschreuter, M. (2005) An empirical analysis of communication flow, strategy and stakeholders' participation in the risk communication literature 1988–2000, *Journal of Risk Research*, 8(6): 499–511.

Gutteling, J. (2005) Mazur's hypothesis on technology, controversy and media, *International Journal of Public Opinion Research*, 17(1): 23–41.

Hall, S., Critcher, C., Jefferson, T., Clarke, J. and Roberts, B. (1978) *Policing the Crisis: Mugging, the State and Law and Order*. London: Macmillan.

Hansen, A. (ed.) (1993) *The Mass Media and Environmental Issues*. Leicester: Leicester University Press.

Hansen, A. (1994) Journalistic practices and science reporting in the British press, *Public Understanding of Science*, 3: 111–34.

Hargreaves, I. and Ferguson, G. (2000) Who's misunderstanding whom? Bridging the gulf of understanding between the public, the media and science. Report prepared for the ESRC.

Hargreaves, I., Lewis, J. and Speers, T. (2003) Towards a better map: science, the public and media. Report prepared for the ESRC.

Hilgartner, S. and Bosk, C.L. (1988) The rise and fall of social problems: a public arenas model, *American Journal of Sociology*, 94(1): 53–78.

Hill, A. (2001) Media risks: the social amplification of risk and the media violence debate, *Journal of Risk Research*, 4(3): 209–25.

Hornig, S. (1993) Reading risk: public response to print media accounts of technological risk, *Public Understanding of Science*, 2: 95–109.

Hornig, S. (2005) Risk reporting: why can't they ever get it right?, in S. Allan (ed.) *Journalism: Critical Issues*. Buckingham: Open University Press, 199–209.

Hudson, R. (2005) How they triggered war on the web, *The Sunday Times*, 11 September.

Internet World Statistics (2005) *Internet Usage Statistics: The Big Picture*. http://www.internetworldstats.com/stats.htm.

Kasperson, R.E., Renn, O., Slovic, P., Brown, H.S., Emel, J., Goble, R., Kasperson, J.X. and Ratick, S.J. (1988) The social amplification of risk: a conceptual framework, *Risk Analysis*, 8(2): 178–87.

Kitzinger, J. (1999) Researching risk and the media, *Health, Risk and Society*, 1(1): 55–69.

Kitzinger, J., Henderson, L., Smart, A. and Eldridge, J. (2003) *Media Coverage of the Social and Ethical Implications of Human Genetic Research*. Final Report to the Wellcome Trust, February, Award no. GR058105MA.

Kitzinger, J. and Reilly, J. (1997) The rise and fall of risk reporting: media coverage of human genetics research, 'false memory syndrome' and 'mad cow disease', *European Journal of Communication*, 12: 319–50.

Lichtenberg, J. and MacClean, D. (1991) The role of the media in risk communication, in R. Kasperson and P. Stallen (eds) *Communicating Risks to the Public: International Perspectives*. London: Kluwer Academic.

Lupton, D. (2004) A grim health future: food risks in the Sydney press, *Health, Risk and Society*, 6(2): 187–200.

McCallum, D.B., David, B., Hammond, S.L. and Covello, V.T. (1991) Communicating about environmental risks: how the public uses and perceives information sources, *Health Education Quarterly*, 18(3): 349–61.

Manning, P. (2001) *News and News Sources: A Critical Introduction*. London: Sage.

Mazur, A. (1981) Media coverage and public opinion on scientific controversies, *Journal of Communication*, 31(2): 106–15.

Miller, D. (1999) Risk, science and policy: BSE, definitional struggles, information management and the media, *Social Science and Medicine*, 49(9): 1239–55.

Miller, D. and Dinan, B. (2000) The rise of the PR industry in Britain, 1979–98, *European Journal of Communication*, 15(1): 5–35.

Miller, D. and Reilly, J. (1994) *Food Scares in the Media*. Glasgow University Media Group. http://homepages.strath.ac.uk/~his04105/publications/Foodscares.html.

Miller, D. and Williams, K. (1993) Negotiating HIV/AIDS information: agendas, media strategies and the news, in J. Eldridge (ed.) *Getting the Message: News, Truth and Power*. London: Routledge.

Miller, M. and Riechert, B.P. (2000) Interest group strategies and journalistic norms: news media framing of environmental issues, in S. Allan, B. Adam, and C. Carter (eds) *Environmental Risks and the Media*. London: Routledge, 45–54.

Morley, D. (1980) *The Nationwide Audience*. London: BFI.

Murdock, G., Petts, J. and Horlick-Jones, T. (2003) After amplification: rethinking the role of the media in risk communication, in N. Pidgeon, R.E. Kasperson and P. Slovic (eds) *The Social Amplification of Risk*. Cambridge: Cambridge University Press, 156–78.

Mythen, G. (2004) *Ulrich Beck: A Critical Introduction to the Risk Society*. London: Pluto Press.

Nelkin, D. (1995) *Selling Science: How the Press Covers Science and Technology*. New York: W.H. Freeman.

Nisbet, M., Brossard, D. and Kroepsch, A. (2003) Framing science: the stem cell controversy in the age of press/politics, *Harvard International Journal of Press/ Politics*, 8(2): 36–70.

Nisbet, M.C. and Lewenstein, B.V. (2002) Biotechnology and the American media: the policy process and the elite press, 1970 to 1999, *Science Communication*, 23(4): 359–91.

Pauwels, L. (2005) Commentary – websites as visual and multimodal cultural expressions: opportunities and issues of online hybrid media research, *Media, Culture and Society*, 27(4): 604–13.

Petersen, A. (2001) Biofantasies: genetics and medicine in the print news media, *Social Science and Medicine*, 52: 1255–68.

Petts, J., Horlick-Jones, T. and Murdock, G. (2001) *Social Amplification of Risk: The Media and the Public, Contract Research Report*. London: Health and Safety Executive.

Petts, J. and Niemeyer, S. (2004) Health risk communication and amplification: learning from the MMR vaccination controversy, *Health, Risk and Society*, 6(1): 7–23.

Philo, G. (ed.) (1999) *Message Received*. Harlow: Longman.

Pidgeon, N., Kasperson, R.E. and Slovic, P. (eds) (2003) *The Social Amplification of Risk*. Cambridge: Cambridge University Press.

Reilly, J. and Kitzinger, J. (1997) The rise and fall of risk reporting: media coverage of human genetics research, false memory syndrome and mad cow disease, *European Journal of Communication*, 12(3): 319–50.

Renn, O. (1991) Risk communication and the social amplification of risk, in R.E. Kasperson and P. Stallen (eds) *Communicating Risks to the Public*. Dordrecht: Kluwer Academic Publishers.

Renn, O., Burns, W.J., Kasperson, J.X., Kasperson, R.E. and Slovic, P. (1992) The social amplification of risk: theoretical foundations and empirical applications, *Risk Analysis*, 48: 137–60.

Ryan, C. (1991) *Prime Time Activism: Media Strategies for Grassroots Organizing*. Boston, MA: South End Press.

Schanne, M. and Meier, W. (1992) Media coverage of risk, in J. Durant (ed.)

*Museums and the Public Understanding of Science*. London: Science Museum Publications.

Schlesinger, P. (1990) Rethinking the sociology of journalism, in M. Ferguson (ed.) *Public Communication*. London: Sage.

Schlesinger, P. and Tumber, H. (1994) *Reporting Crime: The Media Politics of Criminal Justice*. Oxford: Clarendon Press.

Schneider, S.M. and Foot, K.A. (2004) The web as an object of study, *New Media and Society*, 16 (1): 114–22.

Schoenbach, K., de Waal, E. and Lauf, E. (2005) Research note: online and print newspapers – their impact on the extent of the perceived public agenda, *European Journal of Communication*, 20(2): 245–58.

Singer, E. and Endreny, P. (1987) Reporting hazards: their benefits and their costs, *Journal of Communication*, 37(3): 10–26.

Slovic, P. (1987) Perception of risk, *Science*, 236: 280–5.

Stallings, R.A. (1990) Media discourse and the social construction of risk, *Social Problems*, 31: 23–31.

Thirlaway, K. and Heggs, D. (2005) Interpreting risk messages: women's responses to a health story, *Health, Risk and Society*, 7(2): 107–21.

Tulloch, J. and Lupton, D. (2001) Risk, the mass media and personal biography: revisiting Beck's 'knowledge, media and information society', *European Journal of Cultural Studies*, 4(1): 5–27.

Wahlberg, A. and Sjoberg, L. (2000) Risk perception and the media, *Journal of Risk Research*, 3(1): 31–50.

Wilkinson, I. (1999) News media discourse and the state of public opinion on risk, *Risk Management: An International Journal*, 1(4): 21–31.

Williams, C., Kitzinger, J. and Henderson, L. (2003) Envisaging the embryo in stem cell research: rhetorical strategies and media reporting of the ethical debate, *Sociology of Health and Illness*, 25(7): 793–814.

Wilsdon, J. and Willis, R. (2004) *See-through Science: Why Public Engagement Needs to Move Upstream*. London: Demos.

Wolfsfeld, G. (1997) *Media and Political Conflict: News from the Middle East*. Cambridge: Cambridge University Press.

## Further reading

Allan, S. (2002) *Media, Risk and Science*. Buckingham: Open University Press.

Allan, S., Adam, B. and Carter, C. (eds) (2000) *Environmental Risks and the Media*. London: Routledge.

Anderson, A. (1997) *Media, Culture and the Environment*. London: UCL.

Mythen, G. (2004) *Ulrich Beck: A Critical Introduction to the Risk Society*. London: Pluto Press.

Pidgeon, N., Kasperson, R.E. and Slovic, P. (eds) (2003) *The Social Amplification of Risk*. Cambridge: Cambridge University Press.

# 8    Environment and risk

## Phil Macnaghten

### Introduction

This chapter examines debates around risk and the environment including a case study addressing ways in which environmental issues resonate better with the ways in which people experience politics, nature and everyday life. Through empirical research on environmental concerns and everyday practices, this chapter sketches a framework through which the values associated with contemporary environmental risk debates might be developed in a more reflexive relationship to wider transformations in society. In particular, the chapter critically evaluates the standard storyline of a 'global nature' under threat and in need of collective action by a global imagined community. In contrast to rhetorics of the global environment, this chapter explores ways in which the environment is being embodied, valued and experienced in an array of social practices. The chapter further outlines the significance of such embodied practices as significant yet undervalued points of connection for wider, global environmental risk issues.

### The environment at risk

Beck famously defined the move in which modernity, having freed itself from the contours of classical industrial society, is emerging in a new form, dubbed the 'risk society' (1992b, 1995, 1999). In such societies, he argued, everyday life is increasingly governed by risks that have become incalculable, uncompensatable, unlimited, unaccountable and, most important of all, invisible to our senses. The paradigm case of such invisible risks is that of nuclear radiation, a risk which cannot be directly touched, tasted, heard, smelt or, especially, seen. As Beck (cited in Adam 1995: 11) notes of the situation post-Chernobyl:

> We look, we listen further, but the normality of our sensual perception deceives. In the face of this danger, our senses fail us. All of us ... were blinded even when we saw. We experienced a world,

unchanged for our senses, behind which a hidden contamination and danger occurred that was closed to our view.

And yet we know from a variety of forms of scientific and other information that nuclear radiation is an astonishingly powerful risk of contemporary society, a risk whose long shadow is cast over everyone, rich and poor, male and female, black and white. It is a risk that knows no borders, takes no prisoners, knows no senses. It is no coincidence that many of the exemplary cases of the risk society lie broadly in the environmental domain, including in recent years the almost unfathomable risks surrounding anthropogenic climate change. Environmental risks are increasingly seen as flowing across national boundaries, creating a sense of global environmental threat (Beck 1992b). Thus it seems that the emptying of time and space establishes something of a single world, in which through the extraordinary institutions of the global media, people have begun at least to imagine themselves as part of a single 'community'. Giddens (1991: 27), for instance, claims that 'humankind in some respects becomes a "we", facing problems and opportunities where there are no "others"'. As Beck (1992a: 109) argues, in a similar vein: 'with nuclear and chemical contamination, we experience the "end of the other", the end of all our carefully cultivated opportunities for distancing ourselves and retreating behind this category'.

To develop the argument it is necessary to outline some key aspects underpinning the framing of contemporary environmental risk debates. It has become a commonplace that there exists a single term – 'the environment' – which embraces a wide diversity of risk issues, from traffic congestion to global warming, from air pollution to genetically modified organisms, from acid rain to the loss of rare species, from toxic waste to the decay of inner cities. However, the contemporary configuration of 'the environment' in political and civic life is of relatively recent origin. The environment, as a set of diverse problems, had to be gathered up and presented as all symptomatic of a wider overarching environmental crisis (Szerszynski 1993). Through the 1970s and early 1980s a succession of issues emerged which became constituents of an 'environmental agenda'. In the UK, these included the proliferation of chemicals in the 1960s, resource and energy scarcity in the early 1970s, nuclear power and motorways in the late 1970s, agriculture and countryside issues in the early 1980s, and more recently acid rain, ozone depletion, biodiversity and climate change (Grove-White 1991; Hajer 1995). Indeed, a core activity for the environmental movement throughout this period was engagement in a 'struggle for proof', progressively raising the stakes of diagnosis both in spatial and temporal terms (Rose 1994: 287). By the early 1990s, it had been argued that the constituents of a more or less commonly agreed environmental agenda had become largely shared by states and business alongside environmental groups. Within the new discourse of sustainability, everyone appeared to be committed to acting in a manner that respected the finite limits of the planet, agreeing to improve the 'quality of life', but at the same time, 'living within the carrying capacity of living eco-systems' (IUCN 1991). A concern for the future was also endorsed, with an active commitment to 'meet the needs of the present without compromising the ability of future generations to meet their needs' (WCED 1987).

The cultural context in which 'the environment' emerged is of critical importance. Throughout the 1970s and 1980s environmental organizations saw themselves as struggling against denial, 'denouncing the industrial, consumerist, growth-oriented, technocratic and scientific system as damaging to the planet and to people, unacceptable and unsustainable' (Rose 1994: 287). Against the backdrop of the Cold War, the rhetoric of a single world facing shared environmental problems and hence 'a common future' also the title of the Brundtland Report (WCED 1987), helped propel the environment to centre stage within the international arena (see Finger 1993). The global conception of the environment thus fitted a geo-political need, creating a momentum that famously culminated in the Rio Earth Summit in 1992, the site at which working definitions of sustainability became endorsed by governments, non-governmental organizations (NGOs) and business. Of course the discourse of sustainability is riddled with ambiguity and conflict: between the twin goals of environment and development, between the often opposing demands of justice and equality, between the demands of the South and those of the North, and between the technocratic approach of managers to treat environmental issues as essentially engineering and administrative problems and those who argue for more profound shifts in human–environment relations (Redclift 1993; Jacobs 1997; Grove-White 1997; Munton 1997). Furthermore, the institutionally recognized discourse of sustainability can be seen as a marked shift in environmental discourse, replacing previous 'green' anti-growth ideologies with a more benign model of economic and social development (Jacobs 1999). But what remains a constant across discourses of sustainability and previous versions of environmentalism is a core belief that we share the same global environment, that it comprises a set stock of issues, and that these are all symptoms of the same malaise, namely human society's over-exploitation and abuse of the natural world. As Sachs (1999: 37) succinctly points out, 'the fragility of the biosphere under stress by human action, is the storyline of this approach'. The same storyline is further supported by conventional polling techniques, including those sponsored by government organizations and business. Tracking research, including MORI's annual Business and the Environment survey, SCPR's annual British Social Attitudes survey, NOP's periodic survey on the environment for the UK government, and the European Commission's Eurobarometer all proceed on the presumption that the environmental agenda can be delineated into more or less the same specifiable environmental 'risks', which act as the unambiguous object of individual perceptions, attitudes and values. Indeed, surveys often reinforce such distinctions by asking people the relative importance of 'the environment' (elsewhere configured as 'pollution and environmental damage') as opposed to other issues such as 'the economy', 'health' or 'education'. Such environmental issues are further presumed to exist 'out there', independently of social practices and beliefs, defined in universal terms that transcend the local cultural and historical contexts in which particular issues gain their meaning.

So far we have outlined the emergence of a particular configuration of 'the environment at risk'. Yet, how does such a discourse bear upon everyday social life and what does the history of research into environmental perceptions tell us about approaches to risk? As Wilkinson noted in Chapter 2, early risk research tended to imply that the public were behaving 'irrationally' if they did not behave in accordance with expert conclusions about particular risks and risk probabilities (Royal Society 1983, 1985). More recent research suggests that the framing of risk problems by experts, including the mass media, employs tacit assumptions about controlling institutions that many people may not share (Burgess and Harrison 1993). For example, public environmental information campaigns, by their nature, rely on the public identifying with and trusting such institutions (Macnaghten and Jacobs 1997; Blake 1999). However, this may conflict with people's experiences, either directly or through the media, of the past behaviour of the same institutions, their honesty, competence, independence, and so on, which 'rationally' influence people's receptions of the present claims of those organizations. The crucial question then concerns the texture of people's relationship with, and dependency on, those expert institutions that are supposed to be in control of the risks but to which most people have only mediated access. Hence, a neglected dimension of research on public perceptions concerns the very basis of trust: 'Who to believe?' and 'How to decide who to believe?' Such issues of trust are central to whether or not people believe media stories about environmental risks, and the extent to which they will be likely to identify with, or participate in officially defined environmental initiatives. In the following section we examine how social theory might be utilized to develop a comparative framework in which environmental risk perceptions can be related to broader shifts in contemporary society. A richer understanding of key social dynamics around globalization, individualization and risk may yield a more robust framework of analysis. Particular attention will be given to the continuing resilience of the 'global environmental risk' discourse highlighted above.

## A framework of risk and the environment

Heightened risk of environmental degradation is one of the features of globalization, and is amplified by greater levels of awareness and more rapid
networks of communication. Since the mid-1980s a wide variety of environmental issues, including ozone depletion, species destruction, global
warming, chemical pollution, nuclear radiation, BSE and GM foods have
become widely recognized as risks which transcend national borders. Such
risks are seen as complex, long-term and often incalculable (Beck 1992b;
Adam 1998; Macnaghten and Urry 1998). As a result, we are increasingly
dependent on national and, increasingly, global systems of experts – including environmental NGOs, companies, governments and the media – for
information, knowledge, images and icons that enable us to make sense of
such processes (Wilson 1992; Anderson 1997). The crucial question then
concerns people's relationship with, and dependency on, these experts. We
need to understand better the changing relationships of trust between individuals and expert institutions, and how these affect the ways people understand and respond to environmental risks. A second dynamic of social
change, often seen as intimately tied up with globalization, is the rise of
individualism at the expense of tradition and custom in everyday life (Giddens 1994, 1998). How environmental concerns relate to these trends has
received little attention. Arguably, in an ever-more individualized society,
environmental concerns are likely to be felt most acutely when they impinge
upon the body, typically in relation to questions of food and health (Jacobs
1999). Such dynamics coincide with powerful cultural discourses around
health and well-being. Yet they can also operate in tension with parallel
pressures for 'choice', convenience and disposability. As globalization makes
an almost infinite variety of foods, therapies, medicines, lifestyles, diets, and
so on available, we are forced to make active choices about what we eat and
how we live. The spectre of a new and apparently expanding array of both
'visible' and 'invisible' environmental risks, out there, impinging more directly on the body, gives rise to additional forms of insecurity and anxiety
(Beck 1992b; Dunant and Porter 1996; Adam 1998; Franklin 1998). This raises
the possibility that life in the 'risk society' may itself be transforming how
people are experiencing nature and the environment. In a more individualized society, the experience of environmental risk may be becoming
less about 'saving the planet' and the plight of remote others, such as the
rainforest, the whale or the tiger. Rather, the environment becomes most
acutely significant in terms of how it confronts the individual: when it meets
'me' head on, 'in here'.

More conventional forms of engagement with the environment as 'nature' are widely seen to be in decline, particularly in a local setting. For

example, recent research by Demos and the Green Alliance draws attention to the dramatic decline in outdoor play and nature-based school trips by children over the past decade (Thomas and Thompson 2004). For adults, too, the environment is increasingly commoditized: it is something we 'purchase' as part of a luxury holiday or a rural mini-break, rather than being stitched into the rhythms of our lives. Increasingly, we are divorced from nature in our everyday routines: we drive to work, and exercise in the gym, rather than walking to work or running in the nearby park. The paradox is that even as our connections to the local environment as nature are weakening, the presence and force of 'the environment' as a factor in personal consumption and health choices loom ever larger. More personal, internalized representations of 'what nature is' are becoming far more significant. The environment is perceived less as a global good and more as an individualized realm of purity and moral power, located in the context of our bodily practices (Macnaghten 2003). In this sense, people are meeting 'the environment' on a more intimate level, not as part of universal and generalized abstractions, but as connected to their daily practices, leisure pursuits and identities.

To summarize the argument so far, it is argued that wider societal trends – especially those arising from processes of globalization and individualization – are impacting on people's identities as political subjects. People's experience of globalization is simultaneously making people feel more interconnected with the world *and* more vulnerable to global forces increasingly perceived as beyond their control. Individualization is simultaneously increasing personal choice and autonomy *while at same time* contributing to new levels of insecurity and anxiety. Such transformations raise provocative questions on the changing structure of environmental concerns, values and political beliefs, indicating a series of attitudinal shifts:

- from a concern with societal issues 'out there' (e.g. global warming, ozone depletion, rainforest destruction) towards privatized issues 'in here' (e.g. risks such as GM foods and synthetic chemicals that are pervasive, global, and which threaten the health of the body);
- from a concern with the environment as needing to be 'saved' towards an embracing of an environment that 'saves us' from the pressures and insecurities of modern living;
- from a political engagement through formal civic structures and networks towards a political engagement based on personal identity expressed in lifestyle bodily practices.

## Perceiving risk and the environment

In this section I shall examine the utility of the conceptual framework elaborated thus far, using empirical examples taken from UK public perception research conducted at Lancaster University over the past decade (see also Macnaghten 2003). I shall argue for its usefulness in three ways. First, such a framework provides theoretical weight to contemporary research findings indicating that public engagement with environmental problems may be shifting from distant threats 'out there' to more proximate threats 'in here' (Jacobs 1999). Issues such as whales, the Amazon and acid rain, that were prevalent in the 1970s and 1980s, now appear to be migrating towards issues which impinge more directly and more immediately on 'me', my body, my family and my future – such as allergies, traffic, BSE and genetically modified foods. In our research study, people were asked to respond to a variety of images of environmental risks variously depicted in 'global, physical' and 'human, relational' forms. Our findings were striking. Global icons of 'the natural environment' had initial emotive appeal but tended to remain distant and abstract. People recognized such iconic images and their implied relationship to global threats – such as global warming, ozone depletion, deforestation, loss of biodiversity, resource depletion, and so on – but tended to perceive such threats as a problem 'out there', detached from everyday life, making it easy for them to turn off. Alternatively, images depicting a range of environmental threats and risks in terms of their 'human' and 'personal' connections afforded a different tenor of response. While people's responses tended to be less immediate and visceral than the 'non-human' global iconography set out above, the images tended to be seen as more credible, more thought-provoking and, at times, more connected to their 'lived-in world'. These images appeared to contribute to a more enduring sense of a shared 'global imaginary' but one where people's moral sensitivity tended to be at its highest when they are able to establish empathetic connections with others that suffer on a person-to-person basis. Images of 'the environment' were experienced most intensely when they were connected to the 'personal' realm of everyday life. Direct connections to the local and personal environment tended to 'hit home' and matter more. Indeed, it is often through personal, rather than abstract and mediated encounters, that people saw themselves as most likely to become involved in environmental matters. Related research suggests that such evident disconnection is even more pronounced in disadvantaged groups (Burningham and Thrush 2001).

Second, such theoretical resources highlight 'trust' and 'agency' as key organizing concepts in understanding contemporary environmental concerns. Indeed, even though a body of public perception research points to the reality of global environmental issues as having become almost a commonplace in everyday life, it indicates too that a perceived lack of 'felt' agency militates against collective action (Christie and Jarvis 2001; Gordon 2002). In one recent Europe-wide survey, for example, 73 per cent of people said they were more aware of problems than of solutions (Eurobarometer 2002). In the same UK research project highlighted above, across a variety of group settings, people expressed little sense that much could be achieved – either at the level of the individual or through existing avenues for collective action – to mitigate global environmental threats (Macnaghten 2003). Individual action tended to be seen as largely ineffective, due to the global scale of the problems and the perception of powerful commercial interests intractably embedded in systems of self-interest antithetical to global sustainability. Indeed, this whole domain of thinking about the environment tended to be clouded in gloom and despondency, a finding that parallels previous public perceptions research on the environment (see Macnaghten et al. 1995; Macnaghten and Jacobs 1997).

However, what appeared distinctive in more contemporary discussions were the strategies adopted. In different ways people were now *choosing not* to dwell on global environmental threats, as a pragmatic response to apparently intractable problems, and in order to maintain a positive outlook on life (Macnaghten 2003). Reflexive strategies of non-engagement with 'the big picture' – a term which embraced global environmental risks alongside other global issues such as poverty, AIDS, debt, 'the future', and so on – were commonly adopted reflecting how such issues tended to be grouped together as 'negative issues' where personal engagement is felt as likely to be both inconsequential and personally damaging. Such a perceived lack of agency is exacerbated by a collective lack of faith in the effectiveness of those institutions regarded as theoretically responsible for such issues, and hence the apparent intractability of such issues in the face of what Giddens (1990) aptly calls the 'juggernaut of modernity'. Furthermore, the acknowledged complexity of solving environmental problems in an apparently unsympathetic institutional climate appeared to be connected to the scepticism many people expressed towards those who advocate simple solutions, including certain environmental NGOs. For our participants, the portrayal of environmental problems in simple black and white terms lacked credibility and contradicted their own acknowledged ambivalent responses. Indeed, many felt both implicated in global environmental problems and constrained by competing and more immediate demands. For many people there were no easy answers; there was no longer a clear 'good guy' and 'bad guy', nobody to blame and no one beyond blame. Bound by everyday pressures of work and parenting, people accepted their own partial guilt as consumers, as motorists, as employees of business, as travellers, as outdoor enthusiasts, and so on.

Third, the conceptual context above points to a shift in emphasis from a concern with the environment as needing to be 'saved' towards an embracing of an environment that 'saves us' from the pressures and insecurities of modern living. Indeed, a body of literature points to the dangers of assuming that there exists 'one big environment' that is the same for everyone (Cooper 1992; Macnaghten and Urry 1998). In the empirical research highlighted above, we found there were *many different 'environments'*, each connected to people's particular concerns, priorities, social relationships and responsibilities. Three different kinds of encounter were expressed in the group discussions. For many people 'the environment' was perceived as a source of pleasure and transcendence from the burdens and stresses of everyday life. Activities of walking in the countryside, outdoor swimming, mountain biking, rock climbing, gardening, beekeeping and fishing were discussed as ways of 'being in the environment', in proximity to nature, removed from modernity (see also Edensor 2001; Lewis 2001). In these situations, the expressive purity and moral power of nature arise from a practice in which one can experience a nature that is fundamentally 'other' to that familiar in industrial modernity. Such an experience can be seen as emblematic of what Thrift (2001) terms 'immersive' practices, often encountered in contemplative and mystical developments, which constitute a 'background' within which nature is encountered as a means of gathering stillness, both inside and outside the body. In contrast to practices premised on a non-intrusive encounter with nature were those dependent on a more active mode of participation in nature, such as angling, beekeeping and gardening. Again such practices tended to be warranted as contributing to a lifeworld in which people could transcend the pressures of contemporary life through a more intimate and interactive relationship with nature. For other people, the environment was encountered more indirectly, as a set of problems, such as pollution, food safety and personal health, whose putative effects had to be tackled as part of people's evolving responsibilities as mothers and parents. This was especially the case in the group of local community involvers, where the experience of the environment was mediated through their identity as mothers and as carers. The environment was very much an issue in relation to its known or unknown effects on oneself or one's family. Health and food issues were particularly prominent and many of the women were familiar with and concerned over an apparently unending succession of food-health scares in recent years: from Salmonella in eggs to BSE to pesticide residues to GM foods.

To summarize, three different ways in which people encounter the values and benefits of nature and the environment in everyday life have been highlighted: nature as a source of pleasure and transcendence from the burdens and stresses of everyday life; nature as a setting for maintaining important social ties and bonds; and nature as a set of problems whose effects had to be tackled as part of people's evolving responsibilities as mothers and parents.

## Conclusion: beyond the risk society

I conclude by pointing to directions for future research for new ways of thinking through the relationship between risk and the environment and indicating how such refreshed thinking may help advance more socially resilient public policies. Above, I have suggested that global environmental risk discourses may appear distant, abstract, and even disempowering. In the case study set out above, we found that the encounter of a threatened 'global nature' in need of concerted action from an 'imagined global community' – one which embraces government, business and NGO actors alongside the wider public – had the effect of dislocating and detaching people from institutional rhetorics and initiatives on global environmental change. Such findings may seem to endorse the thesis that environmental risk issues are beyond the grasp of individuals, that the differentiation of society leaves little scope for meaningful collective action, that contemporary strategies of individualization are stressing the personal solution to what are structural problems, and that this is leading to withdrawal, apathy and resignation (Bauman 1995, 1999; Beck and Beck-Gernshein 2002). But is this necessarily the case? An alternative interpretation paints a more complex and potentially more uplifting picture. It points to the potential for mobilizing additional public support through deploying a different iconography of 'the global environment' set out in terms of its human dimensions; through focusing on the kinds of experience in the course of which people come into bodily contact with the environment; and through recognition of the texture of people's relationship with those mediating expert institutions reportedly responsible for the management and reporting of environmental risks. A key task for research is to scrutinize and further elaborate these competing interpretations. In our studies, we found that for many people concern about environmental risks begins with personal experience. The environment is commonly experienced not simply as a set of physical issues but tangled up as part of social life. People come to the issues through particular things that matter to them. The 'human' and 'relational' aspects of the environment are often what are resonant. The environment becomes meaningful when it engages with social life, inhibiting or facilitating the development of ongoing human relationships, whether in the context of the family, friends or communities of interest.

Research is required to interpret to what extent these responses can be read as part of an ongoing trend towards the 'personalization' of environmental concerns. And, as Anderson (1997) has pondered, if this is the case, how do we understand the role of the media in such personalized encounters with the environment, given that the personal dimension to environmental risk is often itself more or less completely indebted to mediation? Boltanski

(1999) has usefully analysed the dynamics of a media situation in which concerns for the 'distant other' connect to everyday proximate concerns. People may want to be a small part of the imagined community concerned about the plight of the Amazonian rainforest, international whaling, the burning of fossil fuels, and so on, but such concern may appear fleeting and short-lived if it remains dislocated from everyday life concerns. This implies that those outside traditional communities of supporters are likely to become involved in 'the environment' only when their lifeworld is touched. Hence, rather than talking about 'one environment', might it be more appropriate to talk according to the versions of the environment that are meaningful for different groups of people (see also Cooper 1992; Burningham and O'Brien 1994)? In many ways this reverses the traditional storyline of a 'global nature' under threat and in need of protection from a global imagined community. By contrast, do institutional strategies need to start from people's concern for themselves, their families and localities as points of connection for the wider, 'global' environmental risks and issues? For example, universals such as de-forestation, biodiversity, global warming, pollution, and so on, are more likely to resonate when they are expressed through lived particulars in their (non-universal) local terms. An angler is likely to become politically involved in pollution issues when this is connected to the state of the Atlantic salmon; beekeepers are likely to be stirred by the threats posed by genetically modified agriculture when expressed in terms of the likely effects of cross-pollination; mothers are likely to become actively involved in local environmental in-itiatives when a direct link is made between such activities and the future health of the locality.

Further research is also necessary to enhance understanding of the re-lationship between societal trends of globalization and individualization and public responses to global environmental risk issues in the context of their identities as political subjects. For example, in the research outlined above, there was tentative evidence to indicate that the texture of the relationship between individuals and expert institutions may be shifting, with implica-tions for how people sense, understand, live with and respond to environ-mental risks. The results here are suggestive and exploratory but point towards a heightened form of reflexivity. On the one hand, people clearly remain detached from 'expert' rhetorics on the environment and remain sceptical of the motives of both government and business in this regard. Moreover, people feel similarly ambivalent to those proposing simple solu-tions, including some environmental NGOs, an orientation compounded by the fact that people themselves feel implicated in contributing towards global environmental problems. Such reflexivity has extended further into daily life as people self-consciously are choosing not to reflect on global environmental risk issues. Yet, at the same time, people do not appear to have fully rejected the possibility of shared and collective action. Partly, people are seeking credible solutions, 'in bite-sized chunks', where the material effects of individual action become visible and enduring. And partly, people are seeking relationships with institutions that enable them to feel part of a genuine partnership, individually and collectively 'doing the right thing'. The lack of such a sense of partnership may further explain the move away from 'public' and collective forms of action towards 'private' environmental behaviour such as recycling (Christie and Jarvis 2001). There is also the need to address further how environmental concerns and values become embodied in everyday practices, and the wider implications of the embodiment thesis for developing publicly attuned environmental policies, campaigns and initiatives (Bhatti and Church 2001; Macnaghten and Urry 2001). In the research outlined above, there were many indications of the appeal of a nature that was embraced as a source of intense pleasure and transcendence from the burdens and stresses of everyday life. Through a wide variety of embodied practices and leisure activities, nature clearly had the role of 'saving us' from the pressures and insecurities of modernity (Szerszynski 1996). However, again, this does not imply that the ability to develop widespread participative strategies aimed at global environmental betterment has receded. Rather, it implies the clear need to engage with people *in their own terms*, as responsible and capable individuals, resonating with different lifeworlds through lived particulars. Finally, more conceptual research is needed to link the literature on environmental risk perceptions to the sociology of the body: research which focuses on embodied practice to ascertain how identity is articulated with the natural world, the ways in which this leads to reflexive praxis by social actors, and how this could cultivate an empowered politics of the environment.

## Study questions

1  How are wider societal trends – especially those arising from processes of globalization and individualization – impacting on public responses to environmental risk?
2  What are the strengths and weaknesses of a politics of the environment premised on global environmental risk discourses?
3  What, if any, is the relevance of the sociology of the body to the literature on risk perceptions?

## References

Adam, B. (1995) Radiated identities: in pursuit of the temporal complexity of conceptual cultural practices, Theory, Culture & Society Conference. Berlin, August.

Adam, B. (1998) *Timescapes of Modernity: The Environment and Invisible Hazards*. London: Routledge.

Anderson, A. (1997) *Media, Culture and the Environment*. London: UCL Press.

Bauman, Z. (1995) *Life in Fragments: Essays in Postmodern Morality*. Oxford: Blackwell.

Bauman, Z. (1999) *In Search of Politics*. Oxford: Blackwell.

Beck, U. (1992a) From industrial society to risk society: questions of survival, structure and ecological enlightenment, *Theory, Culture & Society*, 9: 97–123.

Beck, U. (1992b) *Risk Society: Towards a New Modernity*. London: Sage.

Beck, U. (1995) *Ecological Politics in an Age of Risk*. Cambridge: Polity Press.

Beck, U. (1999) *World Risk Society*. London: Sage.

Beck, U. and Beck-Gernshein, E. (2002) *Individualization: Institutionalized Individualism and its Social and Political Consequences*. London: Sage.

Bhatti, M. and Church, A. (2001) Cultivating natures: homes and gardens in late modernity, *Sociology*, 25(2): 365–83.

Blake, J. (1999) Overcoming the 'value–action gap' in environmental policy: tensions between national policy and local experience, *Local Environment*, 4(3): 257–78.

Boltanski, L. (1999) *Distant Suffering: Morality, Media and Politics*. Cambridge: Cambridge University Press.

Burgess, J. and Harrison, C. (1993) The circulation of claims in the cultural politics of environmental change, in A. Hansen (ed.) *The Mass Media and Environmental Issues*. Leicester: Leicester University Press.

Burningham, K. and O'Brien, M. (1994) Global environmental values and local contexts of action, *Sociology*, 28: 913–32.

Burningham, K. and Thrush, D. (2001) *Rainforests Are a Long Way from Here: The Environmental Concerns of Disadvantaged Groups*. York: Joseph Rowntree Foundation.

Christie, I. and Jarvis, L. (2001) How green are our values? in A. Park, J. Curtice, K. Thomson, L. Jarvis and C. Bromley (eds) *British Social Attitudes: The 18th report*. London: Sage.

Cooper, D. (1992) The idea of environment, in D. Cooper and R. Walford (eds) *Horizons in Human Geography*. London: Routledge.

Dunant, S. and Porter, R. (1996) *The Age of Anxiety*. London: Virago.

Edensor, T. (2001) Walking in the British countryside: reflexivity, embodied practices and ways to escape, in P. Macnaghten and J. Urry (eds) *Bodies of Nature*. London: Sage.

Eurobarometer (2002) *The Attitude of Europeans towards the Environment*. Brussels: European Commission.

Finger, M. (1993) Politics of the UNCED process, in W. Sachs (ed.) *Global Ecology: A New Arena of Global Conflict*. London: Zed.

Franklin, J. (ed.) (1998) *The Politics of the Risk Society*. Cambridge: Polity Press.

Giddens, A. (1990) *The Consequences of Modernity*. Cambridge: Polity Press.

Giddens, A. (1991) *Modernity and Self-identity: Self and Society in the Late Modern Age.* Cambridge: Polity Press.

Giddens, A. (1994) *Beyond Left and Right.* Cambridge: Polity Press.

Giddens, A. (1998) *The Third Way.* Cambridge: Polity Press.

Gordon, W. (2002) *Brand Green: Mainstream or Forever Niche?* London: Green Alliance.

Grove-White, R. (1991) The emerging shape of environmental conflict in the 1990s, *Royal Society of Arts*, 139: 437–47.

Grove-White, R. (1997) The environmental 'valuation' controversy: observations on its recent history and significance, in J. Foster (ed.) *Valuing Nature: Economics, Ethics and the Environment.* London: Routledge.

Hajer, M. (1995) *The Politics of Environmental Discourse: Ecological Modernization and the Policy Process.* Oxford: Clarendon.

IUCN (International Union for Conservation of Nature) (1991) *Caring for the Earth.* Gland, Switzerland: IUCN, UNEP and WWF.

Jacobs, M. (ed.) (1997) *The Greening of the Millennium.* Oxford: Blackwell.

Jacobs, M. (1999) *Environmental Modernisation: The New Labour Agenda.* London: The Fabian Society.

Lewis, N. (2001) The climbing body, nature and the experience of modernity, in P. Macnaghten and J. Urry (eds) *Bodies of Nature.* London: Sage.

Macnaghten, P. (2003) Embodying the environment in everyday life practices, *Sociological Review*, 51(1): 63–84.

Macnaghten, P. and Jacobs, M. (1997) Public identification with sustainable development: investigating public barriers to participation, *Global Environmental Change*, 7(1): 5–24.

Macnaghten, P. and Urry, J. (1998) *Contested Natures.* London: Sage.

Macnaghten, P. and Urry, J. (eds) (2001) *Bodies of Nature.* London: Sage.

Macnaghten, P., Grove-White, R., Jacobs, M. and Wynne, B. (1995) *Public Perceptions and Sustainability: Indicators, Institutions, Participation.* Preston: Lancashire County Council.

Munton, R. (1997) Engaging sustainable development: some observations on progress in the UK, *Progress in Human Geography*, 21: 147–63.

Redclift, M. (1993) Sustainable development: concepts, contradictions, and conflicts, in P. Allen (ed.) *Food for the Future: Conditions and Contradictions of Sustainability.* London: John Wiley.

Rose, C. (1994) Beyond the struggle for proof: factors changing the environmental movement, *Environmental Values*, 4: 286–98.

Royal Society of London (1983) *Risk.* London: Royal Society.

Royal Society of London (1985) *Public Understanding of Science Report.* London: Royal Society.

Sachs, W. (1999) Sustainable development and the crisis of nature: on the political anatomy of an oxymoron, in M. Hajer and F. Fischer (eds) *Living with Nature.* Oxford: Oxford University Press.

Szerszynski, B. (1993) Uncommon ground: moral discourse, foundationalism and the environmental movement, PhD thesis, Dept of Sociology, Lancaster University.

Szerszynski, B. (1996) On knowing what to do, in S. Lash, B. Szerszynski and B. Wynne (eds) *Risk, Environment and Modernity: Towards a New Ecology*. London: Sage.

Thomas, G. and Thompson, G. (2004) *A Child's Place: Why Environment Matters to Children*. London: Demos/Green Alliance.

Thrift, N. (2001) Still life in nearly present time: the object of nature, in P. Macnaghten and J. Urry (eds) *Bodies of Nature*. London: Sage.

WCED (World Commission for Environment and Development) (1987) *Our Common Future*. Oxford: Oxford University Press.

Wilson, A. (1992) *The Culture of Nature: North American Landscape from Disney to the Exxon Valdez*. Oxford: Blackwell.

## Further reading

Franklin, A. (2002) *Nature and Social Theory*. London: Sage.

Irwin, A. (2003) *Sociology and the Environment: A Critical Introduction to Society, Nature, and Knowledge*. Cambridge: Polity Press.

Jacobs, M. (1999) *Environmental Modernisation: The New Labour Agenda*. London: The Fabian Society.

Macnaghten, P. (2003) Embodying the environment in everyday life practices, *Sociological Review*, 51(1): 63–84.

Macnaghten, P. and Urry, J. (1998) *Contested Natures*. London: Sage.

# PART III
## PUTTING RISK IN ITS PLACE

# 9 Politics and risk

## Jane Franklin

## Introduction

Over the past ten years or so, political debate has increasingly focused on risk. From the food we eat, to global warming and terrorist attacks on New York and London, risks cannot be predicted or accurately assessed. Risks unsettle the stability of life and make choices difficult. They generate a level of uncertainty that poses a challenge for politicians, who are often unable to guarantee safety and security. As individuals, we also have to decide what to do in the face of increased risk and insecurity. Do we carry on taking the tube or subway, for example, or is it more rational either to stay at home, or cycle to work? An increased awareness of risk calls for political decisions for governments, and for each of us making choices about how to live our lives.

In a sense, politics has always been about managing risk. As McMylor points out in Chapter 11, from early times political thinkers have imagined different ways of controlling the potential chaos of uncontrolled human existence. They have searched for the ideal political system that enables the 'good' and curtails the 'bad' aspects of human life. Over the past two hundred years, politics has been framed by a range of debates, largely between liberal thinkers who have argued for individual rights and freedoms, and socialists for the quest for social and economic equality. These political ideologies, at different times, have spoken to those who wanted to change the world they lived in. They provided both the critique of existing regimes and the means through which people could act individually and collectively to create change. Most notably, they were concerned with the recognition of in-dividual rights and identities and with the fair distribution of material re-sources. Political reform was associated with the idea of progress and of technological invention, which was in part to harness natural resources to overcome scarcity so that human needs could be met. Social reforms at the turn of the nineteenth century, culminating in the welfare state, were to provide security from the cradle to the grave, to guard against material or external contingencies that affect people's lives and their capacity to par-ticipate in society. It is these assumptions of modernity, of principle and practice, that come into question as risk increasingly becomes a defining feature of political life.

This chapter explores the dynamic between politics and risk. Its focus is on politics with a capital 'P', on how risk, in a variety of forms, influences the emphasis of political ideas and practice. Taking the risk society thesis as a centrepiece, I begin with a sketch of those aspects of risk that impact on politics: ecological, institutional, social and individual. I then outline the different approaches of Beck and Giddens to understanding politics in risk societies. Giddens's work in particular has been influential in shaping New Labour's Third Way politics in Britain. The Third Way has also been influenced by communitarianism and the idea of social capital. This 'politics of community' is then examined as an example of how risk/security dynamic shapes politics in practice (Fraser and Lacey 1993; Everingham 2003). Following an outline and critical assessment of this work, the chapter concludes by drawing out some of the themes and issues that may shape the agenda of politics in and beyond risk societies.

The risk society thesis, in the work of Beck and Giddens, has been influential in shaping the way we think about risk and politics (Giddens 1991; Beck 1992; Franklin 1998). Key to their analysis is the idea of social change, processes of modernization and the transition from early to late modernity, from industrial to risk societies. They argue that as a consequence of change, traditional or accepted patterns of life become less predictable (Heelas et al. 1996), making life seem more uncertain and insecure. At the core of the risk society thesis is the idea that the risks and uncertainties we face today are new and particular to late modern societies. It is important, however, to unpack the different aspects of risk that may affect politics.

Risk can mean hazard or danger, and in this way calls for some kind of prediction and insurance against risk. As Kemshall noted earlier, the welfare state has been described as an insurance state, protecting people from the risks of poverty and ill health. Risk can also refer to the existential notion of contingency, relating to the inherent insecurity of the human condition, to identity and 'ontological insecurity'. The risks most prominently discussed today are ecological or environmental risks, in relation to food and health, global warming and climate change. These, Giddens (1990) argues, have been 'manufactured' in processes of agricultural and industrial production methods over the past two centuries. For Beck, manufactured risks cannot be predicted or insured against since they arise from decisions taken in the past and we have no way of knowing what may happen next. Since they defy prediction, they pose a problem for politicians in relation to public safety. Decisions about how to deal with risks based on established strategies seem inadequate, revealing the fallibility of expertise. In this way, new risks expose the inadequacy of power and traditional forms of authority to contain them (Giddens 1990; Beck 1992). Another layer of risk emerges though the process of political and institutional change. Political reforms, especially since the early 1980s, have reshaped the ideals and institutional practices of the welfare state. Since the end of the Second World War, the welfare state had instilled a level of social security by containing and alleviating risks of unemployment, lack of education, material want, ill health and inadequate housing. While those on the left argued that this went some way to alleviating the risks associated with inequalities, reformers on the political right pointed to how the welfare state undermined individual responsibility and action. They argued that it made people docile and less able to care for themselves. As institutions of the welfare state have disengaged from the containment of social and economic risks and insecurities, individuals have had to take this on for themselves by conforming to the model of the 'prudential citizen'. Those who have resources have been able to make the most of political and market freedoms to make choices about their health, education and family lives. For others the relationship between risk and inequality has becomes starker. It is harder to take this responsibility when lack of access to information technology, adequate housing, good transport and economic resources act as a barrier to participation. The impact of this kind of risk has been seen in the aftermath of Hurricane Katrina in New Orleans and surrounding areas in 2005 (Younge and Campbell 2005). Those who did not have the resources to move out of the area were worst hit. As Beck (1992) suggests, the distribution of 'bads' in risk society leans towards the poor. The hurricane exposed a stratum of deprivation, previously invisible and much more subject to risk.

Risk as social and economic insecurity relates to 'social' risk. The dismantling of the institutions of the welfare state, which contained and alleviated social and economic risks places responsibility on those who do not have the resources to cope. The resultant rising crime, 'bad' neighbourhoods and family breakdown result in what is seen as a breakdown in social order. Media reports of 'no-go areas' in major cities, riots, binge drinking and gun crime can contribute to a belief, or a fear, that society is getting out of control. While some argue that this is a consequence of the rolling back of the welfare state, others point to a lack of individual responsibility causing bad behaviour and to a crisis of morals and values in society. Social risk is perhaps more politically defined than other forms of risk and can lead to an authoritarian political response. It can: encourage moral panic and stimulate social policies that crack down on bad behaviour; seek to shore up families and communities as the bedrock of social stability; instil traditional moral values, seen to be lacking. In risk societies, individuals can become a risk to others and, it is argued, welfare states become 'safety states', more focused on social control than on social justice (Delanty 1999: 151). An awareness of social risk strengthens the arguments for a politics of community discussed later.

So far we have looked at environmental, institutional and social aspects of risk. A fourth, interconnected layer, relates to the ways we experience risk as individuals. This is risk as contingency or 'ontological insecurity' (Giddens 1991, 1992), which refers to our sense of self and identity and thus to political agency. In the past, people were born into a fairly fixed set of identities and social relationships were defined by structures of class and gender. The women's movement and reforms of the welfare state have undercut these traditional identities and life patterns (Giddens 1991; Beck 1992). People no longer feel compelled to conform to the traditional family model, or to the working lives that earlier generations took for granted. However, the time lag between 'old' patterns dissolving and 'new' patterns becoming established can also disrupt the social equilibrium. Without traditional roles and values, individuals have to make important decisions about work and relationships for themselves, without solid traditional patterns to follow. In effect, they are forced to make choices about who to be and how to live, to 'write their own biographies'. With this process of 'individualization' (Beck and Beck-Gernsheim 2001) the structures and institutions that represent a degree of continuity in life begin to dissolve such that individuals may experience a sense of release or freedom, alongside feelings of insecurity and uncertainty. So, for Beck and Giddens, risk is implicated in the unravelling of the political, social and personal framework of the modern social order. To explore this in more detail, we outline their different interpretations of how these risks transform political ideas and practices in risk societies. While both thinkers argue that manufactured risks make traditional politics seem out of date and inappropriate, they present quite different arguments as to the impact of risk on conventional politics and the new forms of political engagement that risk generates.

## Beck and the politics of the risk society

Beck's idea of risk society is of a society characterized by its confrontation with contingency and uncertainty, a new social order that emerges as the structural safeguards of modernity begin to dismantle (Beck 1992). This does not mean that the structures of modern society brought complete safety and certainty, but that they gave enough of a sense of security to allow for the economic and political systems of capitalism and liberal democracy to work. The politics of industrial societies was characterized by conflicts of interest between capital and labour, the desire for wealth and the risk of hunger. The risks that accumulated during this period were contained by the political and institutional framework of modernity. As capitalist economies grow and become successful, the environmental damage and the depletion of natural resources on which capitalist production depends become increasingly evident. It is precisely this increased awareness of risk that redraws the political map and generates new forms of political action in the second phase of modernity.

In his book *The Reinvention of Politics* (1997), Beck contrasts two models of politics that emerge in response to risk. The first is 'reflexive'. For Beck (1998: 9), reflexivity refers to the 'shock' of living in a risk society, the stark confrontation with contingency. A reflexive model of politics would be open to the changing patterns of life and is up to the democratic challenge of living with risk. Beck argues that in risk society, industrial institutions and language of politics no longer fit, but we continue to use them as though they were still alive and relevant. They have become 'zombie categories' (Beck 2000b). Reflexive politics is critically aware of the passing of known institutions and traditional structures of thought and action. We need, Beck (1997) suggests, to reflexively reinvent politics for the conditions of second modernity, to think differently in relation to risk. In contrast, Beck outlines a 'counter-modern' approach that also recognizes that the structure of the social world is changing, but is pessimistic about declining values and social disorder. This kind of politics looks to recreate and re-embed the certainties of the past in order to deflect risk and insecurity. It draws on the nostalgic communitarian approach that is mournful of the loss of community, traditional values and ways of living. Neither of these two models fits the politics of industrial society, this new politics does not reflect a left/right opposition, but one of freedom – in a new sense – and security. For Beck (1994) in the risk society, freedom is not the individual freedom of liberalism or individualism, but is reflexive, existential and forced upon us. Further, these models not only refer to debates within the nation-state, but also like risk, transcend national boundaries. While governments continue to manage risk and build strategies for security, Beck (1997) argues that the agenda of politics is increasingly generated by decisions and actions in the public sphere. This 'sub-politics' shifts the focus from central government to civil society. He draws attention to the activities and decisions taken by scientists, corporations and consumers that increasingly shape government policy and people's lives. Scientific and technological innovation raise ethical issues for governments and individuals, as with the example of stem cell research or human cloning. The campaigns of Greenpeace and other ecological groups harness the power of consumer choice towards boycotting certain goods, buying organic food that is grown without pesticides; or cars that run on hydrogen rather than petrol. These 'seemingly un-political actions and decisions' have political effects (Holzer and Sorensen 2003: 82). For Beck, the site of sub-politics is not the factory or the street, as it was in industrial society, but is symbolic, working through the media, information and communication networks. Thus, the political subject of risk society is not the working class but risk itself. People pick up ways of confronting risk, finding answers to the questions that 'slip through the political agendas of nation states' (Beck 1999: 15).

Risk also mobilizes social movements and campaign groups in relation to global issues of injustice and inequality (Beck 1992; Cohen and Rai 2000).

While the experience of risk is shared across the world, the solutions to risk can create global divisions and conflicts. For example, 'industrial societies seek to protect the rainforest in developing countries, while at the same time appropriating the lion's share of the world's energy resources' (Beck 2002: 42). The poorest in the world find themselves in the most hazardous of places. People's lives are no longer shaped predominantly by economic factors, since it is 'not what one has or is able to do that determines one's social position and future, but rather where and from what one lives' (Beck 1999: 62).

Beck (1999) takes a global view of politics with his understanding of 'world risk society'. In this context, he argues for a multilateral response to risk, against what he describes as the unilateral politics of 'the new American empire' or 'new world order' (Beck 2002). Reflecting his counter-modern/reflexive model, he contrasts the 'surveillance' and 'cosmopolitan' state. The concern of the surveillance state is to build security at the expense, Beck argues, of freedom and democracy (2002: 49). A kind of 'democratic authoritarianism' ensues with this model encompassing flexibility in relation to world markets, and a controlling approach to public policy (Beck 2002: 50). Against this, Beck argues for a 'cosmopolitan agenda' that understands and focuses on transnational risk conflicts. The cosmopolitan state will emphasize solidarity with others in the struggle against the causes of terror, and will renew democratic means of building transnational solutions based on human rights and global justice (Beck 2000a; 2002: 50). What is significant for Beck is that politics now rides on a balance between freedom and security. How much freedom can we give up in the interests of stability and safety? Crucial in this is our understanding of freedom in late modern societies. It is not the liberal version of freedom that has underpinned modern political projects for human rights, democracy and market economics. Rather, it is an existential version where freedom is the human condition. For Beck, and indeed for Giddens (1994), individuals in late modern societies are forced into a reflexive, existential confrontation with contingency. It is from this position, rather than from a search for security, he argues, that a more reflexive and democratic politics might flow.

## Giddens and the revival of social democracy

Anthony Giddens is more optimistic than Beck about how politics adapts to the changing circumstances of risk. Giddens's model is rooted in his commitment to left-of-centre politics, and in arguments for a revival of social democracy in the light of social and political change. He argues that risk offers opportunities and challenges for politics: opportunities in that the individualization of life choices and globalization open the way for new forms of democracy in intimate and public spaces; challenges, in finding ways to embed a new social order capable of containing the uncertainties unleashed in times of change. Like Beck, Giddens (1998) argues that risk redefines traditional political goals and principles. He makes a distinction between the 'old' and 'new' style of social democracy. Old-style social democracies worked towards a more socially just and equal society by alleviating the worst effects of capitalist production. With an economic focus, the aim of post-war social democracies was to redistribute wealth and social resources in the interests of social justice. This emancipatory politics is 'concerned above all with liberating individuals and groups from constraints which adversely affect their life chances' (Giddens 1991: 210). Now that social and economic conditions that produced emancipatory politics have been uprooted by globalization, risk and individualization, it is time to re-think the political goals of the left. Concerned 'to carry on the reform of emancipatory politics' (2000: 31), Giddens wants to continue in the social democratic tradition, while changing and redefining it to chime with social and economic change. If the goal of the old social democracy was emancipation from material poverty through economic intervention, the goal of new social democracies is to build a fair, inclusive and economically vibrant society fit for the challenges of the new century. Crucially, this depends on Giddens's understanding of a new kind of political agency in late modern societies. As individuals experience freedoms from the structural constraints of a class-structured society, there is also less need for a politics of 'life chances'. As an extension of emancipatory politics, 'life politics' depends and builds on a certain level of individual freedom from traditional ways of life and patterns of domination. As we begin to lose trust in the expertise of those in traditional positions of authority, such as doctors, politicians and scientists, we recognize that they do not know everything and that they can make mistakes. As Heelas reasons:

> A working definition [of] detraditionalisation involves a shift in authority: from 'without' to 'within'. It entails the decline of a belief in pre-given or natural order of things. Individual subjects are themselves called up to exercise authority in the face of disorder and contingency which is generated. 'Voice' is displaced from established sources, coming to rest with the self.
>
> (Heelas et al. 1996: 2)

Life politics is a politics of choice and decisions, in relation to 'how we should respond to a world in which tradition and custom are losing their hold over our lives' (Giddens 2000: 40). On one level, this entails a 'coming to terms' with the risks and insecurities that change brings. It is about the choices we make in order to reconcile the split between our internal expectations of what life may bring and the uncertain world we live in. On another level the decisions and choices we make about our lives also have an external effect. For example, in challenging traditional ideas about gender, women have destabilized and changed expectations of their role in families and in the workplace. The term 'life politics' captures this process of adapting to a changing world and of making life choices that propel that change. The goal of life politics is not to achieve freedom and choice, Giddens (1991) says, but is to do with what kinds of choices are being made. Giddens (1998) models his new social democracy as the 'Third Way', a politics that moves beyond the oppositions of the old social democracy. It involves a distinctly different interpretation of the relationship between the state and civil society from that of either traditional left or right. The idea at the core of the old social democratic model was that people invested their collective responsibility in the state. With a strong egalitarian ethos, through its policies and practices, the state takes on the role of providing social and economic security for its citizens. In contrast, the neo-liberal model, espoused by the Thatcher government in Britain in the 1980s, accepts inequality as inevitable. It believes that individuals should take back responsibility from the state for their well-being and that the free market will provide those services that individuals require. Giddens argues that these two models, and debates between them, are part of an old political pattern where egalitarianism belongs to the left and the market belongs to the right. In the third way, these ideological conflicts and differences become less significant, and models of mutuality and partnership more important. For example, Giddens (2000: 33) urges us to think beyond the 'old' incompatibilities between state and market provision: 'markets do not always increase inequality, but can sometimes be the means of overcoming it'. This opens up the possibility for the state and market to work together in a new mixed economy involving 'a synergy between public and private sectors' (Giddens 1998: 100). Further, Giddens (1998: 79) advocates a 'social investment state', a new partnership between the state and civil society that has neither the direct involvement of the old social democratic state nor the minimal state of the neo-liberal model, but a relationship of mutual responsibility. With the old model of social democracy, the focus of critique was the economy. It was the economy that needed to be adapted in the interests of a more fair and just society or social order. With Giddens's new model, critical focus turns on society. In times of change, social disruption is detrimental to market economies that thrive on social stability and a flexible workforce. Arguably, this new model of politics is focused on the social world, and more particularly on the responsibilities of families and communities. Giddens's new social democracy has been influential on New Labour's Third Way politics. He supports their arguments for social inclusion as a means to equal opportunity (Giddens 1998: 104) and calls for a renewal of civil society, and for governments to foster the capacity for communities to reinvigorate forms of solidarity and mutual support (Giddens 1999: 81). However, the New

Labour government in Britain has also been influenced by communitarian and social capital approaches to support its strategy for building strong families and communities and a stable social order. We now turn to this 'politics of community'. We can see how this reflects both Beck and Giddens's arguments for how politics deals with social risk and insecurity.

## The politics of community

Like the politics of risk society, the politics of community is broadly concerned with social change, though the emphasis tends to be on its detrimental effects. The argument runs that liberalism has gone too far and that rights-based politics have created an individualistic society. To counter this tendency and to build a more cohesive and settled society, the architects of New Labour in Britain drew on communitarian ideas in development of the Third Way. Communitarianism offers an alternative to a liberal political agenda concerned with individual rights, liberties and opportunities, stressing the ways people co-operate and reciprocate, and have responsibility for each other, rather than how they exist as isolated, rights-bearing individuals (Etzioni 1993). In Blair's (1999) words: 'in place of an atomised, individualised, selfish society, people yearn for a society that heals itself, a politics that reduces division, intolerance, and inequality ... individuals realise their potential best through a strong community based on rights and responsibilities'.

In more recent years, the idea of 'social capital' has also been influential in shaping political debate in Britain and the United States (Putnam 2000; Halpern 2004). In his book *Bowling Alone: The Revival of American Community* (2000), Putnam refers to social capital as the connections among individuals, and the social networks and the norms of reciprocity and trustworthiness that arise from them. He offers an account of what he sees as the decline in social capital in America since the Second World War, and argues that this is due to society becoming more individualized – interested in the 'quest for the ideal self'. Putnam suggests that the 'free agency' of the 1960s generation has had a high social cost, not least the breakdown of traditional family life and the isolation of individuals in society. The vitality of communities is reduced, he argues, when there is less volunteering, less trust, less shared reciprocity. To revive civic communities, he encourages participation in local associations, such as bowling clubs, PTAs, church choirs, which open up channels for the flow of philanthropy and altruism, which in turn, he argues, foster norms of individual and general reciprocity.

Putnam argues that the 'low stock' of social capital held by communities or nations contributes to economic decline, so that governments need to intervene to build social capital through policies such as family-friendly workplaces and supporting local participation in politics and decision-making. This approach to understanding how societies work is situated within a wider conservative perspective on social change and a sense that the norms and values that once held society together have been gradually eroded over the past 50 years or so and need to revitalized. He draws on a critique, both of the welfare state – that is said to have taken too much responsibility for people's lives – and of the New Right emphasis on individual rights over social solidarity. This is further compounded by the social effects of second-wave feminism and identity politics, which loosened the bonds and securities that keep families and communities together (Putnam 2000).

In the UK, New Labour has been drawn to the concept of social capital (Gamarnikow and Green 1999; Baron et al. 2000; Baron 2004, Halpern 2004). The combined influence of communitarian and social capital approaches have contributed towards the redefinition of social democracy, with a stronger emphasis than Giddens has on community. New Labour's Third Way incorporates a neo-liberal approach to economic policy and a communitarian emphasis on social policy, towards a stable social order that underpins a globalizing economy. This generates a coincidence of needs and a partnership between economy and society, rather than tension. Reflecting Giddens's approach, this co-operative synthesis expresses New Labour's desire to move beyond the oppositional politics of left and right, where social and economic interests were often in conflict, towards a consensus politics where partnership overcomes strife. Thus, the emphasis of political debate shifts from earlier political concerns with equality and redistribution, towards safety and security. We can see how the politics of community supports this shift, taking the example of policies to tackle social exclusion. The idea of social exclusion draws on a communitarian logic that understands poverty and deprivation in terms of localized exclusion which arises from the dynamics of particular communities. The Social Exclusion Unit targeted local and specific aspects of social exclusion: street sleeping, teenage pregnancies and youth crime. They worked towards 'joined up solutions' to alleviate inequalities in particular localities drawing attention away from the 'Old Labour' belief in redistribution. The old-style politics focused on the economy. New-style politics focuses on community, to building social capital and encouraging social entrepreneurialism, community action and individual responsibility. Critics of the politics of community argue that – with an eye towards social order and cohesion – there is a tendency to focus on the behaviour of the less privileged in society in their ability to access the resources and opportunities, provided by government, that would initiate their social mobility and economic success (Levitas 1998; Portes, 1998; Baron 2004). As issues of poverty and inequality are increasingly framed in relation to social capital rather than social justice (Everingham 2003), individuals become responsible for their own inequalities. In a twist of the risk society thesis, social capital shifts from understanding inequalities in relation to class or social structure, towards individual agency. Everingham (2003) shows how the distinction made by Giddens of the old and new social democracy is reflected in policy-making. In the 'old consensus' the conflict between the needs of society and the needs of the economy was managed through the concept of social justice and social democracy. In the new consensus, she argues, social justice is replaced with social capital. Social capital reconfigures the dynamic between society and economy, conflating interests previously seen as oppositional. Social relationships, rather than the social effects of capitalism, become a key factor in explaining levels of inequality, economic prosperity and political participation (Gamarnikow and Green 1999). By thus informing policies that focus on social behaviour, social justice as social capital reduces the cost to government providing 'non-economic solutions to social problems' (Portes 1998; Everingham 2003). Thus, the political focus on community is arguably a response to social and individual risk and instability, focusing on families, streets and neighbourhoods and away from wider social and economic contexts. For Beck, this response to risk and contingency has the goal of reasserting the power of traditional institutions to provide security, drawing on 'the invocation of "we-feelings", the disassociation from foreigners, the tendency to pamper family and feelings of solidarity, turned into a modern theory: communitarianism (Beck 1997: 96). While, in practice, the Third Way is a complex amalgam of political ideas and practices, to an extent it seems to reflect aspects of Beck's critique and Giddens's new social democratic consensus.

## Social change, risk and political theory: an assessment

Both risk society and community approaches to political change are based on the premise that traditional structures of power and inequality are being transformed and are no longer useful in understanding the contemporary world. Beck and Giddens share the view that globalization and individualization undermine the traditions and certainties of modern politics and society. Giddens's focus is on the capacity of individuals and institutions to change and adapt to risk, and on the development of a politics that reaches beyond the left/right opposition of old-style social democracies towards a new social democratic consensus. Beck is concerned with the unintended side effects of modernization which generate new points of conflict and new forms of reflexive and counter-modern politics in risk societies (Lash 1994). For Beck, the desire for certainty seeps into politics and political rhetoric, closing off alternative possibilities and legitimizing authoritarian policies designed to shore up a system in decline. He sees the potential for a new global democratic, cosmopolitan politics, but also is alert to the tendency towards the authoritarian containment of risk and insecurity.

In a sense, risk and security are two sides of the same coin. Indeed, Rose (1999) argues that both the politics of risk and the politics of community constitute the current political discourse of risk that operates to order and govern individual lives. He draws attention to how the 'problematic of risk' has become a central organizing principle of politics. The risk society thesis paints a picture that we can recognize. We can identify with their ideas: we do seem to face new and increasingly unpredictable risks in our day-to-day lives; the world does seems more uncertain, the possibility of terror ever closer. As Lupton illustrated earlier in the book, the language of risk resonates with and constructs the ways that people experience and talk about their lives. Rose (1999: 472) argues that with the discourse of community, the social world is redefined, turning attention away from society. It describes a space of inter-action based on neighbourhoods and networks within which people's lives can be contained and structured. In communities, we now understand our-selves to be not members of social classes but of networks and relationships of trust. In this way, citizens can be 'governed through community' (Rose 1999). Rose (1999: 472) quotes the communitarian writer Etzioni, who says that community is 'a space of emotional relationships through which individual identities are constructed through their bonds to micro-cultures of meaning and value'. Individual subjects are redefined by reference to life politics, an individualized responsibility for health, wealth and welfare. What Rose (2001) refers to as 'the politics of life itself' replaces the politics of emancipation and social justice. In tune with the authors of the remaining chapters in this book, for Rose, discourses of risk work in the strategic, economic interests of gov-ernment. The language of community, of obligation, morals and responsi-bilities, he suggests, provides an ethical framework for governing individual behaviour in the construction of an ethical and ordered citizenry. The ques-tion raised by Rose (1999) is significant: to what extent are discourses of risk and community constructed or 'invented' in the strategic economic interests of governments? Is the external, and internal, world that we live in really more unpredictable and dangerous, or have we just assumed a 'way of thinking' that makes it seem that way? Politicians may find it useful to generate a sense of fear, for example, to legitimize social or environmental policy initiatives, or decisions to go to war. What kinds of risks are identified and how they are defined may carry political significance. Beck (2000c: 211) argues that viewing risks as either real or constructed may not be helpful in understanding new social and political forms as they emerge. Indeed, categories of 'reality' and 'construction', he suggests, belong to modern and postmodern ways of thinking that are out of step in the emerging context of second or reflexive modernity. Where poststructural and post-modern accounts deconstruct the taken-for-granted aspects of the social order, theories of reflexive modernization reconstitute, re-conceptualize, to find the 'new rules of the social game' as they emerge

(Beck et al. 2003: 3). Beck points out that he wants to recognize both the substantive material realities of living in a late modern world *and* the cultural interpretations that surround them. So he 'oscillates between realism and immanentism' (Lash 2003: 55) to move beyond them and the old oppositional dilemma they perpetuate.

Another major criticism of the risk society thesis is that it puts too much emphasis on the split between old- and new-style politics, and the distinction between industrial and risk society. By paying too much attention to the difference, we are less able to see overlaps and discontinuities between the two (Heelas et al. 1996). Although Giddens argues that emancipatory politics is still significant, the tendency is towards moving beyond left and right (Giddens 1994). Beck also argues that risk changes the 'coordinates of politics' from left/right to freedom/security. Similarly, the Third Way is constructed on the premise that the 'old' politics of left and right is no longer valid. Those who argue that 'old' inequalities based on economics and class persist are seen to be 'out of date' compared with this analysis (Rustin 1994; Hall 1998). Suspicious of those who argue that we have moved beyond left and right politics, Mouffe (2002) argues that the inclusive politics of the Third Way makes it increasingly difficult to paint alternative political pictures of the problems facing our societies. She argues for the importance of dissent, passion and disagreement in politics, for an adversarial rather than consensual polity which brings dynamism and creativity to political life. Rather than conflicts of interest or lively debate, current political discourse places morality and behaviour at its centre. Similar to Rose, she argues that '[M]orality is rapidly becoming the only legitimate vocabulary: we are now urged to think not in terms of right and left, but of right and wrong' (Mouffe 2002: 1).

The question of how we should live and relate to each other is also central to Bauman's (1999) 'search for politics'. In modernity, he believes that the political project was to make life predictable and certain, to remove contingency and insecurity from people's lives. The welfare state provided this predictability and its institutional and moral framework shaped and contained the social world. In 'liquid modernity', this contingency, disorder and discontinuity, always under the surface, is again acutely felt by everyone as institutions no longer provide secure boundaries to our choices and actions (Bauman 2000). Without traditional or given values to fall back on, 'the tyranny of moral choice returns'. This is why, Bauman argues, the new age of contingency is also the age of community (Morris 1996). We yearn for and lust after community, searching for and inventing it. As Bauman states:

> Community is a warm place, a cosy and comfortable place ... in a
> community, we all understand each other well, we may trust what
> we hear, we are safe most of the time ... We are never strangers to
> each other ... in short, 'community' stands for the kind of world

which is not, regrettably available to us – but which we would dearly like to inhabit and which we hope to repossess.

(2001a: 1–3)

Rather than the politics of community, Bauman calls for a politics that depends on collective action, on an ethical version of living with others. Taking the view that the moral and existential condition which defines human nature is 'responsibility for the other', he stresses that being responsible for, or 'being for' is the beginning of a new kind of politics (Delanty 1999: 115). The politics of community, paradoxically, individualizes and separates people from each other:

> If they fall ill, it is because they are not resolute or industrious enough in following the health regime. If they stay unemployed it is because they failed to learn the skills of winning an interview or because they did not try hard enough to find a job or because they are purely and simply work-shy.
>
> (Bauman 2001b: 47)

In contrast, Bauman (1992: 190) offers the idea of 'sociality', which is not a fixed notion of how individuals interact with each other, but suggests a fluid, ethical process, 'the dialectical play of randomness and pattern ... which treats instead all found structures as emergent accomplishments'. Bauman searches for a politics that accords with new and emerging forms of solidarity and difference in a world where we are increasingly becoming strangers to each other. Arguments that suggest structural inequalities such as class, race and gender are beginning to dissolve, as Adkins (2002) and Lash (1994: 130) argue, fail to recognize new forms of inequality as they emerge in late modern societies:

> In the shift from the manufacturing to informational production a new class is created which is structurally downwardly mobile from the working class. In terms of relations to the information and communication structures ... this underclass includes the 'ghetto poor', but also includes much of the information society's 'excluded third'.

Just as old social structures are dissolving, inequalities such as gender and sexuality are being reconfigured through new forms of social domination such as community, networks, new ways of knowing and forms of communication, advocated by a contemporary conservative agenda (Adkins 1998: 47). The risk society thesis in the work of Beck and Giddens, and the politics of community, stresses the fading of tradition and social structure and the emergence of risk and insecurity as a backdrop to individual choice as a marker of identity. Research that points to the 'reconfigurations' of class and gender recognizes links between new kinds of economic insecurity and shifting forms of traditional structural inequalities (Adkins 2004, 2005).

In practice, the politics of risk tends towards a communitarian response to insecurity and uncertainty. A response that supports policies which focus in on the social world and sideline the wider context of power and economics. Two main themes emerge from this brief assessment, both of which turn attention away from hierarchical notions of power. First, that discourses of risk and community play a significant role in framing political ideas and practices in late modern societies (Rose 1999, 2001). In this view, power operates or flows through discursive strategies and techniques (Foucault 1988). Second, that the politics of risk and community are built on an assumption that structural inequalities are either dissolving or becoming less significant. In the politics of community, it is assumed that individuals can access opportunities through network connections, and their potential for social mobility and moving out of disadvantaged positions is high. This embeds a horizontal understanding of the relationship between structure and agency that airbrushes vertical inequalities out of the picture, without any argument or rationale as to why they are being ignored. While Beck recognizes the inequalities risk generates and Giddens holds onto a commitment to equality and social justice, in the politics of community neither hierarchical nor discursive forms of power are directly addressed (Molyneux 2002).

Despite discursive connections between risk and community politics, however, the links between them are not straightforward. Beck eschews communitarian solutions to risk, arguing that they are comfort-seeking and backward-looking, stimulating an entirely different kind of political practice. For Beck, risk edges in between traditional politics of left and right, and generates a kind of intermediary opposition between liberal freedoms and communitarian securities. As we have seen, neither of these positions represents his reflexive approach. Further, to talk of risk as a construction fails to recognize what he sees as an ambivalent interplay between the real and discursive practices. In the 'real' world of global politics, of risk and fear, new lines of conflict are drawn 'uniting the world against the other, the terrorist' (Beck 2002: 47). This has the effect, Beck argues, of increasing the power of the state in its Hobbesian role as the provider of security and, ironically challenging the neo-liberal economic agenda for global capital. In times of threat, risk and insecurity, Beck (2002) points out that the market has no answers and the state increases its power, finding a new legitimacy for taxation, for the importance of civil society, and a new project, to work towards transnational co-operation between states for shared security. It is hard to untangle, and impossible for individuals to assess, the degree to which terror is played up or played down in the strategic interests of the state.

## Conclusion: beyond the risk society

This chapter has set out and explored the dynamic between risk and politics in late modern societies. Providing a platform for the remaining chapters in the volume, it has outlined the key themes of the risk society thesis in the different interpretations of Beck and Giddens. The politics of community has subsequently been evaluated as a way of addressing how politics adapts to uncertainty and risk in practice. What we can say is that a new political paradigm has emerged in the UK in the past decade, constructed in a dialogue between a critique of individualism, Giddens's new social democracy, and communitarian/social capital approaches. This new politics seeks to manage and respond to social and environmental risks and has had an impact on the change from a left/right to a liberal/communitarian political agenda in Britain. What is perhaps significant about the literature explored here is that it crosses between traditional disciplinary boundaries. The risk society thesis, in the work of Beck, Giddens and Bauman, draws on social theory to develop an understanding of politics in late modern societies. The politics of community rests on conversations between politics, economics and sociology (Edwards et al. 2003). Much of the critical engagement with communitarian and social capital theory has come from feminists working in political philosophy (Fraser and Lacey 1993), political science (Lowdnes 2004) and economics (Tonkiss 2000), in development studies (Molyneux 2002), and sociology (Kovalainen 2004; Adkins 2005). Feminist engagement with the concept has been largely generated in research and policy contexts. There are those who broadly accept social capital as providing a useful insight into understanding women's lives, in its regard for informal political creativity and affective relationships. They work with the idea while recognizing and correcting its universal quality and gender bias (Lowdnes 2004). Feminists have also been critical of the theoretical and political assumptions that infuse the social capital concept, ranging from its neo-functionalist sociology and political conservatism, to its adherence to a troublesome communitarian perspective (Molyneux 2002; Arneil 2003; Everingham 2003). More recent work has looked at how the 'social sphere' is constructed in late modern societies across political, economic and sociological accounts (Adkins 2005; Franklin and Thomson 2005; Misztal 2005).

Overall, the politics of community is largely seen by critics as a reaction to the current landscape of risk and uncertainty, offering answers that are simple, nostalgic and conservative (Franklin and Thomson 2005). This approach fails to recognize persisting inequalities of class, gender and ethnicity, and does not point to fresh inequalities as they emerge in relation to new economic forms of risk. At the same time the issue of freedom in relation to security is increasingly one of global concern. Human rights, civil liberties and social justice of the old kind are defended by liberal politics now that old-style socialism is discredited. In this sense, liberalism is responding defensively to a conservative agenda at national and global levels. To paint a picture of what kind of politics may emerge beyond risk societies, we might look to new lines of political conflict that have been alluded to in the chapter, to sub-political activity, to social movements that coalesce around issues of globalization and poverty. We might also look to the informal decisions made in scientific and corporate fields, perhaps also to an ethical responsibility for strangers and new forms of 'sociality', to changing configurations of inequality and finally, to rethinking the dynamic between freedom and security in the context of the continuing presence of political, economic and strategic power.

## Study questions

1 What kinds of risks do the politics of community address?
2 Is risk a 'real' or a politically constructed phenomenon?
3 To what extent do you think the balance between freedom and security has replaced the politics of left and right?

## References

Adkins, L. (1998) Feminist theory and economic change in S. Jackson and J. Jones (eds) *Contemporary Feminist Theories*. Edinburgh: Edinburgh University Press.

Adkins, L. (2002) *Revisions: Gender and Sexuality in Late Modernity*. Buckingham: Open University Press.

Adkins, L. (2004) Gender and the post-structural social, in B. Marshall and A. Witz (eds) *Engendering the Social: Feminist Encounters with Sociological Theory*, Maidenhead: Open University Press.

Adkins, L. (2005) Social capital: the anatomy of a troubled concept, *Feminist Theory*, 6(2): 195–211.

Arneil, B. (2003) Just communities: social capital, gender and culture, paper presented at the Gender and Social Capital conference, University of Manitoba, 2–3 May.

Baron, S. (2004) Social capital in British politics and policy making, in J. Franklin (ed.) *Politics, Trust and Networks: Social Capital in Critical Perspective*, Working Paper No. 7. London: Families & Social Capital ESRC Research Group.

Baron, S., Field, J. and Schuller, T. (eds) (2000) *Social Capital: Critical Perspectives*. Oxford: Oxford University Press.

Bauman, Z. (1992) *Intimations of Postmodernity*. London: Routledge.

Bauman, Z. (1999) *In Search of Politics*. Cambridge: Polity Press.

Bauman, Z. (2000) *Liquid Modernity*. Cambridge: Polity Press.

Bauman, Z. (2001a) *Community: Seeking Safety in an Insecure World*. Cambridge: Polity Press.

Bauman, Z. (2001b) *The Individualized Society*. Cambridge: Polity Press.

Beck, U. (1992) *Risk Society: Towards a New Modernity*. London: Sage.

Beck, U. (1997) *The Reinvention of Politics*. Cambridge: Polity Press.

Beck, U. (1998) Politics of Risk Society in J. Franklin (ed.) *The Politics of Risk Society*. Cambridge: Polity Press.

Beck, U. (1999) *World Risk Society*. Cambridge: Polity Press.

Beck, U. (2000a) The cosmopolitan perspective: sociology of the second age of modernity, *British Journal of Sociology*, 51(1): 79–105.

Beck, U. (2000b) Zombie categories, in J. Rutherford (ed.) *The Art of Life*. London: Lawrence and Wishart.

Beck, U. (2000c) Risk society revisited: theory, politics and research programmes, in B. Adam et al. (eds) *The Risk Society and Beyond: Critical Issues for Social Theory*. London: Sage.

Beck, U. (2002) The terrorist threat: world risk society revisited, *Theory, Culture & Society*, 19(4): 39–55.

Beck, U. and Beck-Gernsheim, E. (2001) *Individualization: Institutionalized Individualism and its Social and Political Consequences*. London: Sage.

Beck, U., Giddens, A. and Lash, S. (1994) *Reflexive Modernization: Politics, Tradition and Aesthetics in the Modern Social Order*. Cambridge: Polity Press.

Beck, U., Bonss, W. and Lau, C. (2003) The theory of reflective modernization: problematic, hypothesis and research programme, *Theory, Culture and Society*. 20(2): 1–33.

Blair, T. (1999) 'Third Sector, Third Way', paper presented at NCVO Conference at Chiswell Brewery Conference Centre, London.

Cohen, R. and Rai, S.M. (2000) *Global Social Movements*. London: The Athlone Press.

Delanty, G. (1999) *Social Theory in a Changing World: Conceptions of Modernity*. Cambridge: Polity Press.

Edwards, R., Franklin, J. and Holland, J. (2003) *Families and Social Capital: Exploring the Issues*, Working Paper No. 1. Families & Social Capital ESRC Research Group, London South Bank University.

Etzioni, A. (1993) *The Spirit of Community*. New York: Crown.

Everingham, C. (2003) *Social Justice and the Politics of Community*. Aldershot: Ashgate.

Fine, B. (2001) *Social Capital Versus Social Theory: Political Economy and Social Science at the Turn of the Millennium*. London: Routledge.

Foucault, M. (1988) *Politics, Philosophy, Culture: Interviews and Other Writings 1977–1984*, edited by L.D. Kritzman. London: Routledge.

Franklin, J. (ed.) (1998) *The Politics of Risk Society*. Cambridge: Polity Press.

Franklin, J. and Thomson, R. (2005) (Re)claiming the social: a conversation between feminist, late modern and social capital theories, *Feminist Theory*, 6(2): 161–72.

Fraser, E. and Lacey, N. (1993) *The Politics of Community: A Feminist Critique of the Liberal Communitarian Debate*. Hemel Hempstead: Harvester Wheatsheaf.

Gamarnikow, E. and Green, A. (1999) The third way and social capital: education action zones and a new agenda for education, parents and community? *International Studies in Sociology of Education*, 8(1): 3–22.

Giddens, A. (1990) *The Consequences of Modernity*. Stanford. CA: Stanford University Press.

Giddens, A. (1991) *Modernity and Self-Identity: Self and Society in the Late Modern Age*. Cambridge: Polity Press.

Giddens, A. (1992) *The Transformation of Intimacy: Sexuality, Love and Eroticism in Modern Societies*. Cambridge: Polity Press.

Giddens, A. (1994) *Beyond Left and Right*. Cambridge: Polity Press.

Giddens, A. (1998) *The Third Way: The Renewal of Social Democracy*. Cambridge: Polity Press.

Giddens, A. (2000) *The Third Way and Its Critics*. Cambridge: Polity Press.

Hall, S. (1998) The Great Moving Nowhere Show, *Marxism Today*, Special Issue November/December.

Halpern, D. (2004) *Social Capital*. Cambridge: Polity Press.

Heelas, P., Lash, S. and Morris P. (1996) *Detraditionalization: Critical Reflections on Authority and Identity*. Oxford: Blackwell.

Holzer, B. and Sorensen, M.P. (2003) Rethinking subpolitics: beyond the 'iron cage' of modern politics? *Theory, Culture & Society*, 20(2): 79–102.

Kovalainen, A. (2004) Rethinking the revival of social capital and trust in social theory: possibilities for feminist analysis, in B. Marshall and A. Witz (eds) *Engendering the Social: Feminist Encounters with Sociological Theory*. Maidenhead: Open University Press.

Lash, S. (1994) Reflexivity and its doubles: structure, aesthetics, community, in U. Beck et al. (eds) *Reflexive Modernization*. Cambridge: Polity Press.

Lash, S. (2003) Reflexivity as non-linearity, *Theory, Culture & Society*, 20(2): 49–57.

Levitas, R. (1998) *The Inclusive Society? Social Exclusion and New Labour*. Basingstoke: Macmillan.

Lowndes, V. (2004) Getting on or getting by? Women, social capital and political participation, *The British Journal of Political and International Relations*, 6(1): 47–56.

Misztal, B.A. (2005) The new importance in the relationship between formality and informality, *Feminist Theory*, 6(2): 195–211.

Molyneux, M. (2002) Gender and the silences of social capital: lessons from Latin America, *Development and Change*, 33(2): 167–88.

Morris, P. (1996) Community beyond tradition, in P. Heelas et al. (eds) *Detraditionalization: Critical Reflections on Authority and Identity*. Oxford: Blackwell.

Mouffe, C. (2002) *Politics and Passion: The Stakes of Democracy*, CSD Perspectives. London: Centre for the Study of Democracy.

Portes, A. (1998) Social capital: its origins and applications in modern sociology, *Annual Review of Sociology*, 24(1): 1–24.

Putnam, R. (2000) *Bowling Alone: The Collapse and Revival of American Community*. New York: Simon and Schuster.

Rose, N. (1999) Inventiveness in politics: critique of Giddens and the Third Way, *Economy and Society*, 28(3): 467–93.

Rose, N. (2001) The politics of life itself, *Theory, Culture & Society*, 18(6): 1–30.

Rustin, M. (1994) Incomplete modernity: Ulrich Beck's risk society, *Radical Philosophy*, 67: 3–12.

Tonkiss, F. (2000) Trust, social capital and the economy, in F. Tonkiss and A. Passey (eds) *Trust and Civil Society*. London: Macmillan.

Younge, G. (2005) Riots are a class act – and often they're the only alternative, *The Guardian*, 14 November.

Younge, G. and Campbell, D. (2005) Still alive amid the chaos: rescuers arrive at last to discover the forgotten survivors, *The Guardian*, 7 September.

## Further reading

Baron, S., Field, J. and Schuller, T. (eds) (2000) *Social Capital: Critical Perspectives*. Oxford: Oxford University Press.

Bauman, Z. (1999) *In Search of Politics*. Cambridge: Polity Press.

Beck, U. (1997) *The Reinvention of Politics: Rethinking Modernity in the Global Social Order*. Cambridge: Polity Press.

Giddens, A. (1998) *The Third Way: The Renewal of Social Democracy*. Cambridge: Polity Press.

Rose, N. (1999) *Powers of Freedom: Reframing Political Thought*. Cambridge: Cambridge University Press.

# 10 Work and risk

## Steve Tombs and Dave Whyte

## Introduction

According to a now dominant body of knowledge across a range of social sciences, our world is becoming reordered in line with a new logic of risk distribution. As has been illuminated in this collection, literature on the 'risk society' has sought to reconstitute the way in which we understand the very basis for governmental and institutional practices, and the foundations of individual identity formation. This chapter seeks to develop an under-standing of the political significance of Beck's risk society thesis by analysing subject matter that is notable for its complete absence in Beck's work – namely the production and regulation of workplace risks. Work poses massive risks to human health and well-being in contemporary societies. The most recent global estimate puts the total figure at about 2.2 million people killed by work every year (Takala 2005: 2).

Since issues of workplace health and safety are absent both from Beck's own considerations of 'the risk society', as well as from most commentaries, supportive or critical, of this thesis, then, by definition, some of the ground covered here may not be familiar to students of risk debates. We begin, however, on familiar terrain, by reviewing some of the key aspects of Beck's claims regarding the risk society, in particular those that we wish to pursue critically through this chapter – and these focus mostly on Beck's claims regarding the nature, distribution and responses to hazards, rather than with his intimately connected thesis regarding individualization. We then go on to consider risk in relation to work, detailing a series of empirical observations regarding the extent to which productive activity routinely kills, injures and makes sick workers and local communities; we also note some of the wider effects of this routine devastation. We then turn to consider the ways in which, and the extent to which, such effects of production are distributed not randomly, but highly differentially: that is, in ways which reflect long-standing structures of vulnerability constructed upon the modernist cleavages of class, gender and race. Two subsequent sections consider responses to the systematic production of, and vulnerability to, such risks and harms. In these sections we indicate why, and the extent to which, organized labour remains the central counter-weight to the untrammelled production of workplace death, injury and illness. We also consider the political attractiveness of many of the claims associated with the 'risk society', arguing that these have gained currency since they cohere with, as well as provide rationales for, realignments in the nature of state regulation of capital. The steady growth of the risk society literature here corresponds to a language of risk that is now central to debates on regulation and regulatory enforcement, in both political and academic discourse. The central aims of the chapter, then, are twofold. First, we consider a specific, yet significant, long-standing and pervasive set of hazards, namely those created through production and faced by workers. Second, we aim to interrogate critically the risk society literature by exploring the absence of occupational safety and health risks from this significant body of work in light of the internal contradictions and shortcomings of the risk society thesis.

## Marking out the risk society

Beck's *Risk Society* is organized around two, interconnected theses: on the one hand, a risk thesis and, on the other hand, an individualization thesis. To develop a thesis around risk, Beck draws an important distinction between 'risks' and 'hazards'. The basis of Beck's claims regarding individualization is that the characteristic – manufactured – risks of the new modernity are beyond the capacity of governmental control. Thus 'the burden of risk migrates from the jurisdiction of institutions to the individualized sphere of personal decision-making' (Mythen 2005: 130). Nowhere is this process of individualization more apparent than in the world of work: 'rapid labour market fluctuations and the de-standardization of employment relations serve as archetypal examples of the "categorical shift" in social experience'; new and increased levels of individualized 'risk' characterizes flexibilized employment, declining collective bargaining, the rise of casualization, and so on, all of which allow 'various employment costs to be transferred from employers to individual workers' (Mythen 2005: 132). For Beck, these changes in employment are to be understood in terms of 'the intersecting processes of individualization and risk distribution ... the articulation of [these] generates a nascent "risk regime" of employment' (Mythen 2005: 131). While what we have to say in this chapter bears more directly upon Beck's claims regarding risk *per se*, throughout we will return to his claims regarding individualization.

Before exploring more fully the relationship between risk and work, it is worth briefly reviewing what we see as the key points originally raised in Ulrich Beck's *Risk Society*. Beck argues that in the current phase of late modernity, traditional divisions of social class and poverty matter less:

Risks display a social boomerang effect in their diffusion: even the rich and the powerful are not safe from them. The formerly 'latent side effects' strike back even at the centres of their production. The agents of modernisation themselves are emphatically caught in the maelstrom of hazards that they unleash and profit from.

(1992: 37)

In Beck's new smog-enveloped democracy, you reap what you sow. So, even the wealthiest cannot keep a safe distance from the risks they profit from. Risk politics therefore transcend the old-style left–right class politics. Wealth distribution and racial and gender inequalities are submerged by the universal risks that threaten us all. A process of individualization has broken down many of the traditional social bonds and forced us to depend upon market mechanisms as opposed to other institutional (family, welfare state) forms of security. Beck (1998: 18) posits that a *logic of risk* rather than a logic of wealth distribution now shapes political decision-making: 'relations of [risk] definition' thus transcend 'relations of production', whereby the 'legal, epistemological and cultural matrix in which risk is conducted' shapes the new power relation. Governments and political leaders are, if they are to retain some influence in policy decisions, forced to engage with questions that were once the sovereign domains of 'expertise'. Since expertise matters more in the risk society, 'the potential for structuring society migrates from the political system into the sub-political system of scientific, technological and economic modernisation' (Beck 1992: 186). Prior to the risk society, we could clearly differentiate between the realms of 'science' ('non-politics') and politics. In the current phase of modernity what is envisaged is a kind of reversal, where 'the political becomes non-political and the non-political political' (Beck 1992: 186). As this process unfolds, politics becomes colonized with the actuarial science of risk calculation, since 'risk definitions open up new political options which can be used to win back and strengthen democratic parliamentary influence' (Beck 1992: 227). In other words, scientific thinking itself is becoming the principal agent of political change (Fagan 1998). In the risk society, politics is concerned principally with highly technical questions and with the calculus of defining, redefining and acting on risks. The reflexive modernization thesis – the idea that industrial society is now confronted by its own limitations – holds that just as risk society lives under the shadow of a growing range of manufactured hazards, the same process has given us the technical capacity to measure and deal with those hazards.

In *The Brave New World of Work* (2000), published several years after *Risk Society*, Beck developed his thesis of the transition from class society to risk society with a sustained discussion of the labour market and the workplace. In this book, Beck talks of 'the deinstitutionalisation of the conflict between labour and capital' (2000: 174), a process whereby the deregulation of the labour market has had the effect of dissipating the opportunities for class conflict and has strengthened

> the political society of individuals, of active civil society here and now ... this society of active citizens, which is no longer fixed within the container of the nation state and whose activities are organised both locally and across frontiers ... in this way communal democracy and identity are given new life in projects such as ecological initiatives, Agenda 21, work with homeless people, local theatres, cultural centres and meeting places for discussion.
>
> (Beck 2000: 5–6)

For Beck, those new institutional assemblages are the new locations of struggles over workers' rights and working conditions. The claim is that traditional, nationally situated institutions that waged capital–labour power struggles in the past, are now being replaced by new civil society institutions, most obviously non-governmental organizations (NGOs) with a global reach. It is those dynamic new organizations that are driving forward the 'deformalization' of politics. As Franklin has shown, those characteristics are for Beck not merely a manifestation of the deformalization of politics, but the foundation of new structures of representation based on transnational interest groups that are 'cosmopolitan' and decoupled from national political institutions. Beck's analysis of the demise of the traditional institutions (trade unions, trade associations and business federations) is a process best described as the 'deinstitutionalization of labour–capital relations'. We will return to this deinstitutionalization process later.

In summary, then, the risk society thesis as developed by Beck implies that it is the latent and actual 'risks' of late modern societies that erect the new structures of vulnerability as traditional social divisions of race, class and gender are rendered less significant in the age of reflexive modernity. The assertion of the demise of the centrality of class struggle to late modern societies is coupled with an insistence that 'traditional institutions' and the institutional locations of class struggle are becoming less relevant as sites of social and political conflict. In this social and political alignment in which 'traditional' forms of political representation and institutional struggle are becoming less relevant, expert knowledge about risk takes on a new political significance, just as politics is forced to engage with the technological debates about the measurement and control of hazards.

## Risk, harm and work

Perhaps what is most remarkable about Beck's *The Brave New World of Work* (2000) is that in all of its 202 pages, there is no discussion of death and injury caused by work. The risks associated with work are, throughout the book, economic risks (how job insecurity is restructuring social relations, the social impact of long-term unemployment, and so on, which of course lead to secondary health problems) rather than threats to health and well-being present in the workplace. The lack of any discussion of health and safety in the workplace is replicated in Beck's earlier work. This is an astounding gap in Beck's narrative and analysis, since, as we have already indicated, death, injury and disease that result from work are by any measure huge risks that most people in the world face on a daily basis. Moreover, the example of workplace risk, because it is an issue that is inevitably framed by debates on 'risk' and 'class', provides us with a useful approach to interrogating the risk society. As a first step in this exercise, this section lays out the parameters of the scale and nature of the harms caused by working under contemporary capitalism.

In contemporary societies, work routinely kills workers and members of the public through acute injury and chronic illness. The scale of this routine killing – deaths occur across all industries, all types of companies – is almost incomprehensible. In May 2002, the International Labour Organization (ILO) estimated that two million workers die each year through work-related 'accidents' and diseases – a figure which it said is 'just the tip of the iceberg' (Takala 2002: 6). Thus, latest ILO estimates for the year 2000 show that annually there are two million work-related deaths – more than 5,000 every day – and for every fatality there are another 500 to 2,000 injuries, depending on the type of job. In addition, the ILO reports that for every fatal work-related disease there are about 100 other illnesses causing absence from work. According to these ILO figures, the biggest killer in the workplace is cancer, causing roughly 640,000 or 32 per cent of deaths, followed by circulatory diseases at 23 per cent, then 'accidents' at 19 per cent and communicable diseases at 17 per cent. Asbestos poisoning alone takes some 100,000 lives annually, while 12,000 children die each year working in hazardous conditions.

Notwithstanding the kind of data presented above, it is important to be clear that, in fact and of importance in itself, relatively little is known about the numbers of people killed by work activities – a lack of knowledge that says a great deal about the priorities of the societies in which we live. To take deaths from work-related disease, the official statistics do not begin to capture the scale of physical harm wreaked by employing organizations. However, it is possible to highlight the sheer scale of deaths involved. We can do so by considering just one category of deaths in one country – deaths from asbestos exposures in Britain. The Health and Safety Executive (HSE) – the body for overseeing health and safety law in England, Scotland and Wales – has noted that in 2002 there were 1,862 deaths from mesothelioma, an asbestos-related cancer, and a further 1,800 deaths from asbestos-related lung cancers (Health and Safety Executive 2004a: 3). In fact, as the HSE itself recognizes, actual deaths related to asbestos exposure are far higher. Asbestos-related deaths continue to rise in this country (not to peak until around 2025, according to the British government), years after the demise of the industry (the worst affected group are men born in the 1940s), and 70 years after the first official recognition of the cancer-causing properties of this magic mineral.

> Excess deaths in Britain from asbestos-related diseases could eventually reach 100,000 ... one study projected that in western Europe 250,000 men would die of mesothelioma [just *one* asbestos-caused cancer] between 1995 and 2029; with half a million as the corresponding figure for the total number of West European deaths from asbestos.
>
> (Tweedale 2000: 276)

A later study extrapolates from current asbestos-related deaths and concludes that more than 3 per cent of men in Europe will die of asbestos-related diseases in the next 10–20 years (Randerson 2001).

It is also worth recalling that such deaths are hardly simply a matter of historical record, a legacy of a now discarded activity – for the industry remains vibrant globally, with almost 150 countries still using it (asbestos is banned in just 25 countries). Even more chillingly, 'asbestos is only one of a number of hazardous substances in our lives' (Tweedale 2000: 277). In many respects, it is one of the 'safest' since there is now generally accepted knowledge regarding its deleterious health effects and its use is highly regulated, at least in most advanced capitalist economies. Of 100,000 chemicals currently registered for use in the EU, for example, 'little is known about the toxicity of about 75% of these' (European Environment Agency 1999: 6), and there is almost no useful information on their synergistic effects. Reference to this point has been to deaths. Yet these fatalities are only the most visible forms of physical harm caused by work-related activities. Much more common are major and minor ('over-three-day') injuries. According to most recent HSE data, there were 30,666 major injuries and 129,143 over-three-day injuries to workers in Britain in 2003/04; members of the public suffered 13,575 non-fatal occupational injuries (Health and Safety Executive 2004b: 4–5). Yet even these official data fail to capture the extent of physical harm caused by working in what is the fourth most developed economy in the world. While the HSE has long been aware of the significant scale of under-reporting of injuries (major and over-three-day), recent use of the Labour

Force Survey (LFS) has produced evidence of levels of injury that far outweigh 'official' injury data. Based upon the discrepancies between 'official' and LFS data, the HSE has concluded recently that less than 43 per cent of non-fatal injuries that should be reported by employers actually are reported; and data for the self-employed captures less than 5 per cent of reportable injuries (2004b: 7). Moreover, even this recognized level of under-reporting in principle excludes three potentially significant – if somewhat overlapping – areas of occupational injuries, namely those incurred by workers in the illegal economy, by homeworkers and by childworkers (O'Donnell and White 1998, 1999).

Of course, to talk of the 'risks' involved in those deaths and injuries is not merely to talk of the *physical* harms. They have widespread, if largely unrecognized, financial, psychological, as well as social effects. However, it is the financial costs of injuries and ill health which have been the focus of recent attention by official organizations and interest groups. Thus, the HSE and governments have, for almost a decade, sought erroneously – (see Cutler and James 1996), to argue the 'business case' for improved health and safety (Health and Safety Executive 1993, 1994; Davies and Teasdale 1994; Health and Safety Commission/Department of Environment, Transport and the Regions 2000), seeing the costs to companies of injuring and causing illness as a lever to raise standards of compliance! In this context, it has been estimated that the costs of injury and ill health is £18 billion a year (see, for example, Health and Safety Commission/Department of Environment, Transport and the Regions 2000). Yet one of the contradictions within such an argument is that employers *do not* actually meet the costs of workplace injuries and illness. In short, Beck's boomerang effect is all too absent here, as in other contexts (Mythen 2005: 141). Most of the £18 billion cost of workplace injury and illness is paid for by the government and the victims. Even the HSE itself estimates that employers, who cause the health and safety risks, pay between £3.3 billion and £6.5 billion (TUC 2003). In other words, costs associated with injuries and illhealth represent a socialization of the costs of private production, in effect a massive redistribution of wealth from the poor to the rich. That is, through supporting the cost of industrial injury benefit, health and other social services, paying higher insurance premiums, paying higher prices for goods and services so that employers can recoup the costs of downtime, retraining, the replacement of plants, and so on, private industry is subsidized on a massive scale by employees, taxpayers and the general public. This in turn has knock-on effects on government's ability to use revenue from general taxation for more socially productive purposes.

Such bald statistics of deaths or losses to corporate profits or GDP mask a wide array of searing, but less quantifiable, social and psychological harms. Families and communities are subjected to trauma in the event of death and injury. Children lose mothers and fathers, spouses lose partners, sports teams lose coaches and players, church and social clubs lose their members, and workers lose their colleagues – to the extent that such psychological and social costs are immeasurable. Moreover, such losses and harms have effects across generations, so that, for example, children who experience poverty following the death of the main wage earner are themselves more likely to grow up in conditions of relative insecurity, a condition then more likely to be experienced by their own offspring. It remains to be noted that the psychological trauma heaped upon the bereaved is often magnified greatly by the consistent inability of the state, through the criminal justice system, to provide 'answers' as to why someone who leaves for work either does not return, or returns in a considerably less fit condition – despite central elements to law's own stated 'promise' being, first, to provide mechanisms for bringing the perpetrators of illegal harms to account, and, second, indeed increasingly, to provide redress for victims of such harms (Tombs 2004).

## Patterns of risk

What the preceding data demonstrate is the enormous – almost unimaginable – scale of risks associated with working. It should also be emphasized that these are long-standing: if, as Beck claims, risk is pervasive within and integral to modern society, then this is nothing new; witness Marx's *Capital* Volume 1, or Engels' *The Condition of The Working Class*. Moreover, what such data fail to convey is the fact that risks faced at work are neither evenly nor randomly distributed: not only are such deaths, injuries and illnesses unequally distributed, but this unequal distribution mirrors well-known structural inequalities within nations – between regions, classes and communities – as well as between nations. To preview our argument here, and to signal immediately our departure from Beck's claims about the democratic effects of contemporary risks, Scott's (cited in Mythen 2005: 142) pithy observation is a useful one: 'smog is just as hierarchical as poverty so long as some places are less smoggy than others'.

Globally, a particularly heavy toll of death and injury occurs in developing countries where large numbers of workers are concentrated in primary and extraction activities such as agriculture, logging, fishing and mining (Takala 2002: 2–3). This unequal international distribution of risk is further exacerbated by the struggle to secure safer and healthier workplaces in developed countries having as one effect the relocation of risk and hazard to developing economies – creating a key advantage for transnational companies in their ability to 'export' hazardous work from more to less regulated economies (Castleman 1979; Ives 1985). The classic and most infamous manifestation of this was the Bhopal 'disaster'. In Bhopal, India, a chemical plant, operated by Union Carbide of India Limited (UCIL), a subsidiary of

Union Carbide Corporation (UCC), used highly toxic chemicals, including methyl iso-cyanate (MIC), to produce pesticides. In December 1984, water entered an MIC storage tank, setting in process an exothermic reaction, and soon a cocktail of poisonous gases, vapours and liquids, including up to 40 tons of MIC, was spewed into the atmosphere. The Indian government initially put the number of acute deaths at 1,700, a figure subsequently revised to 3,329; 20 years after the leak, in 2004, Amnesty International estimated that there had been over 7,000 such deaths, with 15,000 people having since died from longer-term effects; about 100,000 'survivors' will never work again. While the gas leak was the result of a combination of production and cost-cutting decisions (Pearce and Tombs 1998), the very fact that MIC was on-site at all in Bhopal was the consequence of successful resistance by French chemical workers to a prior Union Carbide intention to store and use MIC at its plant in Beziers, France.

The long and still largely unsuccessful struggle of the victims of the Bhopal gas leak to gain compensation for human and environmental suffering also indicates a further structural inequality associated with global risk distribution: for the economic consequences of death, injury and disease associated with working are also differentially distributed. Thus, for example, occupational health and safety compensation schemes differ enormously – while workers in Nordic countries enjoy nearly universal coverage, 'only 10 per cent or less of the workforce in many developing countries is likely to benefit from any sort of coverage. Even in many developed countries, coverage against occupational injury and illness may extend to only half the workforce' (Takala, cited in Demaret and Khalef 2004). As one might expect, these unequal distributions of risk (and harms) at a global scale are reproduced *within* the most developed economies. Here, for example, there are also good theoretical reasons and some empirical evidence to indicate that these deaths, injuries and illnesses disproportionately fall upon members of the lowest socio-economic groups. If we ask *who* gets killed and injured, the answer is to be found in certain manual occupations – and is comprehensible in traditional class terms. Thus about half of the fatalities incurred by employees in Britain occur in two sectors – construction and 'agriculture, forestry and fishing' – which, along with 'recycling of scrap and waste', also have the highest injury rates to employees (Health and Safety Executive 2004b). If we shift from sector to occupation, we find injury rates can be mapped onto traditional class lines: for example, HSE data indicate that 'process, plant and machine operatives' are 15 times more likely to incur a reportable injury than 'managers and senior officials', and more than ten times more likely than those in 'professional occupations'. Now, while it is accepted that there may be greater risks to be faced on a building site than in an office, the idea that certain occupations are so inherently dangerous that they necessarily produce certain levels of injury cannot be sustained – see, for example, the studies by both Carson (1982) and Woolfson and colleagues (1996) of work organization in the UK offshore oil industry. Indeed, these latter studies also demonstrate that, in a sector that has drawn labour from the high unemployment areas of Scotland and northern England, the idea that workers exchange exposure to risk for higher wages is also more myth than reality (Moore 1991). Thus vulnerability and economic marginalization have mutually reinforcing effects that manifest themselves in terms of exposure to workplace risks. This is further highlighted in recent HSE-sponsored research examining the experiences of different ethnic groups of work-related stress (Smith et al. 2005). Nationally, HSE estimates that about half a million people in the UK experience work-related stress at a level they believe is making them ill, with a total of 12.8 million working days lost to stress, depression and anxiety in 2003/04. Stress, of course, has a multitude of causes, but is generally experienced more greatly by those who are least able to exert any control or influence over workplace demands placed upon them. It is, then, a classic disease of workplace marginalization and vulnerability. Thus, while we concur with Mythen's (2005: 140) argument that 'class position remains a fundamental indicator of vulnerability to unemployment', class also remains a crucial indicator of vulnerability *in* employment (Ekinsmyth 1999).

That there are gender and ethnic, as well as class, dimensions to this unequal victimization is evidenced in the work of Wrench (Lee and Wrench 1980; Wrench and Lee 1982; Boris and Pruegl 1996; Wrench 1996). Smith et al. (2005: 8) found a 'significant correlation' between work stress and ethnicity. In summary, they concluded that:

> Racial discrimination, particularly in combination with gender and ethnicity, was identified as having a strong influence on work stress ... certain work characteristics were also associated with work stress: higher effort reward imbalance, greater job demand, and lower control over work were all associated with work stress.

Put simply, despite popular myths about stress being associated with high-flying corporate executives, if you are a minority-ethnic female, low down the occupational hierarchy with little or no control over your work, and both overworked and underpaid, then you are likely to be subject to this form of occupational illness. Understanding exposure to and victimization from risk, and differential responses to and public knowledge(s) of this victimization, thus requires an understanding of various forms of class–race–gender articulations. Such an understanding requires deconstructing traditional representations of workplace risk and hazards. For while these have traditionally been associated with male occupations, and despite the fact that research has mostly ignored women's occupational health and safety issues (Szockyi and Frank 1996: 17), trends in data indicate that those areas in which women are over-represented, notably services, are those which exhibit both persistently high, and rising, rates of injuries and illhealth (see Craig 1981; Labour Research Department 1996). Indeed, both popular and academic understandings or considerations of the relationships between 'risk' and work view these through the prism of declining, hazardous and male-dominated occupations such as mining, shipbuilding, heavier forms of manufacturing, and so on, meaning that much work within this area has highly, if implicit, masculinist connotations.

As this section has demonstrated, exposure to risks through work is a highly concrete element and manifestation of what has been called the structuring of vulnerability – it is one of the means by which the poorest, most disadvantaged people in our society are further, systematically discriminated against in terms of the quality, longevity, even preservation of their lives. At the same time, as is often the case with structured inequalities, these exposures remain relatively invisible, further exacerbating social, economic and political marginalization of those who face them. What this evidence also suggests all too clearly is that rather than wealth distribution and racial and gender inequalities being submerged by the universal risks that threaten us all, the greater part of the burden of health and safety risks generated by work continues to fall upon workers. This dispersal of risk is a process that reinforces rather than transcends existing patterns of vulnerability and inequality (Mythen 2004). Moreover, those burdens are by no means distributed along new social divisions of risk, but intensify traditional racialized and gendered social inequalities.

## Risk and political struggle

How then to respond to the systematic production of, and vulnerability to, workplace risks? Historically, the key source of opposition to workplace risks has been organized labour, and a key political tactic has been to seek more effective regulation, at best regulation involving workers' representatives themselves – in other words, struggles to secure safer and healthier workplaces have historically been classic struggles on the part of labour and its allies to attenuate management's right to manage and expropriate surplus value. As we have noted, for Beck and other proponents of the risk society thesis, such forms of struggle are increasingly anachronistic, and are being replaced by new non-traditional institutional assemblages. Thus, in this, and the following section of this chapter, we wish to concentrate both upon struggles around the level of regulation and upon government initiatives towards regulation, with specific reference to health and safety at work.

There can be no doubt that the relative decline in trade union membership and the erosion of a range of rights held by workers in the post-war liberal democracies has reshaped the balance of power between capital and labour. The internationalization of neo-liberalism has profoundly repositioned labour markets and labour processes in favour of capital, particularly in the developing world, and this has had profound implications for the way that nation-states imagine and act out their relationship to national and transnational capital. It is also clear that, directly as a result of the global march of capital, NGOs are now encouraged to play a watchdog role in the locations where we find the most dangerous and exploitative work. However, in our view, Beck makes a rather bold leap from observing those phenomena as characteristics of neo-liberal capitalism to using them to support his case for a transition to the risk society.

As Franklin posited in the previous chapter, Beck is undoubtedly right to argue that we need to constantly reassess the 'zombie categories' that dominate social science (Beck and Beck-Gernsheim 2002). However, it is our argument that making such great claims as to emergence of a risk society – especially claims of a dawning of a new epoch in the structure of social relations – cannot be made with purely abstract reference points. The aspects of late capitalism that Beck described as risk society can only be understood within the context of a careful analysis of the concrete realities of struggles around the production of risks. We should be clear here that in understanding the distribution of risk at work we need to move beyond the sweeping claims of Beck, and others, that de-standardization and individualization of work – job insecurity – are universal conditions of modern life. For this insecurity – and all that accompanies it, including the increased likelihood of exposure to workplace risk and harm – are structured in quite specific ways. Thus, much more specificity is needed. For example, as Doogan's analysis of labour turnover in the UK in the 1990s indicates, while long-term employment actually *increased* for skilled, managerial and professional groups, job turnover increased 'absolutely and relatively in elementary occupations in lower skilled occupations and absolutely in low skilled agricultural jobs' (Doogan 2001: 432).

HSE research, based upon UK Labour Force Survey returns, has found significant correlations between injury rates and job tenure. The rate of injury to workers in their first six months is over double that for workers who have been with an employer for at least a year (Health and Safety Executive 2000: 3); and higher rates of injury are associated with shorter working weeks, so that 'those working less than 16 hours per week have double the rate of injury compared with those who work 30–50 hours per week'. There is an obvious issue here about the extent to which people learn on the job, but such facts should also raise concerns about the casualization of work: temporary and part-time workers – workers who are likely to enjoy far fewer forms of employment protection than those in full-time, permanent employment – are, once all other factors have been controlled for, more likely to be injured at work. To these conclusions we can safely add that child workers, home-workers and those working 'illegally' are at the same time likely to face extreme risks while also being invisible to almost any 'official' considerations of the distribution of injury and disease. The converse of these arguments is that the safest workplaces in the UK are those with strong trade unions and effective, functioning, union-backed safety representation. This has been confirmed in numerous research studies. What the most recent studies have found is that strong worker representation in the workplace has a markedly beneficial impact upon health and safety performance (Walters et al. 2005) and that trade unions are the key organizations in providing this support. Strong trade union representation reduces injury rates dramatically, by perhaps as much as 50 per cent (Reilly et al. 1995). Moreover, a review of the research confirmed the consistency of those findings on an international basis (James and Walters 2002). This review of evidence underlines two points. First, at the level of the workplace, the crucial risk controls are those that are exerted by well-organized workers themselves. This suggests that rather than having been made redundant in the current phase of capitalism, 'traditional' forms of labour organization remain just as important as they have ever been. Second, it suggests that were a de-institutionalization process to occur, it would, quite literally, have catastrophic effects. Despite the efforts of employers in particular sectors to remove negotiations around safety from the sphere of industrial relations, this strategy has had only limited success (Woolfson et al. 1996). So, regardless of the relative decline in trade union membership and the incursion of new NGOs onto the scene, trade unions and other 'traditional' forms of worker organization remain crucially important to the mitigation of risks in the workplace. Safety conditions remain institutionalized in collective bargaining agreements in the UK.

Despite the incursion into the arena of health and safety politics by new campaign groups (such as the Simon Jones campaign, see http://www.simonjones.org.uk/) and NGOs (such as the Centre for Corporate Accountability, see http://www.corporateaccountability.org/), the most effective and vocal organizations on matters of health and safety remain the trade unions and trade union organizations such as the Hazards movement, a trade union support network for workplace safety representatives. De-institutionalization and the related shift to new forms of political representation (i.e. NGOs and voluntary organizations rather than labour unions) remain unlikely as long as struggles against long hours and dangerous conditions exist. By engaging in belligerent action, whether this means distribution of Hazards literature or organizing to resist new shift patterns in particular workplaces, for example, workers continue to organize around health and safety at a local level. Thus, we can agree with Mythen's claims that Beck is 'conspicuously mute about expressions of work related solidarity. It must be remembered that new forms of collectivism have emerged as a response to job insecurity' (Mythen 2005:

37). We would add to this that 'old' forms of collectivism also remain crucial – perhaps more so in the area of occupational safety and health than in any other.

In the arena of health and safety policy formation, workers' organizations and the organizations that represent capital remain central to the formal decision-making process of risk management and health and safety policy at the national level. Health and safety in the UK is still based upon a tripartite system in which employers, employees and the state are represented. Thus, the Health and Safety Commission must by law include representatives from the employer and the employee side. In practice, this means that the HSC and the various HSE subcommittees are made up of trade union and trade/business association delegates, alongside senior regulatory officials. There are institutions with an interest in health and safety which do not represent directly the interests of capital and labour (including the Royal Society for the Prevention of Accidents, the Institute of Occupational Safety and Health, and the Institute of Employment Rights as well as the organizations mentioned above), and those organizations undoubtedly do have some influence in policy circles. They may be invited to give evidence to parliamentary committees and conduct research on behalf of government, for example. NGOs, campaigning groups and professional organizations may well be rising in influence as trade union influence shows signs of declining, but this is not to say that those organizations have threatened the centrality of organizations representing capital and labour at a national level. To the extent that there has been an ascent of the realm of sub-politics here, it is merely embellishing, rather than undermining, the formal – nationally moderated – political sphere of politics.

The recent trajectory of legislation in the UK is better characterized as a re-institutionalization of labour–capital relations. The various industrial relations reforms implemented by New Labour have enshrined a social partnership agenda in law. Thus, for example, there has been a concerted attempt through three separate Acts and through the government's interpretation of European legislation to establish information and consultation procedures as an alternative to bargaining (Smith and Morton 2005). Although those arrangements have had the effect of weakening the bargaining power of trade unions, it is not accurate to say that the unions' role in the workplace is being eradicated. Unions retain a key role. The foundations of a new system for establishing recognition agreements in the UK were laid by the 1999 Employment Relations Act. The Act lays down new formal bureaucratic procedures that establish new routes to achieve recognition. For all their bias in favour of the employers' side, it is overly simplistic to talk about 'deinstitutionalization' when formal industrial relations arrangements are actually being reframed, albeit in a way that substantially rebalances power in favour of capital.

On this evidence, any talk of the demise of traditional capital–labour relations at an institutional level is premature. Indeed, it is unhelpful to those who wish to effect change in the workplace or for those who strategically seek the most effective pressure points for social change. The deformalization of politics thesis asserts that progressive social change need not involve confrontation with organized capital and the state; strategies are more likely to be more successful if they forge new compromise agreements and 'partnerships' with opposing interests. Talk of the demise of labour–capital in the risk society thesis coheres strongly with the notion of the 'Third Way', perhaps the most famous set of ideas associated with New Labour. Indeed, the risk society is ideologically consistent with New Labour and is therefore convenient for those that seek to convince us that we have moved beyond the politics of left and right (Giddens 1994).

## The political seductions of the risk society

It is in the political attractions of risk society claims that we can partially understand their ubiquitousness – aspects of the risk society thesis can be both used to justify certain dominant political trends as well as to usher in new initiatives. As Doogan (2001: 439) has noted in the context of insecurity in the labour market, the concept of 'manufactured uncertainty' allows us to transcend understandings of risks as a product of something called the 'age of insecurity'. Instead we have to understand processes of individualization and risk reduction/promotion as conscious strategies of government that arise 'from attempts to increase the productivity and competitiveness of the economy' (Doogan 2001: 439). However, to point to those institutional and ideological aspects of the risk society is not to hold Beck or others particularly responsible for the ways in which his, and others', ideas have been used; it is simply to recognize that ideas and claims are more/less likely to gain credence at certain times in relation to specific sets of social, economic and political trajectories and interests (Tombs and Whyte 2003). It is in its class-myopia that the risk literature is revealed for being *defined* rather than *informed* by popular and political priorities. The shift towards risk management, because it claims to offer scientific/technical rather than political solutions to problems, is also assumed to represent the basis for a less partial, apolitical rule. This 'technique fetishism' (Lavalette 1991) is best understood as a self-fulfilling prophecy that encourages the assumption that safety is best left to experts – be these engineers, technicians, risk analysts or ergonomists. Now, this is not to claim that risk of victimization is viewed as entirely apolitical in dominant academic discourses. But it is telling that missing from the risks considered in Beck's arguments are 'such class-specific and yet global risks as unemployment, poverty, organized crime, AIDS and migration' (Engel and Strasser

1998: 94). The failure of the risk society thesis to focus upon the global risks that are inherent to class-based societies is remarkable since, as Fagan has noted in relation to health and safety risks in the workplace, 'broadly speaking, capital and the state are in the business of risk promotion, while labour and communities adopt a risk-averse stance' (Fagan 1998: 17). If this seems like a rather bold and unforgiving statement, it stands up because standard financial regulatory (accounting systems) and social regulatory systems (labour market regulation and hazard controls) enable business to externalize the financial and social burden of risk. Business risk promotion is therefore better understood as a routine feature of systems of capital accumulation. This point remains unrecognized in the risk society thesis, since, as Rustin (1994: 11) has observed, absent from Beck's analysis 'is the concept of capital itself'.

In the passages in which Beck (1995: 129) does discuss capital, the production of risk creates as many new uncertainties for capital as it does for subordinate social groups. Now struggles over how the cake is sliced up are being changed fundamentally because the cake is poisoned. Whereas the production of wealth creates class contradictions between labour and capital, the production of risks leads to the emergence of class contradictions *within* classes (Beck 1995: 137). 'Production' (the ecological risks produced by industrial pollution) and 'product' (toxic hazards associated with consumer products) risks threaten to destroy corporations, to damage markets, and so on, by creating a cycle of bad publicity and/or civil damages liabilities. The argument is explicitly that the risks produced by industrial society are imploding upon the industrial producers of the risks. However, while capital is under siege from the boomerang effects of late modernity, systems of capitalist social relations remain intact. In late modern societies, the epochal shift heralded by the risk society is not predicated by shifts in the social relations of production. The result is a tacit acceptance that changes in social relations are not necessarily related to changes in the mode of domination. Rather than reflecting real changes in social relations, then, the risk society paradigm paradoxically connects to a normative acceptance of capital's pre-eminence in late modern societies (Rigakos 2001; Rigakos and Hadden 2001).

It is an acceptance that is reflected in political constructions of both the possible and the desirable form that the regulation of capital must take in liberal democracies. In the UK, following two major reviews aimed at lightening the regulatory 'burdens' on business that commenced in 2004, Chancellor of the Exchequer Brown made clear the government's policy trajectory in a speech shortly after the election of a third successive Labour government. This speech heralded 'a new, risk-based approach to regulation to break down barriers holding enterprise back'; the 'new' model will entail 'no unjustifiable inspection, form filling or requirement for information. Not just a light, but a limited touch. Instead of routine regulation trying to cover all, the risk based approach targets the necessary few'. This new approach will 'help move us a million miles away from the old belief that business, unregulated, will invariably act irresponsibly' (Brown 2005). There is nothing particularly new in the rejection of enforcement in favour of risk management in debates on regulation. The language of risk merely allows Brown to express this tendency as a renewed effort. In the sphere of state efforts to improve standards of occupational health and safety – that is, to mitigate risks – an approach centred on risk management has always been central (Braithwaite 2000). Risk management approaches rest on the idea that risks can be scientifically managed out of industrial systems by the application of risk technologies such as probability analysis, safety management systems, and so on. In a 'risk society' sense, the risk management approach also accepts that risks are a consequence of human endeavour and stresses that 'human error' and 'risk taking' are natural by-products of human progress in the modern era. By stressing the behaviour side of safety management, the risk management approach locates the control of risks in the proper management of individuals. In this context, risk management is nothing more than a 'scientific management' strategy which aims to extend management control over production.

Thus, the risk society thesis is compatible with political agendas that are explicitly pro-business – for it provides no challenge to the right of managements to manage while conversely extending the technical paraphernalia available to them. In a pro-business climate, governments can reinforce their commitment to boosting profits by offering 'risk' strategies as opposed to enforcement strategies. This is a crucial point, since the risk management paradigm is characterized as the opposite: as a means to control and constrain management decisions to protect workforces and publics. However, this bipolar understanding of 'risk management' is not particularly useful because it obscures the effect of the rise of 'risk' knowledge and professional technique in the workplace. For us, a much more useful question to approach risk management with asks how 'risk management' actually allows for an ideological shift in the way that regulatory intervention is presented. Companies, in the UK or beyond, have never been exposed to highly interventionist forms and punitive forms of state policing in ways analogous to the dangerous classes. Companies have always been – albeit to greater or lesser extents – encouraged to comply, act as responsibilized subjects, utilize risk management techniques internally, and so on – so that regulation has always existed largely beyond the state, and certainly beyond the punitive, or sovereign, state.

In terms of the literature on regulation, the linking of risk and regulation has, in recent years, become much more explicit. Paradigmatic here is the establishment, in 2000, and the subsequent work of, the Centre for the Analysis of Risk and Regulation (CARR) within the LSE and backed by significant ESRC funding. Thus Bridget Hutter, Director of CARR, and one of the key figures in the Compliance-Oriented School of Regulatory Enforcement (Pearce and Tombs, 1998) has emphasized that regulation needs no longer to be seen through any state-directed command-and-control lens, but as a way of managing rather than eliminating risks associated with life in advanced industrial societies, an attempt to effect a specific form of ordering of priorities within economic life (Hutter 2002). Thus, 'in modern life', 'the distinction between regulation and risk management is becoming blurred', and convergence towards this blurring is a trend visible across a range of areas. A key locus where regulatory systems and risk management meet is 'the corporate system of internal control' (Hutter and Power 2000: 1). Alongside such work is a literature, somewhat longer standing and more specifically focused upon the regulation of workplace health and safety, but nevertheless having similar starting points, concerns and likely outcomes (Gunningham and Johnstone 1999). At the heart of this work, we find the advocacy of a variety of forms of twin-track regulation again begins from the premise that existing models of occupational health and safety regulation have outlived their usefulness. Building on previous work by Braithwaite and colleagues, around the idea of a regulatory pyramid, two-track regulation essentially entails offering 'regulated' companies a choice: between 'traditional' (track one) regulation, or the adoption of a safety management system (track two). The latter focuses upon performance and principle-based rather than specification-standards, and places the onus for determining compliance and how to achieve it upon employers – subject to third-party, though not necessarily state-based, oversight. Incentives play a key role within each regulatory strategy. Criminal law and punitive sanctions are said to remain present as options for state regulators, but always as last resort – mattering most when they are least used, as credible tools of deterrence which become less significant to the point that compliance, then health and safety performance above legal minima, become internalized and normalized within organizations. This is precisely the strategy that is being lauded by Brown when he promises the advent of a 'risk-based approach' to target 'the necessary few'.

Translating such promises into reality is likely to see an exacerbation of trends present in health and safety enforcement. Since at least 2004, we have been witnessing changes in regulatory practices – particularly around 'enforcement' – on the part of the HSE. These changes, indicated by policy and strategy statements which represent what has been termed a 'further downplaying' of 'regulatory solutions' (House of Commons Work and Pensions Committee 2004: para. 54), cohere with the trajectory of regulation being advocated by Brown, above. Thus, for example, the Health and Safety Commission's recently launched *Strategy for Workplace Health and Safety in Great Britain to 2010 and Beyond* (2004) further downplays formal enforcement, dedicating two paragraphs of its 17 pages to this issue. This is one index of what appears to be a more radical shift away from enforcement in HSE practice. Both the burgeoning literature on risk and regulation, as well as that on two-track regulation, share assumptions – assumptions which can be found in some of the risk society literature. First, that state capacity has dwindled with respect to the task of overseeing compliance with law on the part of companies that generate risks. Second, that risk management is best left to the risk experts, to insurers, risk professionals and other third-party auditors, normally in a client relationship with risk-regulated organizations. Ultimately, risk is to be left to managements themselves, so that corporations should be encouraged to act as responsibilized, self-managing, risk-mitigating organizations. Third, this is both feasible and indeed desirable, because corporations can and do have moral commitments to prevent and mitigate risks – they are not profit-driven, amoral calculators who will kill, injure and poison based upon cost–benefit analyses. This perspective – which assumes that corporations are capable guardians of the environment, or human rights and of workers' rights – is as widely held in the risk society literature as it is in policy debates on regulation in the UK, and is neatly summed up in the following statement from *The Brave New World of Work*:

> At present, death sentences, torture, political imprisonment and other violations of civil and political human rights are seen as things that can be accepted, so long as they do not have an adverse effect on business. But it is well within the power of big corporations to put a stop to them – for example, by making respect for human rights an integral part of their decision to invest in a country. Such a change in company policy might produce credibility (and good publicity) which its whole advertising budget could never buy for it.
>
> (Beck 2000: 117)

There is nothing to deny in this statement. However, it betrays a selective myopia in relation to the decisions about 'risks' confronted by big corporations operating globally. What the risk perspective, expressed in those terms, masks, is a political economy of risk in which the demand to minimize some forms of risk can create greater risks. Ensuring that workers have few collective representation rights, for example, might significantly reduce the risk of financial exposure for investors, but workplaces with a weakened collective bargaining structure are also the most dangerous. What the risk society perspective glosses over is this economy of risk in which reducing investment risk might thus involve the creation of new hazards within the workplace.

## Conclusion: beyond the risk society

In its failure to provide any basis for a political economy of risk (Fagan 1998: 7; Elliott 2002), the risk society thesis is only one of a number of academic/intellectual trends which reinforces the general marginalization of Marxism as a body of scholarship in general, and the economic category of class in particular, from social science vocabularies. The idealism and abstractions of risk literatures fail to understand the material origins, nature and consequences of particular risks in relation to particular economic, political and social interests. We can indeed agree with Mythen (2005: 144) when he writes:

> What is required, then, is a clearer demarcation between risk as perception and risk as a material force. Although the two entities are not comfortably decoupled, the risk society thesis simply conflates perception with exposure, setting in motion a distorted understanding of the relationship between work and risk.

And the workplace – in its technologies and forms of organization related to these – is a key site within which to understand the inscription of power relations within particular forms of rationality. Further, as we indicated in our earlier sections, risks, inscribed into the social conditions of production, are formally distributed in a legal structure that enables both risk and responsibility for the production of risks to be redistributed. Studying the allocation of workplace risks makes it unavoidable that we understand risk distribution as a means of distributing wealth. It also allows us to see clearly how the unequal distribution of risk relies upon an unequal distribution of responsibility and accountability for the production of risk.

The evidence we have presented here suggests that serious attempts to regulate capital in terms of workplace risks must be informed by class analysis; not least because of the structured sources of vulnerability to workplace risks that we have indicated. Regulation must be seen as a means of mitigating the systematically unequal distribution of various social bads *and* goods. Beck is correct to note that class societies are bound up with issues of scarcity – the distribution of social goods – but he is wrong to claim that it is risk societies that are defined by the problem of 'insecurity', for the latter is, *and always has been*, integral to 'class' societies also. Moreover, strict enforcement styles of regulation involve some attempt to exert external control over capital, ostensibly on behalf of the non-capitalist class – be this in the role of workers, consumers, local residents, and so on. Further, to the extent that regulation entails intervention in the management and control of the production process, it undermines the absolute rights to manage, and involves increased costs for, capital (Szasz 1984; Snider 1991; Tombs 1995) – so that some regulation is an element of struggle over the level and subsequent distribution of the surplus expropriated through the process of production. In so far as the risk society thesis offers us little in the way of effective solutions to the control of risks that result from under-controlled methods of industrial production, it remains of little relevance to those who seek to effect the means of controlling the life-threatening risks that the larger part of the global population confronts in the course of a day's work.

The considerations set out in this chapter lead us to call for three – related – sets of research activities to become much more widespread than is currently the case. First, we would argue that risks need to be explored both concretely and in a relational fashion: rather than simply assuming the risks that are faced by different groups of people, these must be explored, and both their objective and subjective dimensions assessed in relation to each other. Second, we need far greater research on the *power* and *selective deployment* of risk discourses. This will involve concrete analyses of the *dynamism* of risk discourses and their deployment, as well as considerations of the various *interests* that are tied to these deployments, and the consequences of these. Third, given the intimate relationships between risk and regulation, we would urge concrete analyses of the nature and dynamics of specific regulatory regimes, and in particular both descriptions and theorizations of those conditions within which pro-regulatory groups can gain the ascendancy, so that the costs of production are forced back upon those who generate them while vulnerability to risks on the part of those who are most likely to face them are minimized and mitigated. What ties each of the above calls is the need to transcend the abstracted nature of the risk society thesis and its idealism in order to achieve much more concrete, materialist, grounded forms of analysis.

## Study questions

1   To what extent do observable patterns of exposure to health and safety risks in the workplace support or undermine the risk society thesis?
2   How far can it be said that contemporary struggles around health and safety are indicative of a deinstitutionalization of struggles between labour and capital?
3   Why is the risk society thesis convenient for governments keen to promote pro-business strategies?

## Acknowledgements

For their insightful comments and criticisms, we are indebted to the editors of this volume and to Kathrin Leuze and Susanne Strauss.

## References

Beck, U. (1992) *Risk Society: Towards a New Modernity*. London: Sage.

Beck, U. (1995) *Ecological Politics in an Age of Risk*. Cambridge: Polity Press.

Beck, U. (1998) Politics of risk society, in J. Franklin (ed.) *The Politics of Risk Society*. Cambridge: Polity Press.

Beck, U. (2000) *The Brave New World of Work*. Cambridge: Polity Press.

Beck, U. and Beck-Gernsheim, E. (2002) *Individualization: Institutionalized Individualism and its Social and Political Consequences*. London: Sage.

Boris, E. and Pruegl, E. (eds) (1996) *Homeworkers in Global Perspective: Invisible No More*. London: Routledge.

Braithwaite, J. (2000) The new regulatory state and the transformation of criminology, in D. Garland, and R. Sparks (eds) *Criminology and Social Theory*. Oxford: Oxford University Press.

Brown, G. (2005) A plan to lighten the regulatory burden on business, *Financial Times*, 24 May.

CARR (2004) *ESRC Centre for Analysis of Risk and Regulation. Mid-Term Review Report 2000–2004*. London: CARR.

Carson, W.G. (1982) *The Other Price of Britain's Oil*. Oxford: Martin Robertson.

Castleman, B. (1979) The export of hazard to developing countries, *International Journal of Health Services*, 9(4): 569–606.

Craig, M. (1981) *Office Workers' Survival Handbook: A Guide to Fighting Health Hazards in the Office*. London: The Women's Press.

Cutler, T. and James, P. (1996) Does safety pay? A critical account of the Health and Safety Executive document: 'The Costs of Accidents', *Work, Employment and Society*, 10(4): 755–65.

Davies, N.V. and Teasdale, P. (1994) *The Costs to the British Economy of Work Accidents and Work-Related Ill-Health*. London: HSE Books.

Demaret, L. and Khalef, A. (2004) Two million work deaths a year: carnage is preventable, ILO says. *Hazards*. www.hazards.org/wmd/ilobriefing2004.htm.

Doogan, K. (2001) Insecurity and long-term employment, *Work, Employment and Society*, 15(3): 419–41.

Ekinsmyth, C. (1999) Professional workers in a risk society, *Transactions of the Institute of British Geographers*, 24: 353–66.

Elliott, A. (2002) Beck's sociology of risk: a critical assessment, *Sociology*, 36(2): 293–315.

Engel, U. and Strasser, H. (1998) Global risks and social inequality: critical remarks on the risk-society hypothesis, *Canadian Journal of Sociology*, 32(1): 91–103.

European Environment Agency (1999) *Chemicals in the European Environment: Low Doses, High Stakes?* EEA/UNEP. http://reports.eea.eu.int/NYM2/en/tab_abstract_RLR.

Fagan, T. (1998) Power, risk and reflexive modernisation, paper presented to research committee 24, XIVth World Congress of Sociology, University of Montreal, 27 July–1 August.

Giddens, A. (1994) *Beyond Left and Right: The Future of Radical Politics.* Cambridge: Polity Press.

Gunningham, N. and Johnstone, R. (1999) *Regulating Workplace Safety: Systems and Sanctions.* Oxford: Oxford University Press.

Health and Safety Commission/Department of Environment, Transport and the Regions (2000) *Revitalising Health and Safety: Strategy Statement.* London: DETR.

Health and Safety Executive (1993) *The Costs of Accidents at Work.* London: HSE Books.

Health and Safety Executive (1994) *The Costs to the British Economy of Work Accidents and Work-Related Ill-Health.* Sudbury: HSE Books.

Health and Safety Executive (2000) *Key Messages from the LFS for Injury Risks: Gender and Age, Job Tenure and Part-Time Working.* http://www.hse.gov.uk/statistics/keyart.pdf.

Health and Safety Executive (2004a) *Occupational Health Statistics Bulletin 2003/2004, HSE/National Statistics.* http://www.hse.gov.uk/statistics/overall/ohsb 0304.pdf.

Health and Safety Executive (2004b) *Health and Safety Statistics Highlights 2003/04.* Bootle: HSE Statistics Co-ordination Unit.

House of Commons Work and Pensions Committee (2004) *The Work of the Health and Safety Commission and Executive. HC 456.* London: The Stationery Office.

Hutter, B. (2002) *Regulation and Risk. Occupational Health and Safety on the Railways.* Oxford: Oxford University Press.

Hutter, B. and Power, M. (2000) *Risk Management and Business Regulation. CARR Launch Paper.* London: LSE, available at www.lse.ac.uk/collections/CARR/documents/discussionPapers.htm.

Ives, J. (ed.) (1985) *The Export of Hazard: Transnational Corporations and Environmental Control Issues.* Boston: Routledge and Kegan Paul.

James, P. and Walters, D. (2002) Worker representation in health and safety: options for regulatory reform, *Industrial Relations Journal*, 33(2): 141–56.

Labour Research Department (1996) *Women's Health and Safety.* London: Labour Research Department.

Lavalette, M. (1991) Some very peculiar practices: work organisation and safety in the North Sea oil and gas industry, unpublished manuscript.

Lee, J. and Wrench, J. (1980) Accident-prone immigrants: an assumption challenged, *Sociology*, 14(4): 551–66.

Moore, R. (1991) *The Price of Safety: The Market, Workers' Rights and the Law.* London: The Institute of Employment Rights.

Mythen, G. (2004) *Ulrich Beck: A Critical Introduction to the Risk Society.* London: Pluto Press.

Mythen, G. (2005) Employment, individualization and insecurity: rethinking the risk society perspective, *Sociological Review*, 53(1): 129–49.

O'Donnell, C. and White, L. (1998) *Invisible Hands: Child Employment in North Tyneside.* London: Low Pay Unit.

O'Donnell, C. and White, L. (1999) *Hidden Danger: Injuries to Children at Work in Britain.* London: Low Pay Unit.

Pearce, F. and Tombs, S. (1998) *Toxic Capitalism: Corporate Crime and the Chemical Industry.* Aldershot: Ashgate.

Pickvance, S. (2005) A little compensation, *Hazards*, 90(April/June): 18–19.

Randerson, J. (2001) Lingering death, *New Scientist*, 23 October.

Reilly, B., Pace, P. and Hall, P. (1995) Unions, safety committees and workplace injuries, *British Journal of Industrial Relations*, 33(2): 273–88.

Rigakos, G. (2001) On continuity, risk and political economy: a response to O'Malley, *Theoretical Criminology*, 5(1): 93–100.

Rigakos, G. and Hadden, R. (2001) Crime, capitalism and the 'risk society': towards the same old modernity, *Theoretical Criminology*, 5(1): 61–84.

Rustin, M. (1994) Incomplete modernity: Ulrich Beck's risk society, *Radical Philosophy*, 67: 3–12.

Smith, A., Wadsworth, E., Shaw, C., Stansfeld, S., Bhui, K. and Dhillon, K. (2005) *Ethnicity, Work Characteristics, Stress and Health*, Health and Safety Executive Research Report 308. London: HSE Books.

Smith, P. and Morton, G. (2005) *Eight Years New Labour: The Third Way Management Prerogative and Workers' Rights.* Keele: Keele University, 4 May.

Snider, L. (1991) The regulatory dance: understanding reform processes in corporate crime, *International Journal of the Sociology of Law*, 19(2): 209–36.

Szasz, A. (1984) Industrial resistance to occupational safety and health legislation: 1971–1981, *Social Problems*, 32(2): 103–16.

Szockyi, E. and Frank, N. (1996) Introduction, in E. Szockyi, and J.G. Fox (eds) *Corporate Victimisation of Women.* Boston: Northeastern University Press.

Takala, J. (2002) *Introductory Report: Decent Work, Safe Work.* Geneva: International Labour Organization, at www.ilo.org/public/english/protection/safework/wdcongrs/ilo_rep.pdf.

Takala, J. (2005) *Introductory Report: Decent Work, Safe Work.* Geneva: International Labour Organization, at www.ilo.org/public/english/protection/safework/wdcongrs17/intrep.pdf.

Tombs, S. (1995) Law, resistance and reform: regulating safety crimes in the UK, *Social and Legal Studies*, 4(3): 343–65.

Tombs, S. (1999) Death and work in Britain, *Sociological Review*, 47(2): 345–67.

Tombs, S. (2004) Workplace injury and death: social harm and the illusion of law, in P. Hillyard (ed.) *Beyond Criminology? Taking Harm Seriously*. London: Pluto Press.

Tombs, S. and Whyte, D. (2003) Researching the powerful: contemporary political economy and critical social science, in S. Tombs and D. Whyte (eds) *Unmasking the Crimes of the Powerful: Scrutinizing States and Corporations*. New York: Peter Lang.

TUC (2003) Employers are not meeting the costs of workplace injuries and illness. *TUC Press Release*, 18 March. www.tuc.org.uk/pressextranet.

Tweedale, G. (2000) *Magic Mineral to Killer Dust: Turner & Newall and the Asbestos Hazard*. Oxford: Oxford University Press.

Walters, D., Nichols, T., Conner, J., Tasiran, A. and Cam, S. (2005) *The Role and Effectiveness of Safety Representatives in Influencing Workplace Health and Safety*, HSE Research Report 363. London: HSE Books.

Woolfson, C., Foster, J. and Beck, M. (1996) *Paying for the Piper: Capital and Labour in Britain's Offshore Oil Industry*. London: Mansell.

Wrench, J. (1996) Hazardous work: ethnicity, gender and resistance, paper presented at the British Sociological Association Annual Conference, University of Reading, 1–4 April.

Wrench, J. and Lee, J. (1982) Piecework and industrial accidents: two contemporary case studies, *Sociology*, 16(4): 512–25.

## Further reading

Beck, U. (2000) *The Brave New World of Work*. Cambridge: Polity Press.

Hutter, B. (2002) *Regulation and Risk: Occupational Health and Safety on the Railways*. Oxford: Oxford University Press.

Nichols T. (1997) *The Sociology of Industrial Injury*. London: Mansell.

Pearce, F. and Tombs, S. (1998) *Toxic Capitalism: Corporate Crime and the Chemical Industry*. Aldershot: Ashgate.

Tweedale, G. (2000) *Magic Mineral to Killer Dust: Turner & Newall and the Asbestos Hazard*. Oxford: Oxford University Press.

# 11 Economics and risk

## Peter McMylor

> Where the market is allowed to follow its own autonomous tendencies, its participants do not look towards the person, to each other, but only towards the commodity; there are no obligations of brotherliness or reverence, and none of those spontaneous human relations that are sustained by personal unions.
>
> (Weber 1978: 636)

> The law of markets must dictate.
>
> (Peter Mandelson, Britain's European Commissioner, *Channel 4 News* 23/6/05)

## Introduction

This chapter is not written by an economist, but rather by a sociologist who seeks to place the economic in a set of wider social relations that is perhaps best captured by the idea of an economic sociology. In regard to risk itself and its relationship with this broader economic sociology, it does seem as if there has long been in the Western world an intimate relationship between patterns of economic thought and activity and the conception of risk. Luhmann (1991), in his influential book *Risk: A Sociological Theory*, points to the relatively unclear origins of the word, but is surely on safe ground in pointing out that it is a term that emerges out of the late medieval transition to early modernity and notes significantly that 'it first occurs relatively rarely ... [but] finds significant application in the fields of navigation and trade. Maritime insurance is an early instance of planned risk control' (Luhmann 1991: 9). He goes on to note also that the term begins to occur in particular legal documents as to who is to bear a loss if specific events occur. In general, then, risk is one of number of terms that have undergone dramatic development with the gradual emergence of capitalism. Indeed, in a significant sense the term 'risk' has to be understood as being part of a shared semantic field of terms and concepts which includes trust, chance, interest, opportunity, calculation, gamble and even, I would suggest, excitement – but this latter term can be seen as a relatively late development (Elias and Dunning 1986). All these terms undergo significant change in the early modern period and they both assist in the formation and in turn are formed by the emergence of capitalist modernity, a process caught most powerfully in Hirshmann's (1977) classic work *The Passions and the Interests*.

In essence, the concept of risk, at least in its early modern form, has a crucial economic dimension that centres on 'the realization that certain advantages are to be gained only if something is at stake' (Luhmann 1991: 11). However, in the twentieth century, with the general elaboration of economic and financial regulatory discourse, risk is subject to more specific definition that attempts to mark it out from general issues of uncertainty as in the influential account of the Chicago economist, and staunch free marketeer, Frank Knight (1921). In his book *Risk, Uncertainty and Profit*, Knight famously made the distinction between 'risk' and 'uncertainty', whereby risk refers to situations in which mathematical probability can be allocated to account for the perceived randomness of outcomes, and uncertainties refer to situations in which randomness cannot be expressed in terms of mathematical probability. John Maynard Keynes summed up the idea much later when he wrote:

> By 'uncertain' knowledge, let me explain, I do not mean merely to distinguish what is known for certain from what is only probable. The game of roulette is not subject, in this sense, to uncertainty ... the sense in which I am using the term is that in which the prospect of a European war is uncertain, or the price of copper and the rate of interest twenty years hence ... About these matters there is no scientific basis on which to form any calculable probability whatever. We simply do not know.
>
> (Keynes 1937, cited in Fonseca and Ussher 2005)

This distinction has been very influential and is still used by some economists and insurers today. However, the distinction has in many real-world situations been quite difficult to sustain. As Mythen (2004: 14) notes, 'contemporary risks contain residual uncertainties which render quantification problematic'. It is in this context that Beck (1992) in his extraordinarily influential work on the risk society refuses any simple definition of risk. Mythen (2004: 13) notes the caution in Beck's later work, indicating that risk refers to the consequences of both individual and institutional decisions and stressing that 'risks are forms of institutionalized reflexivity and are fundamentally ambivalent'. This gives, in one way, expression to what Beck calls 'the adventure principle' but on the other hand,

> risks raise the question as to who will take responsibility for the consequences, and whether or not the measures and methods of

precaution and of controlling manufactured uncertainty in the dimensions of space, money, knowledge/non-knowledge and so forth are appropriate.

(Mythen 2004: 13)

This broader conception of risk that can be linked to both natural and manufactured risks and their deep mutual connections to issues of reflexivity are well taken. However, as I have argued elsewhere (McMylor 1996), what remains problematic in Beck's work is the emphasis on the epochal transformation from something defined as 'industrial society' to that of the 'risk society'. Industrial society is defined as the old society of class, filled with distributional conflict over 'goods' – that is, largely material resources, income, social welfare, employment – while the new risk society is dominated by conflicts over the 'bads' of natural and manufactured risks. Moreover, these new risk issues are seen to have an equalizing effect because we were all apparently threatened by the same issues, such as environmental degradation, nuclear warfare and genetic technology. Bauman (1992: 23) locked onto a key problem in his initial review of Beck's book, when he wrote that ours was 'a society notorious for re-forging every human desire and horror into a stratifying device. All too often the struggle against risks boils down to the resourceful dumping their problems into their weak neighbour's backyard.'

Since the appearance of Beck's work, further empirical analysis and theoretical discussion has certainly cast doubt on his claims to an epochal transition and suggests the continuing saliency of the structural inequalities that Beck assumed were passing with the decline of industrial society (Mythen 2004). Indeed, we might well now understand at least these elements of Beck's original work on risk as a product of a particular period of West German development in which it enjoyed social and economic stability and prosperity. It is, I think, hard to imagine any writer articulating within the present German context claims such as 'the struggle for daily bread has lost its urgency' (Beck 1992: 20) with unemployment in Germany in 2005 standing at around 10.5 per cent and the former leader of the ruling SPD Franz Muentefering, prepared to use the language of anti-capitalism in speaking of private equity firms as a 'swarm of locusts' (*Der Spiegel*, 5/5/05). Clearly in modern societies we do have distributional conflicts over both goods and the bads that potentially have a dangerous reinforcing tendency with quite uncertain outcomes. However, it seems that the resources of classical social thought are not exhausted by this new situation as the forces of socially structured market risk and the social structural outcome of these processes are reshaping the social world around us. It is this context of structured uncertainties that can be explored by relating them to resources of economic sociology in terms of both its classical sources and its more recent revival.

## What is economic sociology?

Given that this chapter is focused on economic sociology and risk, the reader might well legitimately ask what exactly economic sociology is and what is to be gained from linking together the two distinct academic social science disciplines. To answer this, I intend to start by spelling out the distinction between economics and economic sociology. I then proceed to look at the classical resources of economic sociology and conclude by looking at how they have been applied to explore aspects of our present-day 'transformations'. What follows will be schematic, but will provide a broad orientation to what can and cannot be expected from economic sociology in understanding the concept of risk. Following Smelser and Swedberg (1994a: 4) there is series of key questions we may want to begin with:

1  *Who is the social actor?*
   Conventional economics tends to assume actors are first and foremost individuals and could be described as subscribing to the conception of social order normally called 'methodological individualism'. Economic sociology assumes that actors are more than individuals but rather members of wider and often overlapping groups that make up society. In other words, this tradition assumes a societal affect in understanding action. This could be understood by different sociologies as either 'holistic' that is, part of a social totality or processual in the form of an ongoing flow of interactions.

2  *What is economic action?*
   Conventional economics assumes actions are done for 'rational' purposes, normally to maximize some clearly understandable utility. So in economics, rationality is an assumption. Economic sociology tends to assume a variety of motives for economic action as for other kinds of action. Economic actions might or might not be rational from an economic point of view but might involve other motivations that emerge out of other non-economic spheres of society, for example, what is the economically rational motive for giving to a charity? Rationality, then, is a variable to be studied for the economic sociologist.

3  *What are the constraints or limits on action?*
   Conventional economics assumes that action is constrained by the scarcity of resources, the level of technology and by the individual tastes of the actor. Economic sociologists also see action restrained by scarcity and the level of technology, but also by the very form of the social structure – including the dimensions of class, race and gender – and the pattern of institutional arrangements including the range of

interpretations, meanings and understandings available to social actors.

4   *What is the relationship between economy and society?*
Conventional economics' basic focus is of course on the market and the economic structure and thus it tends to take the wider society as a kind of given which is the source of things like tastes and preferences, but the origins of which are left unexplored. Often societal or so-called 'external influences' – on, say, the behaviour or structure of the market – are viewed as distortions or interferences and implicitly illegitimate. Economic sociology views the economy as always part of the wider society and would view it as a form of social organization that exists and persists only because of non- or extra-economic social activity such as familial socialization and political and governmental supervision and regulation.

5   *What is the analysis for?*
Conventional economics aims directly at prediction and explanation, rarely at detailed description. The apparent possibility of prediction is the attraction of the discipline for those who own, control or depend on the economy – it holds out the potential for power and control and this rather than its actual success accounts for its prestige. There are systematic problems with social scientific prediction to which economics is not immune (MacIntyre 1981). Economic sociology tends to focus on description and explanation and rather rarely on prediction.

6   *What methods of analysis are used?*
Conventional economics generally uses quite formal methods, especially mathematical modelling, sometimes using no data at all or data from official or governmental publications. Economic sociology uses the full range of sociological methods that are generally less formal and mathematical but also include official data from government publications as well as historical and comparative data and also data produced by the research analyst themselves, so-called 'dirty hands' data.

## Economic sociology: classical and contemporary

If we continue for a moment with our contrast between conventional economics and economic sociology to cover issues of intellectual origins and traditions, we can note some significant differences. Conventional economics has of course normally acknowledged its key predecessors in Adam Smith, David Ricardo and John Maynard Keynes, but with its emphasis on maths and modelling it tends not to frequently revisit its progenitors. Economic sociology, like sociology in general, frequently revisits the classics of its discipline in search of inspiration by drawing on new social contexts that provide horizons for reinterpretation of standard works (Alexander 1987). In respect of economic sociology, this emphasis is especially understandable as the major form of economic social organization that has shaped sociology and been the subject matter of its reflection has been capitalism. For all that, there is a trajectory of change and transformation of capitalism as a system. There are recognizable features especially in its forms of private ownership, market structure, dynamic growth and periodic crisis that mark it out as a continuing social system (see Arrighi 1994; Wallerstein 2004).

It is clear then that the central figures for economic sociology are Marx, Weber and Durkheim. They are the well-known touchstones in any introduction to sociology and I will not dwell on the detail of their work. Marx remains the founding figure of economic sociology, even if some very influential contemporary economic sociologists such as Swedberg (1998) see him as rather a background figure, the best of whose work is integrated into the sociology of Weber. As Tombs and Whyte have lucidly reasoned, the centrality Marx gave to economic crisis, exploitation and social conflict makes him a pivotal figure in understanding issues around the economic and social dimensions of risk, especially those dimensions relating to unemployment, the global movements of capital and labour, and the systematically uneven generation of wealth and poverty. Indeed, the whole panoply of what Beck calls 'manufactured risk' in its very broadest sense must take its initial, if not its final, bearing from Marx. Virtually all those who write on these issues, especially critical thinkers, owe an enormous debt to Marx and much of their work would be unthinkable without it (Tilly 1992, 1999, 2003).

Weber, although of absolutely central importance in the formulation of economic sociology (Swedberg 1998), is perhaps key in one respect in relation to issues connected to risk. This is in respect of his conceptualization of the market dimensions of class stratification that laid the basis for the concept of life-chances in modern capitalism. This has some real purchase on class experience because a market position – although prone to fluctuation – has some patterning effect due to prevailing market conditions and the skills and resources that the individual and the group bring to the market arena. This is in many ways a profoundly individualistic starting point and rooted in Weber's relationship to neoclassical economics and methodological individualism (Clarke 1991). This is congruent with the risk society approach and in fact is a major influence in contemporary policy formation around issues of social exclusion, educational attainment, and so forth. Weber was not sanguine about the market and capitalism, as the quotation at the beginning of this chapter makes clear, but he did accept its existence as an unchangeable framework.

With regards to Durkheim, it is helpful to begin with the interesting confession of the *Financial Times* journalist Michael Prowse to his readers in a revealing paper about how he came to admire sociology. In 2001, he claimed,

> My own conversion to sociology was as sudden as St Paul's was to Christianity. In the summer of 1997, I was writing a panegyric on economic liberalism. I regarded the arguments in favour of free markets and individual liberty as pretty near irrefutable, and I confidently expected to finish my book and resume my journalistic career within a few months.

However, in the end, a sense of fair-minded honesty got the better of him and he thought he ought after years of reading the classic British empiricists, Locke, Hume and Smith and their utilitarian descendants, look at the opposition: 'where better to begin than with Durkheim, a noted exponent of holistic, and hence, I thought, nonsensical social theories?' Yet he goes on to concede:

> For me, reading Durkheim was like crossing the Rubicon. He opened my eyes to arguments that I had not previously considered. To my astonishment I found he was taking apart the arguments that I was trying to make in my book. How was this possible, given Durkheim was writing towards the end of the 19th century? The answer is easy: the economic liberal arguments so popular today – even among Labour politicians – and which underlie the global spread of markets – are mostly recycled.

Prowse went on to suggest that Durkheim in his critique of the liberal economic philosophy of his day had

> a more nuanced understanding of the nature of social phenomena than anyone in the market tradition had possessed. He had a vivid sense of the social as a *sui generis* order of things – an order that has to be just as carefully investigated as the realm of physical nature.

There are a number of interesting aspects about this commentary: in the first place the fact, unthinkable in mainland Europe, of a sophisticated financial journalist never having encountered Durkheim until well into his career. Second, the unassailable English prejudice against sociology he indicates he had until then: 'my previous hostility to sociology had been blind prejudice' and that 'Durkheim, I discovered, fitted none of the stereotypes of the discipline's detractors: he was not woolly-headed and he didn't hide behind obscure generalities. He was as compellingly lucid as any empiricist philosopher.' Third, and most importantly, the power and capacity for a classical figure from sociology still having the ability to surprise, shock and persuade in the context of the dominant Anglo-American ideology of free market capitalism. It is, then, in this context that an examination of economic sociology and issues of risk might best be seen as significant. In many respects, free market capitalism is a paradigmatic form of the modern experience of risk. It could reasonably be argued that much of the success of the contemporary discourse around risk lies in its relationship to both the positive and negative presentation of free markets, privatization and deregulation as highly significant modes of social organization. Who does not now realize that a job can disappear abroad, a pension fund can become insolvent overnight, or that the value of their house can balloon upwards or plummet downwards, leaving them with a debt overhang that is given in Britain the euphemistic name of 'negative equity'? Apart from the health issues considered by Flynn in Chapter 5, these are perhaps the most significant risks that those living in Western societies experience in their lives.

So, Durkheim still has the power to shock and stir those who have never encountered sociology as a critical way of looking at conventional economic thought. As Prowse noted, his work on the division of labour is central to understanding the limitations of economic thought (Fevre 2003). But, paradoxically among sociologists, he is often thought of and taught as a figure more closely linked to methodological questions around positivism or as a precursor to functionalism or perhaps more so now appreciated as subtle and profound analyst of religion.

I now wish to turn to a figure who until recently has not been well recognized within sociology: Polanyi (see Polanyi-Levitt and Mendell 1987; McMylor 2003). Polanyi's substantial focus was on the market and its impact upon society especially in regard to the producing of a pervasive set of risk-based social relations that can be conceptualized as centring on the process of the disembedding of the economy. It is this idea that has been truly pivotal in the recent revival of economic sociology and directly inspired the paper that was to act as a kind of manifesto for this revival: Granovetter's (1985) *Economic Action and Social Structure: The Problem of Embeddedness*.

Polanyi, like Durkheim whom he in some respects resembles, sought to oppose ideas in economic thought which had also influenced other disciplines such as historical anthropology, that aimed at a unified economic theory intended to cover all human societies past and present. Polanyi's contention is that those who have attempted to uncover an overall economic science have imposed concepts derived from their understanding of market economies onto non-market ones. In this process, he maintains that they imposed a vision of past societies as filled with acquisitive individualists with a natural tendency 'to truck and barter' and thereby supporting the theory of human nature held by Adam Smith and his followers. Polanyi sets out his basic theoretical orientation both in *The Great Transformation* and in a lengthy essay *The Economy as Instituted Process*. Here Polanyi makes the distinction between 'substantive' and 'formal' economies:

> The substantive meaning of economic derives from man's dependence for his living, upon nature and his fellows. It refers to the interchange with his natural and social environment, in so far as this results in supplying him with the means of material want – satisfaction ... the formal meaning of economic derives from the logical character of the means–ends relationship as apparent in such words as 'economical' or 'economising'. It refers to a definite situation of choice, namely that between the different uses of means induced by an insufficiency of those means.
>
> (1971: 139)

Polanyi believes the formal definition is readily applicable to the capitalist industrial societies of the West, and that to apply its terms of reference to earlier pre-market societies can only cause grave distortion. Indeed, he goes so far as to argue that

> The two root meanings of economic, the substantive and the formal have nothing in common. The latter derives from logic, the former from fact. The formal meaning implies a set of rules referring to choice between the alternative uses of insufficient means. The substantive meaning implies neither choice nor insufficiency of means: man's livelihood may or may not involve the necessity of choice and, if choice there be, it need not be induced by the limiting effect of a 'scarcity' of the means; indeed some the most important physical and social conditions of livelihood such as the availability of air and water or a loving mother's devotion to her infant are not as a rule, so limiting.
>
> (Polanyi 1971: 139)

It is apparent then that for Polanyi the empirical or substantive economy must in some sense exist everywhere. The crucial difference between market and non- (or pre-)market societies is that in these latter societies the economy is 'embedded' within the overall society, while in the former it is not. What does this embeddedness consist of? Principally Polanyi is referring to a wide range of non-economic institutions such as those of kinship, religion, political/state forms, that provide the context within which economic functions proper are performed. The consequence is that the goals or ends of economic activity are to a considerable degree shaped by these non-economic institutions and values, and it is almost never left simply to small groups or individuals to pursue their own material self-interest. This contradicts the move of the early political economists such as Adam Smith to subsume a whole gamut of human desires and aspirations within the one moment of economic self-interest (Hirschmann 1977). Polanyi's view also has in its favour the fact that it is not based upon a static view of human nature, for, Polanyi argues, in a whole variety of societies, tribal ones, small hunting or fishing communities, and even in the great empires of world history, 'neither the process of production nor that of distribution is linked to specific economic interests attached to the possession of goods, but every single step in that process is geared to a number of social interests which eventually ensure that the required step be taken' (Polanyi 1957: 46). Is such a view based on romantic notions of primitive societies and their altruism? No. For, as Polanyi argues, in the case of a tribal society it is unlikely that most of the time an individual's absolute interest in survival will be put in question, because the community keeps all of its members from starving, unless there is a disaster that threatens all of them. However, for this support to operate, the maintenance of social ties is quite crucial:

> Firstly because by disregarding the accepted code of honour, or generosity, the individual cuts himself off from the community ... second because in the long run, all social obligations are reciprocal and their fulfilment serves also the individual's give-and-take interests best.
>
> (Polanyi 1957: 46)

Polanyi goes on to suggest that the nature of these social relationships may be such that there is pressure 'on the individual to eliminate economic self-interest from his consciousness to the point of making him unable, in many cases (but by no means all), even to comprehend the implications of his own actions in terms of such an interest' (Polanyi 1957: 46). So, in non-market societies the human economy is enmeshed firmly in a variety of institutions both economic and non-economic, and this means that 'religion and government may be as important for the structure and functioning of the economy as monetary institutions or the availability of tools and machines themselves that lighten the toil of labour' (Polanyi 1971: 148). Crucially, therefore, an analysis of the changes of the role of the economy in society turns out to be 'no other than the study of the manner in which the economic process is instituted at different times and places' (Polanyi 1971: 148). Clearly, then, at the abstract level, the corollary of this notion of non-market societies being enmeshed economies within other dominating frameworks, is that in market societies the economy is no longer so embedded. The market means that there is in some sense, a differentiation of economic activity into a separate institutional sphere, no longer regulated by norms that have their origin elsewhere. The individual economic agent is free then to pursue economic self-interest, without 'non-economic' hindrance.

## The double movement: retreat and advance

This, then, is the outline of Polanyi's analytic model of economy. However, in his substantive studies Polanyi takes us further still, examining the significance of the market within the context of the wider social order of nineteenth – and then twentieth-century capitalism and its role in precipitating the great social and political crises of recent European and world history. This analysis is found in Polanyi's famous and significant work *The Great Transformation* (1944), published in the midst of the crisis whose societal roots it sought to find. In essence, Polanyi viewed the problems of Western modernity in the nineteenth and early twentieth centuries as being based on four key institutions. These problems emerged from the nature of the balance of power between states, the international gold standard, the liberal nightwatchman state and, most crucial of all, the self-regulating market system. Polanyi viewed the self-regulating market system as in some respects a kind of nineteenth-century utopianism that in effect had to be created by state policy and action in which land and labour had to be turned into what he termed 'fictitious commodities' – fictitious because they were not originally created for sale. In practice, a struggle ensued to establish and maintain this market system against those who sought to protect the people and society from what we would now clearly see as the 'risks' of poverty and misery ensuing from it. It is this conflict that Polanyi conceptualizes as his famous 'double movement' within society, with the free market radicals of 'Manchester Liberalism' on one side – pushing issues such as land enclosure, the 1834 Poor Law Reform Act and the repeal of the Corn Laws in 1846 – provoking the other side of the double movement in a variety of fairly uncoordinated responses. This 'other side' sought in practice to put limits on the 'manufactured risks' that arise from this form of social change, epitomized perhaps by Chartism and campaigns for the Factory Acts to limit labour exploitation in the 'free market', steady growth of trade unions, the various efforts to rebuild tariff protection for some industries and finally various moves towards a welfare state in the early twentieth century which included programmes such as sick benefit and old age pensions. It is not difficult to see why Polanyi is being read again in the present period, or why a contemporary economic sociology might employ his analysis to illuminate the issue of risk. In essence, the whole issue of Polanyi's concept of the double movement is at the centre of contemporary debates about society and economy, as scholars once more recognize our current situation as being reflected in his writings. Disciplines such as international relations and politics (Inayatullah and Blaney 1999; Blyth 2002), sociology and social policy (Holmwood 2000; Burawoy 2003), and economics (Altvater and Mahnkopf 1997; Harmes 2001) have rediscovered his work, leaving aside the revival in economic sociology proper.

Since at least the 1980s, conflicts over the double movement in society at both the national and international level have been renewed. As Kemshall and Franklin have revealed, in this time welfare states have been retrenched and reformed in the UK. Further, publicly owned industries and services from electricity, gas and water providers to prisons and hospitals have been privatized or at least opened to market pressures (Leys 2001). At the international level, social changes are viewed frequently as an arena to be interpreted in terms of the fierce debate around the concept of globalization (Hirst and Thompson 1996; Held et al. 1999, Sutcliffe and Glyn 1999; Held 2004). We need not enter this debate here, as it frequently goes beyond claims about economic transformations to include cultural interconnections (Giddens 2002). Nevertheless, it is worth noting the enormous significance and influence of the expanded and transformed architecture of the global economy since the late 1970s. This is the result of a combination of economic processes, but also quite crucially of political and state action especially by the USA and the UK in areas surrounding the movement of capital and the reduction of trade barriers. This has created a massive multinationalizing of the economy which is central to the creation of the present UK post-Fordist and largely post-manufacturing economy (Overbeek 1990). As it has materialized, this has created the conditions for a global economy that – in a post-Bretton Woods context – affects the room for manoeuvre of other states who often embrace deregulation of markets in response.

It is in this economic and political context that the discourse around risk and insecurity takes on a renewed salience, as Polanyi's double movement performs yet another twist. To be sure, one of the striking features of the recent past is the way in which various 'gatekeepers', including opinion formers and politicians, deploy the language of both risk and opportunity. Indeed Wheelock (cited in Vail et al. 1999: 38) noted at the end of 1990s 'the widespread view of insecurity as a desirable feature of the economic system'. Going on to quote a representative sentiment from *The Economist*, she states that, 'what works is competition, with its potent mixture of fear and opportunity' (Wheelock, cited in Vail et al. 1999: 38). However, even if some still use this language today, public perceptions are likely to fix on the aspect of fear rather than that of opportunity. It is clear that after the dotcom collapse and the falling stock markets, the new global market can have devastating effects – even on those who thought they had little to do with it. It has been forcibly recognized by tens of thousands – and understood by millions – that what happens to the global market has fundamental consequences on personal pensions.

In a key text within economic sociology, Minns (2001) has pointed out that US and UK commitment to liberalized financial markets has underpinned the development of the pensions industry in those countries. Minns writes about a 'cold war in welfare' between an individualized Anglo-Saxon stock market model and a European model of state provision. Minns (2001: 183) argues convincingly that the Anglo-Saxon model of 'capitalism is actually antipathetic to pensions "welfare" because of its exclusivity and reliance on the most arbitrary mechanism for promotion of the public good – the stock market'. He suggests that the stock market model is more about extending the power and influence of large financial institutions and the stock market itself, than about the promotion of public goods. As Langley (2004: 553) has pointed out in a parallel argument, the crisis of the final salary pension schemes affecting 9 million Britons and 44 million Americans takes place in the context where

> US and UK state managers are committed to furthering the individualisation of responsibility and risk in saving for retirement . . . the neo-liberal economics of welfare and the drive for shareholder value in corporate governance give rise to an economy in which responsibility for pensions does not lie primarily with the state or firm, but instead resides firmly at the door of the individual.

These processes are, of course, in Beck's and Giddens's terms archetypal examples of manufactured risks, but they are risks constructed by visible agents with clear political and economic agendas. These agendas are still explicable in terms of the politics of economic liberalism and social democracy as they have fought out the Polanyian double movement for nearly two centuries. In the UK, the emergence of pensioners' groups seeking redress – plus the British government's new Pension Protection Fund aimed at compensating workers whose pension funds go bust – points up the possibility of once more organizing society so as to absorb the individual within the social whole.

## Conclusion: beyond the risk society

It will be clear from the above that the concerns of economic sociology have always been related to the issue of risk in the broad sense. Economic activity in our global capitalist society has always generated winners and losers and conventional economics has often seen itself as principally concerned with tracing the logic of this process. Polanyi's work is important in many respects – not least because the historical and anthropological cast of his work provides a useful distancing from contemporary assumptions about the nature and purpose of markets. It is also the case that Polanyi's conceptualization of the 'double movement' around the issue of markets and society enables us to makes sense of many contemporary issues, from the activities of the World Trade Organization to attempts to pursue the privatization of public services. In this regard, future research is vital in attempting to broaden our understanding of what we mean by the term 'economic'. A key aspect of this must be on the nature of markets as they really exist as distinctive sets of modern institutional arrangements that include particular organizations, or networks of organizations, stretched along lines of compressed time–space configurations. The upshot of this is that markets have to be understood and studied as local, national and international phenomena. To this end, the work of Strange (1986, 1998) on international financial markets is a vital starting point, especially in relation to the political aspects such as the political structuring of markets (Fligstein 1996). What needs to be unravelled is the process – that inevitably involves political decisions that facilitate the creation of markets – in order to examine what interests and whose interests are at stake and to understand that what was shaped in one form can be reshaped to serve other interests. Such work might well be complex and in some respects quite technical. Yet there are economic sociologists, such as MacKenzie (2000, 2003) who do not shy away from this and elucidate the social basis and consequences of new financial processes and techniques. Nonetheless, as vital as the research on the architecture of modern global capitalism is, it must be complemented by work on the nature of human communities as they relate and negotiate with these economic forms. The full Polanyian emphasis on the double movement, as movement and counter-movement within society, must not be lost or economic sociology will become trapped in the expansionary logic of the economic as a global way of seeing. How communities respond to modern economic forces and build social movements that question dominant forms must be explored. This is the arena that has been called 'infrapolitics' by Scott (1990) and applied by Mittelman (2000). In this analytical space we can see the undeclared forms of practical resistance generated by the understandable resentments produced by large structural transformations that seem to come from beyond the horizon of the community. What we clearly need is a new, updated form of community study that looks at the resources of communities, both material and cultural (see Beynon et al. 2000), to provide a basis for the dynamic renewal of societal protection against the risks of capitalist late modernity.

## Study questions

1   What are the main differences in the way a sociologist and an economist would look at social behaviour?
2   Do you think that conflicts over the distribution of power and resources are still significant in a 'risk society'?
3   How could the citizens and governments of modern societies protect themselves from risks?

# References

Alexander, J. (1987) On the centrality of the classics, in A. Giddens and J. Turner (eds) *Sociological Theory Today*. London: Macmillan.

Alvater, E. and Mahnkopf, B. (1997) The world market unbound, *Review of International Political Economy*, 4(3): 448–71.

Arrighi, G. (1994) *The Long Twentieth Century*. London: Verso.

Bauman, Z. (1992) The solution as problem, *Times Higher Education Supplement*, 13 November.

Beck, U. (1992) *Risk Society: Towards a New Modernity*. London: Sage.

Beynon, H., Cox, A. and Hudson, R. (2000) *Digging up Trouble: The Environment, Protest and Open-Cast Mining*. London: River Orams Press.

Blyth, M. (2002) *Great Transformations: Economic Ideas and Institutional Change in the Twentieth Century*. Cambridge: Cambridge University Press.

Burawoy, M. (2003) For a sociological Marxism: the complementary convergence of Antonio Gramsci and Karl Polanyi, *Politics and Society*, 31(2): 193–261.

Clarke, S. (1991) *Marx, Marginalism and Modern Sociology*. London: Palgrave Macmillan.

Collins, R. (1992) Weber's last theory of capitalism: a systemization, in M. Granovetter and R. Swedberg (eds) *The Sociology of Economic Life*. Boulder, CO: Westview Press.

Elias, N. and Dunning, E. (1986) *The Quest for Excitement: Sport and Leisure in the Civilizing Process*. Oxford: Blackwell.

Fevre, R. (2003) *The New Sociology of Economic Behaviour*. London: Sage.

Fligstein, N. (1996) Markets as politics: a political cultural approach to market institutions, *American Sociological Review*, 61(4): 656–73.

Fonseca, G. and Ussher, L. (2005) *History of Economic Thought* at http://cepa.newschool.edu/het/home.htm.

Giddens, A. (2002) *Runaway World*. London: Profile Books.

Granovetter, M. (1985) Economic action and social structure: the problem of embeddedness, *American Journal of Sociology*, 91(3): 481–510.

Granovetter, M. and Swedberg, R. (1992) *The Sociology of Economic Life*. Boulder, CO: Westview Press.

Harmes, A. (2001) Institutional investors and Polanyi's double movement: a model of contemporary currency crises, *Review of International Political Economy*, 8(3): 389–437.

Held, D. (2004) *Global Covenant*. Oxford: Polity Press.

Held, D., McGrew, A., Goldblatt, D. and Perraton, J. (1999) *Global Transformations: Politics, Economics and Culture*. Stanford, CA: Stanford University Press.

Hirsch, P., Michaels, S. and Friedman, R. (1987) Dirty hands versus clean models: is sociology in danger of being seduced by economics? *Theory and Society*, 16: 317–36.

Hirschmann, A. (1977) *The Passions and the Interests: Arguments for Capitalism before its Triumph*. Princeton, NJ: Princeton University Press.

Hirst, P. and Thompson, G. (1996) *Globalization in Question*. Cambridge: Polity Press.

Holmwood, J. (2000) Three pillars of welfare state theory: T. H. Marshall, Karl Polanyi and Alva Myrdal in defence of the national welfare state, *European Journal of Social Theory*, 3(1): 23–50.

Inayatullah, N. and Blaney, D. (1999) Towards an ethnological IPE: Karl Polanyi's double critique of capitalism, *Millennium*, 28(2): 311–40.

Knight, F. (1921), *Risk, Uncertainty and Profit*. Boston: Houghton Mifflin.

Langley, P. (2004) In the eye of the 'perfect storm': the final salary pension crisis and financialisation of Anglo-American capitalism, *New Political Economy*, 9(4): 539–58.

Leys, C. (2001) *Market-Driven Politics*. London: Verso.

Luhmann, N. (1991) *Risk: A Sociological Theory*. Berlin: Walter de Gruyter.

MacIntyre, A. (1981) *After Virtue*. London: Duckworth.

MacKenzie, D. (2000) Fear in markets, *London Review of Books*, 13 April.

MacKenzie, D. (2003) Long term capital management and the sociology of arbitrage, *Economy and Society*, 32: 349–80.

McMylor, P. (1996) Goods and bads, *Radical Philosophy* 77, May/June.

McMylor, P. (2003) Moral philosophy and economic sociology: what MacIntyre learnt from Polanyi, *International Review of Sociology*, 13(2): 393–407.

Minns, R. (2001) *The Cold War in Welfare: Stock Markets versus Pensions*. London: Verso.

Mittelman, J. (2000) *The Globalization Syndrome: Transformation and Resistance*. Princeton, NJ: Princeton University Press.

Mythen, G. (2004) *Ulrich Beck: A Critical Introduction to the Risk Society*. London: Pluto Press.

Overbeek, H. (1990) *Global Capitalism and National Decline*. London: Unwin Hyman.

Polanyi, K. (1957) *The Great Transformation: The Political and Economic Origins of Our Time*. Boston: Beacon Press.

Polanyi, K. (1971) The economy as instituted process, in G. Dalton (ed.) *Primitive, Archaic and Modern Economics: Essays of Karl Polanyi*. Boston: Beacon Press.

Polanyi-Levitt, K. and Mendell, M. (1987) Karl Polanyi: his life and times, *Studies in Political Economy*, 22: 7–39.

Prowse, M. (2001) How I crossed the Rubicon of social theory, *Financial Times*, 7 April.

Prowse, M. (2005) Emile Durkheim, *Prospect*, 107.

Scott, J. (1990) *Domination and the Arts of Resistance: Hidden Transcripts*. New Haven, CT: Yale University Press.

Simmel, G. (2004) *The Philosophy of Money*. London: Routledge.

Smelser, N.J. and Swedberg, R. (eds) (1994a) *The Handbook of Economic Sociology.* Princeton, NJ: Princeton University Press.

Smelser, N.J. and Swedberg, R. (1994b) The sociological perspective on the economy, in N.J. Smelser and R. Swedberg (eds) *The Handbook of Economic Sociology.* Princeton, NJ: Princeton University Press.

Strange, S. (1986) *Casino Capitalism.* Oxford: Blackwell.

Strange, S. (1998) *Mad Money.* Manchester: Manchester University Press.

Sutcliffe, B. and Glyn, A. (1999) Indicators of globalization and their misinterpretation, *Review of Radical Political Economy*, 31(3): 111–31.

Swedberg, R. (ed.) (1996) *Economic Sociology.* Cheltenham: Edward Elgar.

Swedberg, R. (1998) *Max Weber and the Idea of Economic Sociology.* Princeton, NJ: Princeton University Press.

Tilly, C. (1992) *Coercion, Capital, and European States, A.D. 990–1990.* Oxford: Blackwell.

Tilly, C. (1999) *Durable Inequalities.* Los Angeles: University of California Press.

Tilly, C. (2003) *The Politics of Collective Violence.* Cambridge: Cambridge University Press.

Vail, J., Wheelock, J. and Hill, M. (1999) *Insecure Times: Living with Insecurity in Contemporary Society.* London: Routledge.

Wallerstein, I. (2004) *World-Systems Analysis: An Introduction.* Durham, NC: Duke University Press.

Weber, M. (1978) *Economy and Society.* Berkley: University of California Press.

Wheelock, J. (1999) Who dreams of failure? Insecurity in modern capitalism, in J. Vail, J. Wheelock and M. Hill (eds) *Insecure Times: Living with Insecurity in Contemporary Society.* London: Routledge.

## Further reading

Fevre, R. (2003) *The New Sociology of Economic Behaviour.* London: Sage.

Leys, C. (2001) *Market-Driven Politics.* London: Verso.

Minns, R. (2001) *The Cold War in Welfare: Stock Markets versus Pensions.* London: Verso.

Polanyi, K. (2001) *The Great Transformation: The Political and Economic Origins of Our Time.* Boston: Beacon Press.

Smelser, N.J. and Swedberg, R. (eds) (2005) *The Handbook of Economic Sociology.* Princeton, NJ: Princeton University Press.

# 12 Culture and risk

## Jim McGuigan

## Introduction

This chapter is about risk and culture. In what follows the proposition is explored that a sense of risk has pervasive and acutely cultural manifestations today, ranging from the routinely agonistic experiences of everyday life and the life course to the specialized practices of cultural production and circulation, the dynamics of which are accentuated by neo-liberal globalization. To my knowledge, the risks of creative work and their severe manifestations under conditions of neo-liberal globalization have never properly been considered from the risk society perspective. First, however, and since this is a general chapter on risk and culture, it is necessary to consider the mediation of risk, how risks are represented in contemporary communications media and how popular understanding of societal and global risk is thereby framed.

Mainstream economic perspectives have traditionally seen risk as a matter of scientific calculation of probabilities, not as a cultural matter. While this may seem like a neutral, technical exercise, nonetheless it is bound up with insurance and public policy where values inevitably play their part. In stark contrast, some social scientists, such as Douglas and Wildavsky (1982), see the question of risk as almost entirely a matter of culture, how the world is framed, understood and acted upon. There are problems here of philosophical idealism that underplay the sheer materiality of risk, especially from an ecological perspective. Douglas and Wildavsky (1982) are very much concerned with combating the claims of environmental campaigners and, in effect, give succour to corporations and governments in resisting criticism. A much more critical approach to the cultural impacts of risk is provided by Beck and Beck-Gernsheim (2002), whose work is considered at some length in the present chapter. For them, risk is grounded in environmental concerns, and while it has much more general significance for everyday life and culture in the broadest and the narrowest senses, I shall consider their articulation of risk in the context of the environment in the first instance.

## Culture, the environment and risk

There are both strong and weak senses of risk. The risk society thesis, in its original formulation, represents the strongest version of risk, suggesting that human beings are putting their very existence on planet earth in danger for short-term gain, risking long-term extinction. The risk society thesis warns us of imminent ecological catastrophe resulting from pollution, global warming and the unsustainable use of resources. Nobody may feel personally responsible for any of this: the decisions are made elsewhere. Are there identifiable perpetrators who can be called to account or is it 'the system' that is to blame? Who commands 'the system', anyway, and why do we consent to it? Is the convenience of cheap air travel, for instance, really worth the risk of destroying the environment? According to Beck (1992a) this strong understanding of risk must be distinguished from hazard. Human beings have always had to live with hazardous nature, the vagaries of the weather, extremes of heat and cold, mysterious diseases and being eaten alive by wild animals, to name but a few. Now, these hazards are under greater control than they have ever been, although disastrous eruptions such as the South Asian tsunami at the end of 2004 and earthquakes generally are always likely to happen, however much we know or seek to deal with them. Interestingly, that tsunami was largely addressed as a matter of scientific knowledge (the movement of tectonic plates), relief (charitable aid) and the political economy of recovery and future protection, not an act of God or something equally irrational, as in past responses to such catastrophes (Voltaire 1947). In spite of some discussion about whether or not 'we' were to blame, rationality, in this case, discounted strictly human culpability as well as the work of supernatural forces. Despite being portrayed as 'natural disasters', the devastation of New Orleans on being hit by Hurricane Katrina and the devastating earthquake in the Hindu Kush mountain range of Pakistan certainly had an element of human culpability in their inadequately built environments for protection from such occurrences. Modern risks, on the other hand, are quite different from natural hazards old and new. They arise as a consequence of human actions, mainly resulting from industrialization and capitalist accumulative rationality: modern risks are manufactured. As Beck himself puts it:

> Human dramas – plagues, famines and natural disasters, the looming power of gods and demons – may or may not quantifiably equal the destructive potential of modern mega-technologies of hazardousness. They differ essentially from 'risks' in my sense since they are not based on decisions, or more specifically, decisions that focus on techno-economic advantages and opportunities and accept hazards as simply the dark side of progress.
>
> (1992b: 98)

This argument makes a realist claim, that the risks of industrial modernity do actually exist and are not just a matter of perception or the irresolvable contest between catastrophic and complacent discourses (Lupton 1999); that some people see (hu)man-made hazards and impending disasters all around them and others do not. Beck argues that the unintended consequences of using nuclear power, depleting natural resources, polluting the atmosphere, eroding the ozone layer, and so forth, has deleterious consequences for quality of life. The explosion at the Chernobyl nuclear plant and its aftermath in the 1980s are emblematic for Beck (1995). If you do not think that bad things are likely to happen with the environment, then look at the bad things that have happened already. They are harbingers of a doom-laden future.

There are many criticisms of Beck, not least of which concerns the excessively totalizing character of his risk society thesis. It seeks to explain a great deal and, in effect, too much. The implausibility of such an all-encompassing analytical framework is at risk, it can be said, of undermining Beck's many particular arguments that are exceptionally insightful. That is the basis for a theoretical critique of the risk society thesis. The empirical criticisms are rather more palpable and straightforward. For instance, Beck's writings on risk can be criticized for placing too much emphasis on anecdotal evidence like the Chernobyl disaster (Mythen 2004). Lomborg, the self-styled 'skeptical environmentalist', does not cite Beck in his extensive treatment of the statistical evidence for environmental degradation (Lomborg 2001) Yet, Lomborg's arguments can be taken as the exemplary empiricist critique of widespread alarm at the extent to which we are said to be putting our natural environment at risk. Lomborg was himself once a member of Greenpeace, the environmentalist NGO, and admits to possessing stock left-wing views on the state of the world in general. His is not the work of some American think-tank dedicated to defending the system against its life-world opponents. Lomborg's controversial book, *The Skeptical Environmentalist*, should be required reading for ecological activists who are sympathetic to Beck's risk society thesis in order to test out their arguments and strengthen them against reasonable scepticism or – if convinced by Lomborg – perhaps relinquish them *tout de suite*. Lomborg (2001: 3) questions what he calls 'the litany of our ever deteriorating environment'. This includes: natural resources running out; insufficient food to feed a growing world population; air and water pollution; extinction of species; deforestation; depleted fish stocks; and dying coral reef. Lomborg (2001: 4) responds to dominant assumptions about the deterioration of the environment by asserting:

> We are not running out of energy or natural resources. There will be more and more food per head of the world's population. Fewer and fewer people are starving. In 1900 we lived for an average of 30 years; today we live for 67. According to the UN we have reduced poverty

more in the last 50 years than we did in the preceding 500, and it has been reduced in practically every country.

Lomborg backs up his claims with exhaustively researched statistics. However, he is not arguing a complacent case. For him the evidence suggests that 'things are *better* – but not necessarily *good*' (Lomborg 2001: 5). For example, the effects of global warming are exaggerated, in his opinion, but it is incontrovertibly happening and may have worrying consequences. Lomborg argues that policies for improvement are not helped by blanket condemnation of everything that is occurring on the environmental front. It is necessary to identify the worst problems and do something about them, such as the persistence of mass starvation in an unequally rich world where the material conditions of life are generally improving rather than worsening. He recommends cost–benefit analysis to establish priorities in dealing with problems. From such a point of view, he argues, the eradication of AIDS is a more urgent and tractable problem than containing or reducing global warming.

In spite, or perhaps because of, its dull economism, this line of reasoning amounts to a defence of modernity against myths of a better past and advocacy of returning to traditional ways, exemplified by deep-green politics, while retaining the Enlightenment impulse of fearless criticism in favour of human betterment founded upon reliable evidence and emancipatory reason. The to-ing and fro-ing of claim and counter-claim is characteristic of cultural debate on chronic issues such as risk and environmental degradation. Empirical counter-evidence is also used from the other side of the environmental debate to the one occupied by Lomborg.

For instance, Monbiot (2005: 23) has challenged Bellamy's claim that the world's glaciers 'are not shrinking but in fact are growing', according to the Glacier Monitoring Service in Zurich. Monbiot checked this assertion with the Glacier Monitoring Service and was informed, without reservation, that Bellamy was wrong and that the evidence he quoted for his erroneous claim was not furnished by the Zurich-based monitoring unit at all. On further investigation, Monbiot found that Bellamy's figures, used to back up his claim that since 1980 glaciers have been growing not melting, were derived from a well-organized American lobby, supported by dubious science, against the mounting evidence of perilous climate change and campaigns to halt it. So, in this case and many others, the risk society thesis is by no means lacking in empirical substantiation, even though the evidence is patchily presented by Beck. This debate harkens back to Macnaghten's earlier consideration of public deliberations about who and what to trust. I do not wish to adjudicate between Beck's thesis and Lomborg's counter-evidence: after all, ambivalence is a pronounced feature of late-modern consciousness and sensibility (Bauman 1991). Instead of trying to resolve the contrary views argumentatively, the intention here is to illustrate uncertainty about the present cultural condition and the difficulties of knowing quite what to think and do, which is typical of the current conjuncture; and, moreover, the reason why we should take the risk society thesis seriously.

In his later work, Beck (2000) is keen to stress the ambivalence of risk, a weaker version. It is not exclusively about impending global catastrophe, though that may be so. It is also about a more culturally rooted and pervasive set of phenomena. It is about a sense of risk, uncertainty and chance, in a plethora of weaker senses than the catastrophic, maximalist version of environmental risk. Actually, when we talk of a culture of risk, this is what is probably meant most commonly in the life-world when confronted by an uncertain future, dictated not only at the outer reaches of the system but also in mundane activity. The palpability of the life-world always outstrips that of a remote and apparently unfathomable system over which people ordinarily feel they have little if any control (Habermas 1987), which is not to deny that the operations of the system do have determinate consequences for everyday life, sometimes fatally so. For many, however, impending global catastrophe is too awesome to contemplate whereas there is a sense that the travails of daily and knowable existence can at least be addressed and something done about them by yourself and by significant others in your life-world. This chimes with Macnaghten's earlier observations about the prescience of risk issues that people encounter 'head on' within the zone of routine cultural practices. In what follows the proposition is explored that a sense of risk has pervasive and acutely cultural manifestations today, ranging from the routinely agonistic experiences of everyday life and the life course to the specialized practices of cultural production and circulation, the dynamics of which are accentuated by neo-liberal globalization. As yet, the risks of creative work and their severe manifestations under conditions of neo-liberal globalization have not been properly considered from the risk society perspective. First, however, it is necessary to consider how risks are represented in the contemporary communications media and how popular understandings of societal and global risks are thereby framed.

## Culture, media and risk

Beck appreciates that public understanding and political struggles over risk are hugely dependent on their articulation by modern media of communication. According to Beck, risk issues are defined in the public sphere by the contest of contending forces – most especially between environmental campaigns and corporate public relations – in relation to the processes of mass mediation. As Beck (1998: 18) puts it, however, a 'mismatch exists in risk society between the character of hazards, or manufactured uncertainties, and the prevalent relations of definition'. The major implication here is that, for whatever reason, the media are not up to the job of representing risks adequately and in such a way that public support for policies to eradicate them is mobilized effectively. Media researchers have complained that Beck's account of mediated risk is too vague and imprecise (Cottle 1998). This criticism opened up a busily worked seam of empirical research, closely examining various cases of risk and their mass mediation (Allan et al. 2000). It is an elementary truism of media research that news does not simply reflect reality but instead constructs versions of reality that usually legitimize what is going on politically. In any event, in terms of public understanding, reality is always a mediated affair. Moreover, the political culture in general sets limits on the reportable and so do corporate interests linked to media organizations. Famously, the Soviet news media covered up the Chernobyl disaster as best it could. Such a deliberate omission is less likely in the news media of liberal-democratic countries. However, important issues disappear from view for long stretches of time, such as famine, and reappear intermittently. Furthermore, the news is necessarily selective, so all sorts of risk issues are hardly reported at all. There is a cycle of news reporting whereby an issue remains current only for a comparatively brief period until it goes stale and another issue crops up to take its place. The time of news is incommensurate with the time of 'real' reality, that is, in the realm of prediscursive occurrence from the point of view of the media. As Anderson has previously argued, news is event-driven and, especially in television, impelled by visualization of dramatic incidents. So-called 'real-world' problems, however, remain acute even when news coverage has moved on to something else. Critics complain about the neglect and sidelining of deep and long-term issues in favour of topical events. Additionally, they question the slant on news coverage of selected topics and the particular ways in which different voices are admitted to the news and given greater or lesser credence according to hierarchies of power and authority. Such complaints are routine features of critical media research.

More generally, there is complex exchange and, indeed, frequent confusion between ontology – what exists – and epistemology – what is known. It does not follow that if we do not know about something then it does not exist. Beck has argued persistently that the discourse of proof in environmental debates restricts understanding of subterranean processes that are not immediately observable and measurable. Similarly, Adam (1998) notes how radiation is imperceptible in everyday life. It only becomes manifest to public understanding in its demonstrable effects, which are typically much delayed, as in the case of leukaemia, for example. Proof of harm normally has to be adduced for the risk to be taken seriously enough in mainstream media and public policy, as in claims concerning the effects of radiation from mobile phones and the emplacement of towers (Burgess 2004). Occasionally alarmist reporting and flare-ups of public concern are refuted rapidly when there is no hard and fast evidence of harmful effects, although they may actually exist. In this respect, the use of mobile phones remains a classic risk society issue, a massive real-life experiment on the public, the results of which may not be known for quite a while. The telecoms companies themselves, however, take the putative risks seriously by patenting protective shields that, at the same time, they are reluctant to put on sale since it would incite widespread alarm and, hence, reduce custom and use, which for them has priority over public health (McGuigan 2005a). In this kind of instance, where dire warnings have been issued and largely ignored, the precautionary principle – that potentially harmful action which as yet remains unproven should not be taken – hardly applies at all. So, one of the most mundane features of everyday life now – the heavy use of mobile phones – goes on uninterrupted, oblivious to genuine medical concern about its possible longer-term effects. It is strangely re-miniscent of what used to be thought, said and done about the risks of smoking.

Critical research on news media and risk does not complain so much about lack of coverage: risk issues, in fact, constitute a staple feature of the news. If anything, it might be argued, there is too much news of risk, though much of it is inadequate in its representation. In practice, critical research questions the kind of coverage given to such issues: sensationalism; frag-mentation and atomization; bias towards official witness – positivistic sci-ence, politicians, and accredited spokespeople generally; short span of attention; apparently random selectivity; and so on. Lomborg's (2001: 39) take on news coverage of environmental problems concurs with that of critical media research. He says, 'the basic job of news is to report individual, unrelated events from many different parts of the world . . . hunger in Africa is nowhere near as good news as a plane crash' (Lomborg 2001: 39). Lomborg goes on to note that coverage of the Ethiopian famine of 1984 was almost accidental. The BBC journalists who picked up on it and broke the story were actually in Addis Ababa on their way to reporting a completely different story. Their reports alerted the global media to a humanitarian crisis that might otherwise have been missed. It generated international concern with endur-ing ramifications in global politics and was followed at the time by popular charitable activities such as the Band Aid record, the Live Aid concert and the still running biennial Comic Relief. However, by the time of Live 8, a global network of rock concerts timed to coincide with and put pressure on the G8 summit at Gleneagles in July 2005 – yet actually serving to distract attention from genuine protest – serious questions had to be asked about the value of such events. The role of the former pop star, Bob Geldof, and another ageing rocker, Bono, had transmogrified into that of providing band aid for the leaders of rich countries to cover up their use of hypocritical ploys when ostensibly addressing poverty in the world, especially Africa.

No discussion of media representation, misrepresentation or sheer non-representation is entirely satisfactory without some consideration of how all of this plays with audiences. Audience research, however, is fraught with difficulties and has been dominated by artificially created data of psychological effects on behaviour. Somewhat neglected with regard to risk is Gerbner's (1995) longitudinal research on the American media cultivation of a 'mean world syndrome', which eschews crude demonstration of effects. His argument is that over time the day-to-day violence presented on US television and, most notably, the enormous body count on crime shows, particularly in fiction programming, is not only frightening but encourages a stay-at-home culture since the city streets are understood widely, most acutely so by older people, to be the sites of continuous mayhem. The everyday life-world is thus rendered even scarier than it actually is, though functioning as a self-fulfilling prophecy when the streets are deserted after dark. The public's fear of danger in the USA, not only on its city streets but also from external enemies of the American way of life, especially since 9/11, is deeply felt. A recent BBC and much acclaimed documentary series in the UK, *The Power of Nightmares*, argued that contemporary politics is all about instilling fearfulness into people (McGuigan 2005b). Furedi (2002) has written of 'the culture of fear', which penetrates deeply into everyday life so that everything becomes potentially very scary. In his opinion, demotic talk of risk has moved inexorably from the positive connotations of 'taking a risk' to anxieties over being 'at risk'. Now, as a result, everyone is at risk of becoming the victim of counselling. Furedi's work is an important counterpoint to what might be deemed a neurotic obsession with risk in contemporary culture. Yet, it probably goes too far in casting doubt upon the palpability of intense problems of insecurity – and, not only psychological insecurity – today.

Such arguments concerning a 'mean world syndrome' and a 'culture of fear' are general propositions that go beyond audience research as such and for which the causal connections that are made between media and effect need to be treated circumspectly and located within a much broader cultural context than media-centric research tends to do. Nevertheless, risk consciousness is undoubtedly a discernible phenomenon. There is further confirmation of this phenomenon from empirical research, as the studies reported by Macnaghten in Chapter 8 demonstrate. In their focus group research on attitudes to environmental sustainability, Macnaghten and Urry (1998: 221) found that 'nearly all groups remarked on an emerging climate of uncertainty and the sense that life has become increasingly unpredictable'. Their respondents felt powerless to do anything about the problems that concerned them since these were considered so deeply entrenched yet of long-term consequence. The typical attitude was of resignation faced with terrifyingly uncontrollable forces.

## Living with a culture of uncertainty: on your own in the face of risk

One corollary of the risk society thesis is the thesis of individualization. The prospects of ecological catastrophe may seem remote but the dilemmas and uncertainties of everyday life are much closer to home. The human-made hazards brought upon humankind by global risk society are complemented at the everyday level by individualization, which is both liberating and disconcerting, combining personal freedom and high anxiety:

> Individualization of life situations and processes ... means that biographies become *self-reflexive*; socially prescribed biography is transformed into biography that is self-produced and continues to be produced. Decisions on education, profession, job, place of residence, spouse, number of children and so forth, with all the secondary decisions implied, no longer can be, they must be made. Even where the word 'decision' is too grandiose, because neither consciousness nor alternatives are present, the individuals will have to 'pay for' the consequences of decisions not taken.
>
> (Beck 1992a: 135)

Older ties of tradition and collective identification are loosened and individuals are increasingly responsible for themselves and the consequences of their actions. In that sense, there is a correspondence between societal risk and personal risk. In the risk society, individuals expect to control their fates, to spend their money and time as they so wish, to be in command of their bodies and living spaces. These expectations are increasingly commonplace, though with the highly educated and comparatively well off leading the way in authoring their own biographies, determining career paths, accepting and rejecting social obligations. Older fixities of class and status are less acceptable. The ideals of bourgeois individualist ideology, the dreams of Romanticism and the grim vision of Existentialism are realized for potentially everyone. Are we all existentialists now, condemned to freedom, alone in the world? It is more likely that individualization is experienced in a common rather than a philosophical sense as a kind of Americanization of the self.

Individualization might mean the dissolution of class identity and, hence, class struggle. It has implications for ethnic, gender and sexual identity. Most immediately, it signifies a crisis of familial relations, not the end of the family but a renegotiated contract governing intimate conduct, outlawing masculine dominance and liberating hitherto subordinate members. The 'nuclear family' was a cornerstone of industrial capitalism and simple modernity, reproducing labour power, sustaining patriarchy and serving, ideally, as a safe haven for the individual. Feminism, the rising divorce rate and the virtual emancipation of the child from parental authority have undermined that institution's stability for many members of reflexively modern society. Typically, 'personalized contradictions' are experienced in individual conduct and primary relationships. No role is rigidly prescribed by tradition any longer. Women, in particular, struggle with contradictory aspirations in work, partnerships and childcare. Singlehood, serial monogamy, multiplex families, arising from divorce and remarriage – in none of these arrangements are rules and conventions established. In personal life – and not only in wealth creation, science, technology and official politics – risky decisions have to be taken with no guarantee as to outcome or, normally, sufficient insurance cover. Which is not to say there is no guidance or assurance on offer: it is just that they are unreliable in a chancy social world. In global terms, these features of individualization are most pronounced in problems experienced by the comparatively wealthy, yet they are spreading down and further around. Divorce, for instance, used to be too expensive for the poor as well as stigmatizing for the divorcee; this is not so now in affluent parts of the world. Inevitably, such developments provoke ever-hardening resistance, such as the Islamic fundamentalist reaction to these modern ways. There are also Christian forms of religious revivalism: such as papal edicts confirming the official prohibition on contraception in spite of the spread of AIDS, at its chronic worst in Africa, and the disqualification of women from the priesthood and priests from marriage; and in the extraordinary political clout of Protestant fundamentalism in the USA and its dissemination to South America.

Beck and Beck-Gernsheim (2002: 22–9) have usefully distilled the individualization thesis into a set of basic propositions that are interlinked with one another in their essay 'A life of one's own in a runaway world' (see McGuigan 2006a). There is a 'compulsion', in Beck and Beck-Gernsheim's words, 'to lead a life of one's own' in a highly differentiated risk society (2002: 23). That is, individualization is more pronounced where a modern complex division of labour and separation of spheres of activity exists. Individualization is not an individual matter. Certain kinds of institutional arrangements foster individualization among the many, not just the few. This may be experienced as surviving 'the rat race' by being proactive, inventive and successful in achieving one's goals. Quite possibly, everybody is trying to do the same. Individualized activity, it has to be stressed, does not run counter to social institutions; it is embedded within them and required by them. There is nothing necessarily rebellious about institutionalized individuality. It is a kind of conformity. In the risk society, life is no longer scripted in advance for the individual. The individual is 'free', so to speak, to author the narrative biography of his or her life course. There is always the possibility, however, that one's own life story will go disastrously wrong, for which the individual will be held to account. There is no point in trying to blame, say, your poverty and debasement on 'society'. There is no let up. Not being vigilant about one's own health, for instance, is a personal failing. Illness, addiction, unemployment and the like are no longer seen as blows of fate but deemed to be matters of individual responsibility.

In a globally networked world, the person's position is displaced, that is, affected by forces operating in other places. Moreover, migration is an ever more pronounced feature of life under conditions of increased mobility. Traditions do not exactly disappear in these circumstances but are constantly reinvented. Old classifications have to be discarded and new ones formulated. There are no set rules for conduct; new ones are persistently tried out to see if they will work. Successful self-realization requires the weighing up of contradictory evidence, negotiating one's way in uncertain conditions where older arrangements, such as established family and work relations, are dissolving in a situation of flux. Flexibility in negotiating the uncertain conditions of modern life, being a survivor, becomes the standard of socially approved success. Life is lived in a culture of process rather than in compliance with static tradition. Living with uncertain prospects and no traditional authority to rely upon results in fresh political possibilities. Democratic negotiation and re-negotiation of everything are always on the cards. For example, there is a hidden green message in the thesis of individualization. As Macnaghten posits, the autonomy and defence of the personal life may connect to protecting the environment. Beck and Beck-Gernsheim (2002: 28) claim that 'the dominance of the life of one's own thus leads to an opening and a sub-politicization of society, but also to a depoliticization of national politics'. The old collective identifications of party politics – the party of the working class and so forth – are becoming unhinged. Here, Beck and Beck-Gernsheim refer explicitly to the New Labour project in Britain, a pragmatic politics under the cover of a long-standing front – the representation of labour – that has little substance these days. Sub-politics has a more radical aspect, however, in the shift from party politics to 'single-issue' campaigns, obviously in environmental politics but also in such matters as mobilization of an anti-war constituency in 2003 against the Anglo-American assault on Iraq. These issues resonate with individualization in the sense that one-off campaigns do not necessarily require any permanent sense of collective identity.

Individualization looks very much like the kind of subjectivity and approved way of carrying on called into being by neo-liberal globalization, constructing a type of individual attuned to living in such a harshly modern civilization. Neo-liberalism, first and foremost, is a reaction to post-Second World War Keynesian command management of the national economy and the social wage guaranteed by the welfare state, public protection of the individual from the travails of poverty and unemployment, ill health and old age, from 'cradle to grave'. The shift from Fordist organization and job security to the flexible networking of post-Fordism in a 'global world' is a feature of the neo-liberal political economy that has had a dramatic impact since the 1970s. It is a reversal of nineteenth-century principles of free trade in an international economic order, minimal state intervention except for coercion (police and military), and competitive individualism entailing precious little help for the weak who fall by the wayside and exorbitant rewards for those who bully it out at the top. As former British prime minister Margaret Thatcher noted, the necessary reason why the Good Samaritan could be charitable was that he was rich.

Beck and Beck-Gernsheim (2002: xxi) effectively deny the link between individualization and neo-liberalism, putting it down to a misunderstanding or mistranslation into English of a German meaning:

> One can hardly think of a word heavier with misunderstanding than 'individualization' has proved to have been in English-speaking countries. To prevent the discussion ... from running aground on these misunderstandings, it is necessary to establish and keep in view the distinction between the *neoliberal idea of the free-market individual* (inseparable from the concept of 'individualization' as used in the English-speaking countries) and the concept of *Individualisierung* in the sense of *institutionalized individualism*, as it will be developed.

This is a curious disclaimer since the appropriate neo-liberal subject has two not unrelated roles, the sovereign consumer and the entrepreneurial self, neither of which would seem contrary to the notion of individualization. Admittedly, for the Becks, individualization does mean more than that. It involves liberation as well as subjugation to prevailing imperatives. However, the popular appeal of neo-liberalism is similarly experienced as liberating, albeit somewhat illusory: for everyone, freedom of choice and opportunity to make it on your own. And, surely, that particular imaginary is deeply institutionalized now.

## Taking a chance: culture and capitalism

Capitalism has always been a risky business, involving present investment to produce later profit. The safer the investment, the more modest the likely profit. High-risk investment may yield greater profits or, indeed, greater losses. Historically, capitalism has gone through periods of boom and bust, once regarded as the inevitable fluctuations of the trade cycle. Thus, capitalism, however successful, was always vulnerable to crisis. Speculation was often associated with periodic destabilization and dramatic collapse, such as the Wall Street crash of 1929. The 1930s were a decade of severe disorder, economic recession, mass unemployment and the ascendancy of radical politics: communism, fascism and national socialism. Nazism rose and fell but communism endured much longer, sweeping up Eastern Europe, gaining power in China and spreading its promise to poorer parts of the world generally. The historical insecurities of capitalism and the challenge of an alternative economic system prompted liberal-democratic states to organize society in more stabilizing and socially equitable ways, heralding the period of the welfare state and the mixed economy; the so-called golden age of full employment and the consumer society. Social-democratic principles were, in effect, hegemonic for a while at the nation-state level in the West and even, to an extent, in the bastion of capitalism, the USA. That set of arrangements faltered in the 1970s and the popular gains of the previous 30 years came under siege. In the past 30 years, neo-liberal globalization has triumphed as communism has collapsed and social democracy went into retreat. The effects have been manifold, including the restructuring of industries and labour relations along more capitalistic lines. These and other features of the present condition have impacted consequentially upon cultural industries and cultural work generally.

If capitalism in general is inherently risky, then, capitalist cultural or creative industries and work within them, in particular, are doubly risky and, therefore, exemplary, not least because they are considered to be at the cutting edge of economic development (Rifkin 2000; Florida 2002). Miege (1989) argues that cultural industries are confronted with the problem of regularizing and marketing output, which is difficult to achieve, especially for autonomous works of art that are not easy to pigeonhole. Garnham (1990) points to the contradiction at the heart of the industrially produced cultural commodity: it is not typically used up in the act of consumption. The consumer can view a DVD over and over again whereas a loaf of bread cannot be eaten twice. Cultural industries, therefore, adopt strategies of artificial scarcity and perpetual novelty in order to encourage consumers to seek new products. In fact, most cultural commodities fail in the marketplace. Taste is very difficult to predict. So, hits have to pay for misses. For Bjorkegren (1996), cultural business is characerically postmodern, *avant la lettre*, since it is multirational. Most businesses only pursue a single, commercial rationale. Cultural businesses, however, are obliged to combine a cultural with a commercial rationale. The actual mix of commerce and culture varies between different sectors, with some sectors still putting culture before commerce, which is much harder to do in increasingly fierce market conditions. Yet, it still remains the case that

> A prominent feature of arts-related businesses is ... a high level of uncertainty in the market response to individual products. Because of this uncertainty, the business strategies of arts-producing

> organizations tend to be 'emergent' rather than deliberate, an out-
> come of interaction with the environment rather than the result of
> internally generated business plans.
>
> (Bjorkegren 1996: 43)

While that may be so, it does not stop cultural businesses seeking to perform like any other cost-conscious business. However, certain strategies are pecu-liar to cultural business. Rather like Nike products – which might be regarded as quasi-cultural commodities – more money is usually put into marketing would-be Hollywood blockbusters than making them. However, if there is not a quick return from the initial sales push on release, the product is quickly abandoned as yet another turkey. A past history of spectacular failure, such as the way Cimino's *Heaven's Gate* brought down United Artists (Bach 1985), leads to huge efforts being put into budgetary control, micro-management and product-testing. This is done in order to reduce uncertainty and tame wild creative types like the ill-fated Cimino, whose great success with *The Deer Hunter* prompted him to overspend extravagantly on his next production. The example of cultural business casts some doubt on the sheer novelty of riskiness in the risk society, at least in this area of human endeavour. None the less, it is true that cultural businesses have become more risk-conscious and, indeed, risk-averse. Which has prompted them, in addition to synergistic multiple exploitation of successful properties, to devolve risk in two especially salient ways. First, in post-Fordist structures, the practice of outsourcing by the major corporations so that they continue to command distribution – the locus of power in the cultural industries (Garnham 1990) – while saving their businesses from other risks. Production is done 'independently' and so is research and development by 'indies' of one kind or another. The second way of devolving risk is to lay it on the workers as Tombs and Whyte also argue. Here, we return to the theme of individualization, linked in this particular connection to the uncertainties, anxieties and downright riskiness of cultural work.

Interestingly, the French word, *risque*, has often been used in English language discussion of creativity, signifying artistic daring with an erotic charge. And, while 'creativity' is still worth thinking about (Negus and Pick-ering 2004), it takes back seat to the neo-liberal relations of production and economic imperatives now in charge of the fashionably yet ironically named 'creative industries'. Creative work has never been easy or secure. Many feel the calling, as they do in sport as well, but few enter the elect, leaving large numbers of talented and dedicated people, mostly young, not quite making it and having to find alternative occupations from which to earn a living. In this respect, near success should be distinguished from abject failure. The differ-ence between the successful and those who nearly succeeded may often be just a matter of chance. In spite of the poor odds, a great many ambitious young people are prepared to take a chance on making a creative career for themselves. In her research on young creative workers in London, McRobbie (2002: 516) observes that 'creative work increasingly follows the neo-liberal model, governed by the values of entrepreneurialism, individualization and reliance on commercial sponsorship'. Young creative workers these days are object lessons in the more general process of individualization in response to social and economic change, which is only partly grasped by the risk society thesis since it places too little emphasis on how capitalism has been restructured over the past 30 years.

Crucial here is the isolation of the individual worker from collective representation and the relative absence of solidarity with those in a similar plight. If you do not make it, it is your own fault. During the 1980s in Britain, for instance, Thatcherism attacked 'restrictive practices' in broadcasting, where strong unions had in the old days protected their members and bargained for comparatively high wages for permanent staff. Union power was much weakened, as it was also in other industrial sectors. The 'job for life' was to become something of an anachronism. With the exception of core administrative functions, 'flexible' labour and contractual insecurity became common for most new entrants to the broadcasting industry. For some older broadcasting workers it became harder to sustain their careers, though some of them benefited from new business opportunities that were opening up for those with established reputations and contacts. It became more difficult to build a career for each successive age cohort of broadcasting personnel in this period (Patterson 2002). A sharp division occurred between the securities of higher management – accountants and the like – and the insecurities of 'creatives', who had to manage themselves from project to project. Many are now obliged to move perpetually between temporary jobs, reliant on whatever reputations they have built up or prepared to work for very little, sometimes both. Among other institutional reforms that particularly affected commercial television (Ursell 1998), both the BBC and ITV were required from the 1990s to obtain 25 per cent of their programming from independents, that is, the kind of companies that had sprung up in the heady days of the 1980s to supply the publishing broadcaster Channel 4 with innovative programmes.

Broadcasting in Britain was thus transformed from a bureaucratic and cumbersome Fordist framework to the looser structures of post-Fordism (Arthurs 1994). Costs were driven down in this highly competitive independent sector – now supplying proliferating cable and satellite channels as well – where wages shrank and working conditions were becoming intolerably stressful. Poor pay and overwork all grew apace (Sparks 1994). It is exceptionally difficult for women to sustain a broadcasting career when they have children and for women generally in creative and information industries, not only in Britain (Jones 1998; Beale 1999). Unpropitious conditions are typical of work generally in the creative industries, from the arts world to the fashion industry, despite the glamorous image of such work. Yet, still, 'more and more young people opt for the insecurity of jobs in the media, culture or art in the hope of success' (McRobbie 2002: 521). Below the level of the very successful, many are complicit in their own exploitation, imbued, as they are, with success stories of making it on your own. Club culture, 'cool' yet non-disruptive attitudes and frantic networking to make the big breakthrough deflect attention from the dire circumstances of work for these young people in a neo-liberal cultural economy until they are worn out by it all and go off to do something less risky. In news coverage of the media, there is a steady flow of celebrity stories, rarely relieved by stories of how tough it can be in cultural work, such as union disputes in job-shedding Hollywood and occasional reports of young people literally working for nothing in order to get a foothold in media and cultural occupations. Modern media are self-obsessed but they display remarkably little reflexivity in this sense. Cultural policy today tends to promote rather than resist this state of affairs, so driven is it by the economic imperatives of the creative industries (McGuigan 2004, 2005c).

For Romanticism, the ideal form of work was art. It was creative and made personal expression concrete in the work itself. For the lucky few, fame and fortune were the rewards. For most, however, rewards were meagre and the struggle was hard. Posterity might revalue the work but by then the artist would be dead. The worst kind of work was constant toil and lack of control, which has always been much more common than self-realization in creative activity. Which of these kinds of labour approximates closest to cultural work today? Many are still motivated by its productive pleasures and perhaps also by the prospects of fame and fortune. The wager is high risk and the wages are low. Creative work under neo-liberal conditions embodies the ubiquitous process of individualization in a risky culture.

## Conclusion: beyond the risk society

In this chapter I have sought to demonstrate the applicability of the risk society thesis and its corollary, the individualization thesis, to understanding contemporary cultural process in general and, in particular, from how problems in the world are framed in the media to the struggle to make a creative career for oneself. The risk society thesis is extremely fruitful in generating questions of social and cultural analysis, but both the risk society and individualization theses are not faultless. Several of their flaws have been itemized in the foregoing account or, at least, contrary views that call its cardinal propositions into question have been tabled. Perhaps the natural environment is not at great risk after all and maybe we are too anxious about the supposed risks of everyday life. The risk society thesis does not explain everything. Its greatest fault is the implied suggestion that it does. Other perspectives, combined with aspects of the risk society thesis, offer rich prospects for making sense of what is going on. The publication of Beck's *Risk Society* (1992a) urged Rustin (1994) to complain that it had an insufficient account of the role of capitalism in contemporary social transformation. In this chapter, following that criticism, I have combined analysis of neo-liberal globalization with insights derived from the risk society thesis, especially concerning how risks inculcated by an increasingly fierce mode of capitalism are lived on a daily basis in terms of individualization.

On the surface, particularly in wealthy countries, capitalism today does not look so bad. Capitalism has become 'cool' (McGuigan 1996b). We live in a cornucopia of consumption, drowning deliriously in a sea of branded goods. This is nothing like the miseries of nineteenth-century capitalism in Europe that Karl Marx wrote about so scathingly (1976). That is because the miseries have been devolved to cheap labour markets and sweat shops in poorer parts of the world, to newly developing countries, where conditions of work are every bit as bad – if not worse – than in Victorian Manchester (Klein 2000). This is storing up deep trouble for the future in terms of social injustice, realizing popular aspirations for over-consumption, resource depletion and all the horrors warned of by Beck in the risk society thesis. Back in the already rich countries work is not so much fun either. Even in the ostensibly glamorous 'creative industries', in truth, life can be pretty miserable too.

## Study questions

1 What are the strengths and weaknesses of the risk society thesis as a tool for examining cultural change?
2 How are risk and individualization connected together in the work of Beck and Beck-Gernsheim?
3 In what ways are the typical conditions of creative work in the cultural and media industries today related to risk, individualization and neo-liberal globalization?

## References

Adam, B. (1998) *Timescapes of Modernity: The Environment and Invisible Hazards.* London: Routledge.

Allan, S., Adam, B. and Carter, C. (2000) *Environmental Risks and the Media.* London: Routledge.

Arthurs, J. (1994) Women and television, in S. Hood (ed.) *Behind the Screens: The Structure of British Television in the Nineties.* London: Lawrence and Wishart.

Bach, S. (1985) *Final Cut: Dreams and Disasters in the Making of Heaven's Gate.* London: Faber and Faber.

Bauman, Z. (1991) *Modernity and Ambivalence.* Cambridge: Polity Press.

Beale, A. (1999) From 'Sophie's choice' to consumer choice – framing gender in cultural policy, *Media, Culture and Society*, 21: 435–58.

Beck, U. (1992a) *Risk Society: Towards a New Modernity.* London: Sage.

Beck, U. (1992b) From industrial society to risk society – questions of survival, social structure and ecological enlightenment, *Theory, Culture & Society*, 9: 97–123.

Beck, U. (1995) *Ecological Politics in an Age of Risk.* Cambridge: Polity Press.

Beck, U. (1998) Politics of risk society, in J. Franklin (ed.) *The Politics of Risk Society.* Cambridge: Polity Press.

Beck, U. (2000) Foreword, in S. Allan, B. Adam and C. Carter (eds) *Environmental Risks and the Media.* London: Routledge.

Beck, U. and Beck-Gernsheim, E. (1995) *The Normal Chaos of Love.* Cambridge: Polity Press.

Beck, U. and Beck-Gernsheim, E. (2002) *Individualization: Institutionalized Individualism and its Social and Political Consequences.* London: Sage.

Bjorkegren, D. (1996) *The Culture Business: Management Strategies for the Arts-Related Business.* London: Routledge.

Burgess, A. (2004) *Cellular Phones, Public Fears, and a Culture of Precaution.* Cambridge: Cambridge University Press.

Cottle, S. (1998) Ulrich Beck, 'risk society' and the media – a catastrophic view? *European Journal of Communication*, 13(1): 5–32.

Douglas, M. and Wildavsky, A. (1982) *Risk and Culture: An Essay on the Selection of Technological and Environmental Dangers.* Berkeley, CA: University of California Press.

Florida, R. (2002) *The Rise of the Creative Class – And How It's Transforming Work, Leisure, Community and Everyday Life.* New York: Basic Books.

Furedi, F. (2002) *Culture of Fear: Risk-Taking and the Morality of Low Expectation.* London: Cassell.

Garnham, N. (1990) *Capitalism and Communication: Global Culture and the Economics of Information.* London: Sage.

Gerbner, G. (1995) Television violence – the power and the peril, in G. Dines and J. Humez (eds) *Gender, Race and Class in the Media.* London: Sage.

Habermas, J. (1987) *The Theory of Communicative Action*, Vol. 2. *The Critique of Functionalist Reason.* Cambridge: Polity.

Jones, J. (1998) Passion and commitment – the difficulties faced by working mothers in the British television industry, in S. Ralph, J. Langham Brown and T. Lees (eds) *What Price Creativity?* Luton: John Libbey.

Klein, N. (2000) *No Logo: Taking Aim at the Brand Bullies.* London: HarperCollins.

Lomborg, B. (2001) *The Skeptical Environmentalist: Measuring the Real State of the World.* Cambridge: Cambridge University Press.

Lupton, D. (1999) *Risk*. London: Routledge.

McGuigan, J. (2004) *Rethinking Cultural Policy*. Maidenhead: Open University Press/McGraw-Hill.

McGuigan, J. (2005a) Towards a sociology of the mobile phone, *Human Technology*, 1(1): 45–57.

McGuigan, J. (2005b) The power of nightmares, *Flow: A Critical Forum on Television and Media Culture*, 1(10). www.flowtv.org.

McGuigan, J. (2005c) Neo-liberalism, culture and policy, *International Journal of Cultural Policy*, 11(3): 229–41.

McGuigan, J. (2006a) *Modernity and Postmodern Culture*. Maidenhead: Open University Press/McGraw Hill.

McGuigan, J. (2006b) The politics of cultural studies and cool capitalism, *Cultural Politics* forthcoming 2(2): 137–58.

Macnaghten, P. and Urry, J. (1998) *Contested Natures*. London: Sage.

McRobbie, A. (2002) Clubs to companies – notes on the decline of political culture in speeded up creative worlds, *Cultural Studies*, 16(4): 516–32.

Marx, K. (1976) *Capital*, Vol. 1. London: Penguin.

Miege, B. (1989) *The Capitalization of Cultural Production*. New York: International General.

Monbiot, G. (2005) Junk science, *The Guardian*, 10 May.

Mythen, G. (2004) *Ulrich Beck: A Critical Introduction to Risk Society*. London: Pluto.

Negus, K. and Pickering, M. (2004) *Creativity, Communication and Cultural Value*. London: Sage.

Patterson, R. (2002) Work histories in television, *Media, Culture and Society*, 23: 495–520.

Rifkin, J. (2000) *The Age of Access: How the Shift from Ownership to Access is Transforming Capitalism*. London: Penguin.

Rustin, M. (1994) Incomplete modernity – Ulrich Beck's risk society, *Radical Philosophy*, 67: 3–12.

Sparks, C. (1994) Independent production, in S. Hood (ed.) *Behind the Screens: The Structure of British Television in the Nineties*. London: Lawrence and Wishart.

Ursell, G. (1998) Labour flexibility in the UK commercial television sector, *Media, Culture and Society*, 20: 129–53.

Voltaire (1947) *Candide*. London: Penguin.

## Further reading

Beck, U. (1992) *Risk Society: Towards a New Modernity*. London: Sage.

Beck, U. and Beck-Gernsheim, E. (2003) *Individualization: Institutionalized Individualism and its Social and Political Consequences*. London: Sage.

Bjorkegren, D. (1996) *The Culture Business: Management Strategies for the Arts-Related Business*. London: Routledge.

Furedi, F. (2002) *Culture of Fear: Risk-Taking and the Morality of Low Expectation.* London: Cassell.

McRobbie, A. (2002) Clubs to companies – notes on the decline of political culture in speeded up creative worlds, *Cultural Studies*, 16(4): 516–32.

# 13 Conclusion

## Towards a holistic approach to risk and human security

*Gabe Mythen and Sandra Walklate*

## Introduction

This book has showcased the work of a range of thinkers at the leading edge in their respective disciplines in order to provide an overview of the way in which risk has been approached, researched and theorized within the social sciences. Furthermore, the contributions herein invite us to think hard about under-researched issues and to consider areas ripe for future exploration. We have documented both the possibilities and the limitations of risk theory in understanding contemporary social relations and the processes at play in social change. In this respect, this collection has concerned itself with what lies *beyond* the risk society – both as a conceptual paradigm and as a set of social conditions. In the context of some of the events alluded to in the Introduction – such as 9/11, the train bombings in Madrid and the terrorist attacks in London in July 2005 – an understanding of the nature and im-plications of the risk society is ever more pertinent. The events of 9/11 would seem to have taken a particular toll in terms of both the boundaries seen to be transgressed and people's perceptions of future security (Worcester 2001; Jenks 2003). Despite the analytical commitment made by both Beck and Giddens that current risk preoccupations reflect 'manufactured insecurities'; a preoccupation with what it is that we have done to nature rather than what it is that nature can do to us, it is clearly a view that is no longer a wholly tenable one in the contemporary world. Yet we are still left with the problem of how to make sense of the modern social condition and the dilemmas that human beings encounter in managing their lives on a day-to-day basis. Each of the contributors to this volume has drawn a picture of the impact that the risk society thesis has had on their respective disciplines or in relation to their substantive fields of study. Reflecting on such snapshots, it is hard to deny the powerful influence that both the concept of risk and the theory of risk society has had on the social sciences. But within these pictures it is also possible to discern common presumptions and common predicaments: a palette of risk, while infinite in its range, is also perhaps limited in its profundity and consistency. In this conclusion we hope to add some further depth, texture and maybe even colour to the different social scientific risk agendas that have been presented here.

## Conceptualizing risk: problems and possibilities

As Franklin reminds us in Chapter 9, risk and risk decisions permeate all aspects of social life. Such decisions and choices are not confined to politicians endeavouring to manage the economy or trying to persuade the electorate of the efficacy of their policies, they are decisions that we each differently make over whether or not to use the London Underground to where we might more or less safely park our cars when we visit any major city. So the problems of risk and uncertainty pose dilemmas for all of us, despite the fact that our individual decisions about where to park our cars or whether to travel on the Tube might not be as impactful as a motion to reduce or raise interest rates. Nonetheless, if enough of us choose not to park in a place viewed as particularly risky or to use public transport, that too will take its toll on local retail trade. This example alerts us to one of the intrinsic problems broached by the risk society thesis which has been flagged up by authors in this collection. That problem is how to reconcile the individual process of risk decision-making with that of understanding societal processes, whether these are institutionalized in political, policy or cultural processes, or less visible to the individual and embedded in the structure of society itself. In particular, the chapters by Wilkinson and Lupton admirably draw our attention to the problem of the 'lived reality of experience' (Wilkinson) when put alongside the 'cultural construction of risk knowledges' (Lupton). In many ways this theoretical quandary has been side-stepped by a good deal of the work that has embraced the risk society thesis as it has been currently articulated and/or culturally constructed and as a result concerns itself with tracing the various ways in which the question of individual agency has been translated into individual responsibility. As Kemshall pointed out in Chapter 4, amidst the politics of risk, the responsible citizen is also cast as the prudential citizen. Both Flynn and O'Malley explain how notions of individual responsibility permeate issues pertaining to health and crime. Each of these analyses sets an agenda that places tensions between lay knowledge and professional knowledge, in the case of the first, and constructions of the likely offender in the case of the second – neither of which necessarily results in the equitable delivery of either health services or social justice. Offering a somewhat different understanding of what a prudential citizen might look like, in Chapter 6 Sanders offers us a perceptive understanding of expressions of prudence and responsibility in her appreciation of the way in which sex workers operate reflexively with local situated knowledge to develop their own understandings of a 'continuum of risk'. As the case study discussed by Macnaghten in Chapter 8 illustrates, individuals encounter and interpret issues relating to the environment in different ways that are often not accommodated by either politics, social policy or the risk society thesis. People may well be meeting the environment on a more intimate plain, proselytized through their daily activities and leisure choices. This itself raises all kinds of questions relating to the problems and possibilities associated with the prudential citizen. As this discussion implies, the tensions between locating risk as part of human agency and locating risk as a socio-cultural, political process remain.

Yet, as Anderson argued in Chapter 7, the ability to effectively communicate risk in contemporary society is crucial to national and individual security and fulfils a role in harnessing and ensuring the protection of the prudential citizen. For their part, in Chapter 10, Tombs and Whyte would argue that the tension between structure and agency at the heart of debates about risk remains largely because the risk society thesis reproduces an account of social life that glosses over political economy and conflates risk perception with the material force of risk. Globally, it needs to be remembered that the distribution of risk is both uneven and unequal. Specific regions act as repositories for the risks generated by affluent Western nations – from nuclear waste to the exploitation of labour. It is the people who inhabit such areas who feel the full material force of 'global' risk. As McGuigan suggests in Chapter 12, 'life is lived in a culture of process', so much so that this often mitigates an awareness that the big risk may actually be capitalism itself. This is a theme explored more fully by McMylor in Chapter 11 who argues that the work of Polanyi – especially his concept of the 'double movement' – provides one way of thinking through the relationship between ontology and epistemology that appears to be missing from contemporary risk debates. In Chapter 5 Flynn embraces critical realism as a way of responding to the structure/agency dynamic as articulated and expressed through discourses and forms of risk. It is this embrace that we wish to explore more fully in the furtherance of a holistic social scientific approach to risk.

## Situating risk in contemporary society

This text, and the issues it has addressed, have highlighted the demand that politicians, policy-makers and social scientists alike 'think security' (De Lint and Virta 2004). Furedi (2002), for example, has pointed out that – despite the spectacular quality of the 9/11 strikes on the United States – risk and insecurity are culturally ubiquitous phenomena. As opposed to Beck, Furedi

(2002: 5) believes that the current preoccupation with 'new terrorism' post-9/11 is symptomatic of the trend towards focusing on the negative and destructive features of the modern age:

> Being at risk has become a permanent condition that exists separately from any particular problem. Risks hover over human beings. They seem to have an independent existence. That is why we can talk in such sweeping terms about the risk of being in school or at work or at home. By turning risk into an autonomous, omnipresent force in this way, we transform every human experience into a safety situation.

As McGuigan has shown, it is likely that Furedi's 'culture of fear' has taken root within Western cultures, orchestrated by state institutions and those working within the media and security industries. Further, both McMylor and Kemshall explain how this uncertain context invokes individuals to become active risk managers, responsible for identifying and negotiating risks through the life course. For our purposes, Furedi's thesis usefully highlights the central importance of recognizing the global context of local events in the context of the risk society debate. So, for example, the push to tighten the legal framework in which terrorism is to be managed – as was debated in the UK in the summer of 2005 – relates to the wider movement of populations and the loosening of national boundaries, as well as technological advances and shifting modes of communication. Massive social changes such as these also make their mark on cultural processes. As Young (1999) reasons, over the past 50 years we have moved from being an 'inclusive' to an 'exclusive' society. In the 'inclusive' society of the 1950s questions around citizenship had been resolved, the state was interventionist and the rules of social order were clear and uncontested. The deviant, the law-breaker, was in the minority and once they had paid their debt to society were to be integrated into it. All this certainty began to change in the aftermath of the so-called 'cultural revolution' of the 1960s and the economic crises of the 1970s. Young goes on to suggest that these processes resulted in a social and economic precariousness, experienced by many city dwellers in particular as the rich and poor increasingly lived side by side. As a result, people were made well aware of the huge disparities in the rewards for different occupations. At the cultural level, over this period of time there was also an increase in awareness of diversity from the more public presence of gay communities to appreciation of the needs of those from ethnic minorities. Thus, for Young (1999), the inclusive society was marked by security and tolerance while the time at which he was writing was increasingly marked by insecurity and intolerance. Such insecurity and intolerance offered the mechanisms whereby notions of belonging, who is one of us and who is not, have the potential not only to exclude the stranger, 'the Other', but also to demonize them. It is within this lacuna that Furedi's 'culture of fear' constantly constructs and re-constructs those to be feared, those we avoid, those who are risky. At the present moment in the UK, it is evident that young Asian males are being clumsily cast as 'other' by some right-wing politicians and sections of the media. No great surprise that this group have borne the brunt of stop and search initiatives, questions of fairness and justice notwithstanding (Mythen and Walklate 2005).

So, local and global processes have a compounding impact upon each other, in terms of both what counts as risk and who is considered risky. There is, however, a further dimension to these processes. The governmentality approach to risk has pointed to the ever-increasing surveillance and regulatory procedures that we are all subjected to in the risk society. Those processes are also embedded in the political construction of the risky; hence the drive to push through restrictive legislation that targets those seen to be risky. Such tightening, however, is merely the surface manifestation of wider and deeper strategies of surveillance that have harnessed those same technological developments – CCTV, the Internet and the mobile phone – in the capture of the 'failed terrorists' whose bombs failed to detonate in London two weeks after the initial attacks. The costs and benefits of these strategies of surveillance that regulate us all are laid bare in the aftermath of the events in London. There is logic then in Lyng's (2005: 10) observation that 'the risk society and governmentality perspectives may capture two dimensions of the same social order in the late modern period'. If we add to this the cultural/symbolic perspective, then our prism is complete – a prism that, in the context of criminal justice policy, Garland (2001) has called the 'culture of control' in which strategies of responsibilization exhort us all to play our part in managing responses to risk, as the chapters by O'Malley and Kemshall aptly illustrate.

By cherry picking the fruits of the risk society, governmentality and cultural/symbolic approaches we can gain a decent vantage point on the current socio-cultural context and how this itself shapes and conditions responses to risk. The rudimentary question remains, however, about what exactly people are doing with all of this. As Bauman (2000) ponders, how do we seek biographical solutions to what are clearly systemic problems? To borrow third hand Wilkinson's (2001) reading of Tillich (1952), how do people in the contemporary risk environment prevent their minds from becoming 'factories of fear'? Is there a conceptual apparatus that might enable us to transcend the age-old problem of connecting individual risk assessments with embedded structural conditions? Drawing on the ideas expressed previously by Flynn and the work of Bhaskar (1975), we are going to suggest that wider adoption of a critical realist approach might enable us to overcome the inherent limitations of the approaches discussed above and thereby move us towards a deeper and more coherent understanding of risk.

## Critical realism: one way to take risk forward?

In defining the central tenets of critical realism Bhaskar (cited in Outhwaite 1987: 51) states:

> The conception I am proposing is that people, in their conscious activity, for the most part unconsciously reproduce (and occasionally transform) the structures governing their substantive activities of production. Thus people do not marry to reproduce the nuclear family or work to sustain the capitalist economy. Yet it is nevertheless the unintended consequence (and inexorable result) of, as it is also a necessary condition for, their activity.

Elsewhere, Walklate (1990) has argued that the adoption of this kind of position involves recognizing that human beings actively construct and reconstruct their daily lives; that these constructions reflect both practices of resistance and acceptance of their social reality; these constructions are made in a context of observable and unobservable generative mechanisms that have a real impact on people's lives. Regardless of whether or not people are aware of them, these processes have both intended and unintended consequences that further feed the knowledgeability of human beings and set the scene for future action. As Sayer (2000: 19) points out: 'much of what happens does not depend on or correspond to actors' understandings; there are unintended consequences and unacknowledged conditions and things can happen to people regardless of their understandings'. Flynn adds to this in Chapter 5 by suggesting that

> What is critical about this approach is that it assumes the possibility of alternative conditions, it asks what must and what might happen, and it is critical of existing structures and processes – critical realism aspires to offer a potentially emancipatory analysis associated with normative structures.

So what can be extracted from this approach and fed into a more holistic understanding of risk?

Put rather simply, in the first instance it posits a meaningful, if not straightforward, relationship between individual action and the social conditions of and for action, in other words, the structure and agency conundrum alluded to earlier. This is a relationship that is not many miles away from the theory of structuration posited by Giddens (1984). In the context of risk this means, first, recognizing that there are real risks. Independent of people's knowledge of them, there are actual risks – what happens when people encounter risky situations – and there are the risks that people ex-perience for themselves. To use the example of the terrorist threat, those in positions of power have long known about the real risks of an attack in London which is distinct from the actual risks for those people who en-countered those attacks and how those who survived dealt with that. In ad-dition, there is the empirical reality of what people may choose or choose not to do in the aftermath. The latter two types of risk bear very little – if any – relationship with the real risks of further attack. However in the second in-stance, a critical realist approach, with its intrinsic commitment to the pos-sibility of change, offers not only the opportunity of being critical of structures and processes, it also sets that analytical approach within the realm of the normative: what should and should not be the case.

In the context of the relationship between health and risk, Flynn has offered a persuasive argument as to how this kind of approach might engage medical professionals, institutions and lay people in a constructive debate in relation to health and health care priorities. In other words, meeting full on the political, structural and moral processes that lie embedded within the delivery of health care, thereby opening up the opportunity for change. In a similar way, encouraging a deliberative debate on the nature and causes of 'new terrorism' – which would include listening to those whose views might be contemporarily unacknowledged or absent from such discussions – might provide a way of setting a different kind of political agenda in the response to terrorism. By implication, this means dealing with thorny issues concerning morality, diversity, religion and tolerance. In a different context, these are the very issues that Franklin, McMylor and McGuigan grappled with in preceding chapters. To access the problems and concerns that congregate around risk we need to address the empirical reality of people's perceptions and experiences. Otherwise, as Wilkinson states, grand theories of risk remain but 'castles in the air'. Following Lupton's lead, to properly understand the role of risk within everyday life-worlds, more extensive use must be made of emergent qualitative methods, such as biographical and narrative research.

As Adams (2003: 87) states: 'risk management decisions are moral de-cisions made in the face of uncertainty'. Yet as Hudson (2003) has argued, over the past decade such decisions have also become entwined with ques-tions of responsibility: 'although there may be nothing new about fearful consciousness of risk, there is something new about the placing of responsi-bility for risk so unequivocally on individuals'. Chiming with Sanders' find-ings, Hudson (2003: 53) goes on to suggest that 'what is new, perhaps, is the joining together of the actuarial, probabilistic language of risk and the moral language of blame'. As Franklin reflects, discourses of risk – and notions of community – play a significant role in framing political ideas and practices in contemporary societies. Further, Kemshall sagely reminds us that political distinctions are routinely drawn between 'responsible' and 'feckless' citizens;

the former being deserving of welfare and security, the latter undeserving and excluded. Thus, as Tombs and Whyte propose, the social sciences need to be more attentive both to the power and the selective deployment of risk discourses as well as to the interests that are wrapped up in such deployments. This corresponds with Franklin's caveat that the politics of risk tends to construct a horizontal understanding of the relationship between structure and agency that secretes vertical inequalities.

All of this hints at and taps into a critical issue currently occupying Western neo-liberal cultures: should liberty be traded in the interests of security? If one believes the findings of an ICM poll that 73 per cent of people felt that it was right to give up civil liberties to improve security against terrorism, the question is far from rhetorical (Branigan 2005). In the face of the terrorist threat, the liberty/security paradox has become a very real one, symbolized in the UK by the looming possibility of conflict between politicians and the judiciary over the security of the state and the rights of potential deportees. Hudson's (2003) answer to this kind of dilemma is to argue for an uncoupling of rights from responsibilities; in other words to take the blame out of risk. This, in her view, does not entail 'dissolving wrongness'; 'discourse as a process of justice means that all claims must be listened to respectfully and that denial either of wrongs done or of the humanity of the wronged and the wrong doers is ruled out' (Hudson 2003: 224). Such an emancipatory stance towards justice seems compatible with a commitment to the fundaments of critical realism.

## Conclusion: travelling on a risky road?

We have come a long way in our search for a holistic approach to risk, from identifying the connections between different ways of thinking about risk in the present, to advancing novel approaches for the future. The examples that we have used have inevitably reflected our current interests. It is a moot point as to the extent to which these preoccupations concern us all. The risk issues that people fix on will vary according to – among other things – age, gender, class, ethnicity, sexuality and place (Mythen 2004). Furthermore, as Tombs and Whyte insist, we need to be duly wary about the threat of risk imperialism in social sciences, to ensure that fundamental inequalities and injustices are not allowed to slip off the radar. Clearly a balance needs to be struck between focusing on long-term environmental risks and the everyday risks – around health, work and crime – that habitually confront us. As Lupton prompts, we need to remember too that risks are sometimes voluntarily taken and produce tangible gains and pleasures. By drawing on pertinent examples, it has been possible for us to identify the diverse ways in which the different approaches adopted facilitate our understanding of particular risk incidents and processes. As the chapters in this book have demonstrated, common concerns about individual responsibility, political agenda setting and social welfare are evident in the different disciplinary approaches to risk. What is more, we have argued that the best way to transcend the boundaries between competing disciplines is to propose and take forward overlooked and/or innovative ideas, such as critical realism. What the social sciences must do is look for a way forward on risk. We need not, as Hudson (2003: 224) says, waste time 'deliberating the constitutionality of torture or killing', but instead mobilize the resources available to us in more productive and practical ways. These other ways demand a wider set of discourses than those currently in circulation in order to ensure that the price we pay for security is not our liberty. Debating the shape and merits of a holistic social scientific approach to risk might be one place to start.

## References

Adams, J. (2003) Risk and morality: three framing devices, in R.V. Ericson and A. Doyle (eds) *Risk and Morality*. Toronto: University of Toronto Press.

Bauman, Z. (2000) *Community*. Oxford: Polity Press.

Bhaskar, R. (1975) *A Realist Theory of Science*. Leeds: Leeds Books.

Branigan, T. (2005) Britons would trade civil liberties for security, *The Guardian*, 22 August.

De Lint, W. and Virta, S. (2004) Security in ambiguity: towards a radical security politics, *Theoretical Criminology*, 8(4): 465–91.

Furedi, F. (2002) *Culture of Fear: Risk Taking and the Morality of Low Expectation*. London: Continuum.

Garland, D. (2001) *The Culture of Control*. Oxford: Oxford University Press.

Giddens, A. (1984) *The Constitution of Society*. Cambridge: Polity Press.

Hudson, B. (2003) *Justice in the Risk Society*. London: Sage.

Jenks, C. (2003) *Transgression*. London: Routledge.

Lyng, S. (2005) *Edgework: The Sociology of Risk Taking*. London: Routledge.

Mythen, G. (2004) *Ulrich Beck: A Critical Introduction to the Risk Society*. London: Pluto Press.

Mythen, G. and Walklate, S. (2005) Criminology and terrorism: which thesis? Risk society or governmentality? *The British Journal of Criminology*, advance access at http://bjc.oxfordjournals.org/cgi/rapidpdf/azi074v1.

Outhwaite, W. (1987) *New Philosophies of Social Science: Realism, Hermeneutics and Critical Theory*. London: Macmillan.

MORI/Strategy Unit (2002) *Public Attitudes to Risk*. London: Cabinet Office.

Sayer, A. (2000) *Realism and Social Science*. London: Sage.

Tillich, P. (1952) *The Courage to Be*. Glasgow: Collins.

Walklate, S. (1990) Critical victimology, *Social Justice*, 17(3): 25–42.

Wilkinson, I. (2001) *Anxiety in a Risk Society*. London: Routledge.
Worcester, R. (2001) The world will never be the same: British hopes and fears after September 11th 2001, *International Journal of Public Opinion Research*. www.mori.com.
Young, J. (1999) *The Exclusive Society*. London: Sage.

# Index

# RISK, COMMUNICATION AND HEALTH PSYCHOLOGY

## Dianne Berry

This is the first book to clearly assess the increasingly important area of communication of risk in the health sector. We are moving away from the days when paternalistic doctors managed healthcare without involving patients in decision making. With the current emphasis on patient empowerment and shared decision making, patients want and need reliable, comprehensive and understandable information about their conditions and treatment. In order to make informed decisions, the people concerned must understand the risks and benefits associated with possible treatments. But the challenge for health professionals is how best to communicate this complex medical information to diverse audiences.

The book examines:

- Risk: defining and explaining how the term is used by different disciplines, how its meanings have changed over time and how the general public understand it
- Health communication and the effects on health behaviours
- Effective risk communication to individuals and the wider public
- Effectiveness of patient information leaflets, and strategies for improving oral and written health communications
- The cognitive and emotional issues at stake for patients in understanding risk and health information
- The use of new technologies in risk and health communication
- Ethical issues, and the future of risk communication

Using examples from disciplines including psychology, sociology, health, medicine, pharmacy, statistics and business and management, this book is key reading for students who need to understand the effect of risk in health psychology as well as for health professionals interested in doctor-patient communication, informed consent and patient welfare.

184pp  0 335 21351 0 Paperback     0 335 21352 9 Hardback

**IMAGINING THE VICTIMS OF CRIME**

**Sandra Walklate**

This book situates the contemporary preoccupation with criminal victimisation within the broader socio-cultural changes of the last twenty five years. In so doing it addresses not only the policy possibilities that have been generated as a consequence of those changes but also concerns itself with the ability of victimology to help make sense of this change. Written in the post 9/11 context this book considers the efficacy of theory and policy relating to questions of victimhood to accommodate the current political and cultural climate and offers a critical understanding of both. It adopts an explicitly cross-cultural position on these questions. It will be vital reading for anyone interested in the problems and possibilities posed by criminal victimisation understood in the broadest terms.

**Contents:** *Why are we all victims now? - Theory and Victimology - Structuring Criminal Victimisation - Victimisation, risk and fear - Victimisation, politics and policy - Local victim; global context - The rhetoric of victimhood and the role of the state.*

224pp  0 335 21727 3 Paperback     0 335 21728 1 Hardback